Facing the Crisis

DISLOCATIONS

General Editors: August Carbonella, *Memorial University of Newfoundland*; Don Kalb, *University of Bergen & Utrecht University*; Linda Green, *University of Arizona*

The immense dislocations and suffering caused by neoliberal globalization, the retreat of the welfare state in the last decades of the twentieth century and the heightened military imperialism at the turn of the twenty-first century have raised urgent questions about the temporal and spatial dimensions of power. Through stimulating critical perspectives and new and cross-disciplinary frameworks that reflect recent innovations in the social and human sciences, this series provides a forum for politically engaged and theoretically imaginative responses to these important issues of late modernity.

Recent volumes:

Volume 30
Facing the Crisis: Ethnographies of Work in Italian Industrial Capitalism
Edited by Fulvia D'Aloisio and Simone Ghezzi

Volume 29
Big Capital in an Unequal World: The Micropolitics of Wealth in Pakistan
Rosita Armytage

Volume 28
Fifty Years of Peasant Wars in Latin America
Edited by Leigh Binford, Lesley Gill and Steve Striffler

Volume 27
Brazilian Steel Town: Machines, Land, Money and Commoning in the Making of the Working Class
Massimiliano Mollona

Volume 26
Claiming Homes: Confronting Domicide in Rural China
Charlotte Bruckermann

Volume 25
Democracy Struggles: NGOs and the Politics of Aid in Serbia
Theodora Vetta

Volume 24
Worldwide Mobilizations: Class Struggles and Urban Commoning
Edited by Don Kalb and Massimiliano Mollona

Volume 23
The Revolt of the Provinces: Anti-Gypsyism and Right-Wing Politics in Hungary
Kristóf Szombati

Volume 22
Frontiers of Civil Society: Government and Hegemony in Serbia
Marek Mikuš

Volume 21
The Partial Revolution: Labour, Social Movements and the Invisible Hand of Mao in Western Nepal
Michael Hoffmann

For a full volume listing, please see the series page on our website: https://www.berghahnbooks.com/series/dislocations

Facing the Crisis

Ethnographies of Work in Italian Industrial Capitalism

Edited by Fulvia D'Aloisio and Simone Ghezzi

berghahn
NEW YORK • OXFORD
www.berghahnbooks.com

First published in 2020 by
Berghahn Books
www.berghahnbooks.com

Library of Congress Cataloging-in-Publication Data
A C.I.P. cataloging record is available from the Library of Congress
Library of Congress Cataloging in Publication Control Number: 2020936860

British Library Cataloguing in Publication Data
A catalogue record for this book is available from the British Library

ISBN 978-1-78920-780-4 hardback
ISBN 978-1-78920-781-1 ebook

Contents

Figures and Tables

Figures

Tables

Acknowledgements

Earlier versions of the chapters in this edited volume were originally published by L'Harmattan Italia under the title *Antropologia della crisi* in 2016. We wish to thank Elisa Pellizzari of L'Harmattan Italia for granting clearance to the publication of all the chapters in revised and updated form.

The English version of this book would have never come about without the help and encouragement of Michael Blim. Our biggest thank you goes to him. We also wish to thank Don Kalb in his capacity as coeditor of the Dislocations book series for accepting our invitation to write an Afterword.

We also want to acknowledge some relevant influences underlying our work: Enzo Mingione, Amalia Signorelli (in her memory), Susana Narotzky, Gavin Smith and Sylvia Yanagisako. They were not directly involved in this book, but their works and suggestions have been an inspiration to us.

We would like to thank the anonymous referee for their insightful comments on the draft version of the manuscript. We are grateful to Giuseppe Vittucci for being so helpful and taking his time to find data and update charts and tables. We also want to express our gratitude towards all the contributors who embarked on this project and in particular the economist Andrea Fumagalli for his open-mindedness in debating with anthropologists. Last but not least, we would like to thank all our interlocutors and protagonists of the ethnographies who took time away from their activities to talk to us about their own life and work.

Simone Ghezzi thanks his wife Elizabeth Esteves for her helpful suggestions, critiques and support, and their daughter Emily for her joyful presence. He also dedicates his share of this book to the memory of his father Angelo, who passed away during the drafting of the manuscript. Fulvia D'Aloisio thanks her mother for her helpful support and Francesco for his always intelligent and witty comments.

— Introduction —

The Crisis in Italy

Anthropological Insights on Changes of Work, Enterprise and Life Horizons

Fulvia D'Aloisio and Simone Ghezzi

Economic Crisis and Cultural Crisis: Between Flexibility and Precariousness

During the summer of 2011, the FIAT (Fabbrica Italiana Automobili Torino) factory in Termini Imerese, a small town in the metropolitan area of Palermo (Sicily), closed down, and in 2012 strikes and demonstrations were held in the area attempting to reverse this decision. It was the first (and up until now the only) FIAT factory to be decommissioned. This event marked a watershed that anticipated the new global structure of FIAT, but it also indicated the culmination of a crisis that has had strong repercussions in Italy, in an industrial-capitalist system characterized by specificity and weaknesses. The crisis, which started with the US Credit Crunch of 2007/2008, produced profound transformations that had repercussions on the Italian economic-productive system, which, as a whole and with the due internal differences, is certainly not one of the most solid examples in the European framework. In January 2019, major Italian newspapers reported a relevant figure, namely that Italian industrial production had dropped by 22 per cent since the 2007 crisis; almost a quarter of total production, a trend that is strongly divergent from the general European trend.[1]

FIAT, a microcosm of the great Italian industrial capitalism characterized by family ownership and involvement, can therefore be taken not only as providing an example of some critical aspects of the great interdependence between industry and politics in Italy, but also as a symbol of the general trend in the manufacturing industry: in the context of the general instability and political weakness that have been the subject of frequent reports in the press, the country has become less able to govern the processes of internationalization of the economy and to react adequately to the crisis.

Crisis is an increasingly used term and, since 2007, has become part of the international lexicon. As an Italian anthropologist noted, the image repeatedly broadcast by the media of Lehman Brothers employees leaving their offices with their boxes of personal effects constituted an iconic symbol of the crisis, immediately understandable for everyone, but corresponding however with an equally dense incomprehensibility of the reasons underlying what was happening (Signorelli 2016).

The aim of this work is to reflect in anthropological terms on the effects of the crisis in Italy, choosing industrial-manufacturing, small and medium-sized enterprises organized into districts (in central and northern Italy) as ethnographic field areas and case studies; then providing an example of a large manufacturing company (FIAT, the national automotive industry that has long operated as a sole player in Italy) as an example of the so-called assisted big industry in Italy; and, finally, examining a service sector that is particularly crucial for industrial production, namely the transport of goods by road. This type of freight transport, as illustrated in Chapter 6 of the volume, underwent significant development in Italy after the Second World War, both due to the devastation caused to the railway system during the war and to implicit agreements with vehicle manufacturers, primarily FIAT.

From an anthropological point of view, the 2007/2008 economic crisis and its effects maintain an inextricable link with a cultural crisis. By cultural crisis, we mean both a transformation of knowledge and values linked to work, and a transformation of everyday life practices, which consist of strategies of resistance, reaction and reorganization in the face of the economic crisis, and of the values and ethical principles that influence the organization of daily life, as well as the possibility of overcoming and transcending small and big difficulties which can arise in both the present and the immediate future. As we will show, the theory outlined by the Italian anthropologist Ernesto de Martino can help us to explain the impact of the crisis from an anthropological perspective and the cultural instruments used to tackle the crisis.

There is no doubt that the transformation of work, regarding its roles, functions and techniques, has lasted at least a century – 'the short century', in the famous expression of Eric Hobsbawm (1994). Starting from the writings of Karl Marx and during the twentieth century, the conceptual opposition, explained by Marx as dialectic, between capital and labour was central, and work was classified in the category of paid labour. Although this was not the only type of work possible (and since the late twentieth century, industrial workers have decreased in Western countries and are no longer a homogeneous category), it gave rise to the two specific categories of workers that define the social structure of the West (blue-collar workers, technicians and foremen on the one hand, and entrepreneurs and managers on the other).

However, at the turn of the twenty-first century, we found ourselves faced with a more fluid and heterogeneous category to describe workers, which saw changes in the distribution of workers between sectors (from the production of goods to the production of services and from manual work to so-called cognitive work), but also in the content and organization of the work itself. In the brief outline that we can give here: the result is a more heterogeneous composition, pulverized into a myriad of tasks and types of contracts, more polarized, and in which the definition of professional categories becomes more difficult, generating completely redefined status, identity and class memberships.

Many scholars, within the frame of international debate, have confronted the economic crisis and its outcomes in social life, in the cultural organization of work and subsistence strategies. Indeed, recent ethnographies of industrial work have raised interesting points of view in order to interpret the large-scale changes introduced by the crisis.

In the introduction to *Industrial Work and Life*, Massimiliano Mollona not only considers the central role of ethnography in capturing the variegated forms of contemporary capitalism in its different locations, but also underlines, in the wake of Marxian philosophy, that work is something more than and different from a merely material and individual process: it is mainly 'a social and collective process of imagination, creativity and self-realization' (Mollona 2009: xxv). This is a central point of view for anthropological analysis, which also forms the focus of this volume.

The viewpoint taken by Sharryn Kasmir and August Carbonella (2014) is an even more explicitly Marxian perspective, which is necessary, in the authors' opinion, due to the worldwide increase in protest movements and demands for rights; these reveal the evermore evident contradictions of the capitalist system in its neoliberal form and of the forms of dispossession and delocalization that are capable of producing accumulation by dispossession (Harvey 1989); this, albeit in a heterogeneous form, determines what the authors consider to be a new global proletariat. In thus reaffirming the need for a comparison, the authors underline the fact that dispossession was experienced and articulated in different forms at the end of the twentieth century, and yet the theoretical focus is not so much on the global/local opposition 'that has captured the anthropological imagination in the last twenty years' (Kasmir and Carbonella 2014: 3); instead, they refer to the critical junctions (in the sense of Kalb (2009)) in which the working classes relate to the regional, national and global institutions of power and influence.

At the same time, Kasmir and Carbonella also warn us that the widespread disappearance of the notion of class is linked more to the disappearance of its Fordist form, while the opposition between specialized industrial workers in the North and workers deprived of skills (and racially connoted) in the South also risks obscuring a more fluid and heterogeneous class experience. In addition, the authors believe that the consequences of the great ongoing recession are producing new differences and inequalities within the processes of dispossession. They consider it necessary to place labour policies at the heart of the analysis, as a fundamental step towards a global anthropology of work centred 'on the dialectic of dispossession and incorporation in people's daily lives, as well as the ways working people make new divisions and alliances in the context of global accumulation' (Kasmir and Carbonella 2014: 6). The more interesting point here is the notion of work as politically connoted, which implies a multiplicity of connections with the state and capital as mechanism of regulation on the one hand, and with workers and their living conditions at the local levels on the other.

The introduction by Victoria Goddard to *Work and Livelihoods: History, Ethnography and Models in Times of Crisis* (2017) opens up further interesting scenarios, starting with the crisis in large industrial sectors such as the steel industry, a process symbolized by the bankruptcy of Detroit City Hall in 2013. This process is also identifiable in the move of the central production of US General Motors from the north of the United States to Tennessee (Kasmir 2014), and can be similarly traced easily for the Italian case, via the story of Turin and the decline of the local FIAT Mirafiori plant, which followed the internal relocation with the construction of the Melfi plant in 1993, until the international merger between FIAT and Chrysler in 2014 (D'Aloisio 2003, 2014, 2016, 2017). In view of the enormous changes in the production, work and assets of global capitalism that these sites are both an effect and a cause of, Goddard draws attention to the aspects of continuity in the changing processes, as well as break points, and how the 'old' can recur and remain in the 'new'. In essence, it is difficult to reduce the current issue to the decline of industry, and, vice versa, it is more profitable in Goddard's view (and for previous authors) to pay attention to the coexistence of different forms of inclusion and translation of the dominant capitalist forms: this is because 'it is clear that globalized production strategies have uneven outcomes, producing a complex landscape consisting of different forms of production and particular concentrations of economic activity' (Goddard 2017: 3).

It is beyond the scope of this volume to analyse the changes that occurred globally in terms of employment due to technological innovation, yet a reflection on the consequences of this matter on the global structure of social class is necessary. As noted by James Carrier and Don Kalb, the category of class calls for a very strong redefinition, first because, contrary to a conventional notion of class:

> Exchanges between classes are not restricted to the transaction of labor power and pay. They also include rent for the use of property of various sorts, most obviously housing and land, but also patents or even money (in the form of interest), as well as the purchase of commodities produced by labor power for the profit of the owners of capital. (Carrier and Kalb 2015: 2)

Second, class is increasingly associated with kinship, gender, race and ethnicity, which has produced a proliferation of class-structured social domains that are not always reducible to the categories of income, education and occupational status. The idea of Kalb's regarding the disclaimer of the class category is not independent from a cognitive distortion, due to the hegemony of the Western middle class and the success of capitalism that seems to transcend it. Conversely, Kalb thinks that the long opposition between practice and structure, and between the local and the global situations, has been the most important mistake responsible for separating 'the intimate ethnography of what it means to be human and the big historical process' (Kalb 2015: 11). Instead of the old notion of class, he prefers to talk about a class emerging from class struggles, an interesting point of view that recalls – in our opinion – the role of ethnographic fieldwork capable of outlining several specific situations of class structuring.

With regard to the transformation of work that is directly dependent on technologies, which is one of the areas of focus in our case studies, there is a vast literature. From the metamorphosis of work by André Gorz (1964) to the end of work as proposed by Jeremy Rifkin (1994), which was subsequently taken up by Ulrich Beck (1999) in his idea of the end of traditional working practices, many authors have described, in more or less apocalyptic terms, transformations that evoked the objective reduction of manufacturing work. Furthermore, they evoked scenarios that had become more noticeable at the turn of the twenty-first century and during the 2007/2008 crisis. In brief, they are as follows: the need to free work from the paradigm of cumulative economic growth (Latouche 2006); the possibility of a capitalism paradoxically 'without work' (Beck 2000), in reference to a society that is increasingly divided between holders and non-holders of a job, which also has serious consequences for democratic coexistence; and finally the appearance of a new ideal type of worker, the flexible man, effectively described by Richard Sennett (1998).

Beyond these more or less catastrophic hypotheses, in 2015 the International Labour Organization (ILO), the UN agency responsible for the study and control of work transformation, already noted that in 180 countries with different levels of development analysed, less than a quarter of job contracts were stable and full-time (ILO 2015: 5). Moreover, the trend seemed to continue and it was assumed that, in the coming years, the level of stable labour would have represented an even lower fraction of the total. This data produced new worries, since a reduction in the number of jobs corresponds in the widespread opinion of economists to the risk of a further slowdown in the demand for global goods, due to the fact that workers are the most consumer-friendly category, and so, as a consequence, a further slowdown in the demand for labour could be generated; the danger, clearly, was to perpetuate the negative traits that characterized the global economy in the period following the 2007/2008 crisis.[2]

In this regard, what happened in the twentieth century can be defined, in the words of the Italian sociologist Aris Accornero (2000: 145), as 'the missing work'. According to Accornero, this is the real collapse of the production model and worker profile that characterized the twentieth century, which has produced an almost constant increase in unemployment not only in Europe and the United States, but also in Japan. Well-known processes, such as the financialization of businesses, the expansion of the stock market, the increase in competition and the radical change in protection and the representation of work, have made the constraints and margins of employment more labile; the result is, on the one hand, the increased risk of losing one's job, and, on the other hand, the reduction in laws to protect workers. The most nefarious effects of these processes are felt in the precariousness of work, which has recently increased especially in Europe, but also in what can be defined as pulverization: a multiplicity of forms and contracts that are more difficult to control through legislative protection.

Between work that is lacking and work that is transformed, perhaps the most effective synthesis is given as three parallel processes, as follows: a traditional type of work is moving away from both the European and American continents, based on the shifting of much manufacturing to countries with lower labour costs, and the corresponding expansion of services and the tertiary sector. New jobs arrive with foreign immigration, which often cover areas in which the natives or locals no longer commit themselves (from agricultural labourers to carers for the elderly, to cite just two examples common in Europe). Finally, there is work that remains and that is invested with extensive restructuring processes, in its techniques, purposes, contents and quantitative and qualitative composition (Negrelli 2013). It is also important to add that economic migration towards industrialized countries is increasingly characterized by gender, according to three characteristic trends: the growing feminization of the global workforce; the increase of women working in the informal or more dangerous sectors of the economy; and the increase of women migrating to occupy the service sector in industrialized countries (Sherif Trask 2014: 29; Desai 2010).

In relation to the three categories mentioned above, the distinctive feature of contemporary work therefore appears to be precariousness, which has been analysed recently by Guy Standing, who poses the problem of the nature, causes and outcomes of the creation of a vast number of precarious workers, a true global class in progress (Standing 2011). First of all, Standing clarifies the definition of a category that can be vague and generic, arguing that it is not just casual or poor workers, or workers without protection, while the condition of total lack of control over one's work does not seem sufficient either. More precisely, Standing believes that precarious workers should be understood as those who lack the seven types of occupational safety that social democratic parties and trade unions had prioritized in the postwar period for the working class.[3] Overall, what is missing from the category of precarious workers is professional identity, a lack of belonging to a working community, established practices and a shared memory, alongside a growing sense of alienation and exploitation in the fulfilment of their tasks. This is a condition Accornero

(2000) has effectively encapsulated in the expression 'small-w work', as opposed to typical twentieth-century work: wage-earning, productive and manufacturing, which founded an ethic and an ideology, as well as the status system. This is a form of work that has therefore multiplied in terms of its variety, which has decreased in its overall availability and is more disjointed in its lifespan, with a shorter amount of time necessary for many activities, even if not all people work fewer hours than before. Alongside this, it should also be remembered that work and employment do not necessarily prevent poverty, according to a growing relationship in recent years in EU countries (Ehrenreich 2001; Saraceno 2015).[4]

From the perspective of organizations, and therefore of the establishment, the hallmark of contemporary work appears instead as flexibility. According to the Italian sociologist Luciano Gallino, flexibility is a real keyword, which in recent years has been used in economic research, in speeches and announcements from the Bank of Italy, in economic newspapers and in other sources (Gallino 2007, 2012, 2014). This is obviously not a neutral term, since it implies a precise vision of work, which directs policies on the subject and which, as mentioned above, ends up being similar but politically opposite to the term 'precariousness'; however, before investigating the nefarious effects of the link between flexibility and precarity, it is worth remembering that there are opposing perspectives – between workers that benefit from flexibility and workers that don't – as discussed in the aforementioned essay by Sennett (2000).

In contrast to routine, flexibility is expressed in our contemporaneity, according to Sennett (1998), in three substantial elements: discontinuous reinvention of institutions, flexible specialization of production and concentration of power without centralization. At the individual level, the characteristics of flexibility materialize in the ability to abandon one's own past, in self-confidence and also a strong disposition to accept job fragmentation. However, according to Sennett, it is possible to find in flexibility a new culture of risk (which flexibility necessarily entails), which enhances movement, considers stability to have negative economic and career repercussions, and resorts to movement as a continuous search for new opportunities. This situation, which is perhaps commonplace in the US labour market, is not properly representative of the Italian case, as labour mobility has never been at the core of labour legislation.

According to Ronald Dore, the issue of flexibility, regardless of the positive or negative connotation that one wishes to attribute to it, must be traced back, at least in English-speaking countries and in particular in the United Kingdom, to a collective desire for it as a means to oppose the protection practices operated by the trade unions (Dore 2004). Dore also points out that at least since the 1980s, we must distinguish between internal flexibility and external flexibility: the latter refers to allocative efficiency, achieved through the greater freedom of companies to hire and fire employees, which offers the possibility of downsizing the workforce at minimal cost and, at the same time, the free search for the desired skills in the labour market; the former refers to productive efficiency, which is to improve the organization, to lead to innovation and to increase the efficiency of work. A relevant consequence of this distinction, which opens up a broad debate on the possibility of reconciliation between the two types of flexibility, is a compromise solution, so to speak, that sees companies engaged in creating a core of reliable workers with distinctive enterprise skills and who have been subjected to long training schemes; conversely, there would also be a wide range of functions that require minimal training, with little specific knowledge, for which full-time and long-term jobs are not needed and where it is obviously possible to contain costs (Dore 2004). This solution therefore implies the effect of the polarization of labour, from the moment that the companies use the flexibilization of work as an element in the response to the transformations in the market.

The anthropological focus of this volume is not on the economic issues of the crisis or on proposing possible solutions; rather, it intends to explore the meaning and the (ethical) value of work, to discuss the extent to which work is (or is not) still able to effectively contribute to building and shaping the subjectivities and social identities of men and women, as new forms of production and consumption are emerging, and to think about the structure of roles and tasks in this particular phase of capitalism.

Taking advantage of these reflections, in this work we aim to provide an overview of some case studies of Italian industrial production, their situation during the crisis of 2007/2008 and the strategies of resistance and transformation implemented by the protagonists – male and female workers, entrepreneurs, families linked to the companies, cities and local populations involved in the crises – which together gave rise to specific and original local reorganizations. Special attention has been paid to the industrial districts, systems of organized production which principally developed in north and central Italy.

Difficult Economic Conjuncture and Systemic Crisis in the Made in Italy Industrial Districts

As explained above, a lot of attention has been paid to the transformations of industrial capitalism into more flexible forms of production. Italian capitalism has provided some interesting insights on this subject because it encompasses different and yet intertwined systems of production that have converged towards flexibility. The 'mix' of an informal economy, petty commodity production and mass production in one small region or even a single location attracted the attention of geographers, sociologists, economists and eventually some anthropologists. Thus, it is not accidental that the majority of the chapters in this volume contribute to the anthropological literature by focusing on local production systems.

These local production systems received international recognition in the late 1970s, when the sociologist Arnaldo Bagnasco (1977) coined the well-known term 'the Three Italies'. He proposed a threefold model of Italian development: the 'first' Italy of the industrial triangle (Milan-Turin-Genoa) characterized by the presence of large and vertically integrated factories; the 'second' Italy of the less developed south; and the 'third Italy', former rural areas of northeastern and central Italy that experienced rapid social and economic development due to the mushrooming of small-sized and family firms practising subcontracting and flexible production – a form of production organization quite distinct from the Fordist model of production, in which large vertically integrated firms were dominant. In the same period, two Italian economists, Giacomo Becattini (1978, 1986) and Sebastiano Brusco (1986, 1989), provided empirical evidence of spatial clustering of small firms in Tuscany and Emilia-Romagna respectively. They proposed an explanatory model of the 'third Italy' that bore a strong resemblance to the organization of production described by Alfred Marshall (1919, 1920) in some areas of England: the industrial district. Marshall noticed that commodity production could take place through the division of labour in large factories, as well as by distributing each step of production in localized small firms and workshops. Becattini borrowed the term and defined it 'a socio-territorial entity which is characterised by the active presence of both a community of people and a population of firms in one naturally and historically bounded area' (1990: 38). In their model of the Third Italy, both Becattini and Brusco were well aware that in order to understand the economic efficiency of these localized production models, social and cultural categories had to be included in their analysis. Local outsourcing, flexible arrangements and know-how were embedded in the intricacy of information networks, encouraged by social proximity between entrepreneurs and workers, and by self-organizing forms of local cooperation with relatives and acquaintances.

These pioneering studies catalysed the attention of scholars from different quarters, who speculated at length about the organizational and technological changes that took place in Italian industrial capitalism and that contributed so much to the market success of the so-called Made in Italy production.

Michael Piore and Charles Sabel (1984) examined the regional economies of the Third Italy to argue that craft production supported by technological development and organizational innovation proved to be an effective alternative to mass production. In their analysis, the revival of craft production-cum-computerized machinery was an indication that a solution was about to be found for the crisis of Fordism and mass production. They suggested that the transition to flexible processes of specialization and decentralization of production in some Western economies, resulting in the creation of smaller productive units, represented the 'second industrial divide' in the history of industrialization, whereas the first divide occurred in the nineteenth century when 'the emergence of mass-production technologies – in Great Britain and then in the United States – limited the growth of less rigid manufacturing technologies' (Piore and Sabel 1984: 5). Thus, according to these authors, the second industrial divide partially reversed the technological process that favoured mass production at the expense of craft production in the nineteenth century. In their optimistic view, the skilled worker and labour autonomy, which had been lost in the first transition, would be reconstituted under the new technological conditions.

Others, such as Scott Lash and John Urry (1987), viewed the crisis of capitalism in a different way. They distinguished between an epoch of 'organized capitalism' and a new era of 'disorganized' capitalism, emphasizing not only the economic aspects of this transition but also wider social and cultural changes. According to their view, the Italian industrial districts are an example of disorganized capitalism; they developed as large factories declined and underwent major restructuring, and flexible and deregulated forms of work organization were increasingly implemented in small workshops. David Harvey (1989, 1991, 2005) theorized in Marxist terms the transition from Fordism to a new regime of 'flexible accumulation' regulated by neoliberal policies, stressing the corporate attempt to regain full control over the labour process through the geographical relocation of industrial production. An analogous position was held by the regulation school (Lipietz 1992; Jessop 1992, 2003), which viewed capitalism as a crisis-ridden economic system requiring modes of regulation to sustain it and limit its inherent structural and conjunctural contradictions. Thus, for the regulationists, the current post-Fordism phase – neoliberalism – is a new hegemonic regime of accumulation emerging from the crisis of Fordism during the 1970s and 1980s, after a period of intensive accumulation and mass production. Contrary to Piore and Sabel's view, this new phase of capitalism 'involves the subordination of small and medium enterprises to new forms of monopolistic competition on a global scale' (Jessop 2003: 260).

Another critical, albeit different, position was held by scholars such as Anna Pollert (1988, 1991) and Ash Amin (1989), who raised critical questions about this alleged new phase of post-Fordist production much earlier than any other scholar. Pollert in particular argued that the debate on the contemporary restructuring of capitalist economies created a 'new orthodoxy of flexibility', which is a conflation of meanings, a single typology on a diverse range of social realities:

> The implication of a radical break from the past, in the preoccupation with newness and change and the absence of a historical perspective on the significance of work and labour market flexibility in previous periods, has consolidated a nostalgic picture of past stability and harmony and future stability and growth based on flexibility. (Pollert 1991: 3–4)

The 'fetish of flexibility', as Pollert calls it, seems to have reached an overarching consensus, which emerges clearly in the present relentless commitment of nation-states to search for labour-market flexibility. However, flexible arrangements are not a novelty, as Alfred Marshall had documented; moreover, they seem to raise various concerns in terms of labour exploitation and disguising new rigidities in gender relations (Gibson-Graham 2006). This is an issue that has seldom been fully explored in the industrial district literature, with some noticeable exceptions in anthropology (Yanagisako 2002).

The criticism by these scholars is relevant to our discussion as they foresaw some of the emerging critical issues that will be examined in this volume. We began by presenting an almost idyllic, perfectly functional image of the Italian model of small-scale production, as illustrated by Piore and Sabel's work, and we concluded by mentioning critical approaches that compellingly challenge a much of the mythology of competitiveness, cooperation and social stability embodied in the industrial districts. Their economic success contributed to portraying them as a highly functional model of production to measure against others, and at the same time it blurred and obscured faults and contradictions that only the recent crisis has managed to bring to the fore. Indeed, an early important contribution to this critique has been Michael Blim's *Made in Italy* (1990), an ethnographic work on the emergence of small-scale industrialization in the Italian region of Marche. Blim clearly suggested that this model of capitalism, which has become 'the darling of neo-liberal development theory' (1990: 3), offers a rather mixed view, with the spectre of economic decline always present. His chapter in this volume seems to confirm his early foresight, as we will illustrate shortly. On the whole, further signs of economic decline and significant transformation in the social setting of the industrial districts became apparent at the turn of the millennium (Whitford 2001; Ghezzi and Mingione 2003; Hadjimichalis 2006). Indeed, since Bagnasco published his provocative work, much has changed in all three Italies. Areas of localized production are widespread throughout Italy, from north to south, like a fragmented patchwork; large factories have been shut down, downsized and relocated to the Mezzogiorno (such as the FIAT plant at Melfi) or abroad; family enterprises and self-employment are persistently dynamic, but seem to have lost part of their enterprising vitality. And finally, the argument that industrial districts are 'communities of people', homogeneous systems of values and views, with widespread social consensus is no longer tenable, as all of the contributions to this volume seem to imply.

All of the chapters in this volume on the industrial districts make the argument that the recent economic downturn was not simply the manifestation of the worst economic crisis since the Second World War. What on the surface appeared to be prolonged economic crisis was actually a crisis of a different kind. The analysis that the authors have carried out in their own case studies indicates a consistently convergent path towards a systemic crisis. In other words, the transformations that have occurred and are still occurring suggest a more complex picture that these contributions have just begun to outline.

To categorize the crisis as 'systemic' is not just a mere question of semantics. This term allows us to consider the interdependence of various elements and the frailty, rather than the resilience, of the system when one or more of these elements falls apart. The crises that periodically hit the empirical contexts discussed in this volume have left visible marks or, rather, scars that are reflected in the ambivalence of small enterprising households towards precisely the very craft production that receives so much praise from a number of scholars. Indeed, the very idea of labour as an individual asset upon which industrial districts founded their economic prosperity has been called into question principally by those who contributed to shaping that same idea and benefited from it. Work is now imagined in a wider and precarious global economy, and not simply embedded in the local territory or conceptualized within the boundaries of the family. The dislike and distrust of a future following in the footsteps of and the same trade as one's parents do not cause dismay in the household, but nonetheless are creating a 'transitional vacuum' and a future loaded with uncertainties. This same sense of uncertainty is similarly perceived among employees. The increasing cross-boundary transactions of coveted locally produced commodities have exposed the industrial districts to international capital that has no links to the territory. This capital may indeed breathe new life into mature sectors, but it also raises some concerns. The new management of these factories is not compelled to establish moral obligations with the local labour force; therefore, as a trade unionist argues in Zanotelli's chapter, the recourse to lay-offs has turned into an impersonal procedure, whereas in the case of autochthonous employers, the lay-offs of their workers would be experienced as a painful choice and as a last resort after everything else has failed. By the same token, the new management of these firms may alter the network of the local suppliers to establish new forms of labour exploitation and precarious work.

The emergence of new leaders among the most successful medium-sized Italian firms in the industrial districts is also causing remarkable changes in the local economy. Some of these firms, which are well known in the global market, have created their own global networks, bypassing the structural organization of the industrial district. Others, by contrast, have chosen not to renounce local resources in terms of knowledge, skilled workers and outsourcing in general; however, in order to remain competitive, they have imposed their own business model based on strong investments in technology and managerial resources. Hence, it is likely that this kind of endogenous reorganization has triggered other restructuring processes as far as labour is concerned – that is, work precarity and flexibility. Following this reorganization undertaken by the industrial districts, the embeddedness that had characterized the older system of production – then an essential ingredient of competitiveness and development – is now being called into question by the new industry leaders.

As a result of these recent changes, there seem to be two major forms of labour precarity in the current Italian capitalist model. The first is the precarity generated in the manufacturing industry, which has affected traditional forms of occupation, such as craft labour in the industrial districts and elsewhere. Skilled labour that was achieved through continuous working experience is now becoming increasingly jeopardized by fragmented work experiences and precarious job positions. The second is the precarity regarding intangible (i.e. cognitive and linguistic) production that is widespread in the flexible environment of the service industry of large urban centres, as discussed by Fumagalli in this volume. These new jobs, which are inherently precarious, have begun to spread among highly educated freelancers and professional workers following the organizational transformations of biocognitive capitalism. In both cases, organizational and technological innovation leads to various forms of (self-) exploitation.

The crisis in craft production means not only that the younger generations are no longer committed to the manufacturing sector, but also that the transmission of skills and know-how, and consequently the reproduction of a skilled labour force, is undermined. The cases of the jewellery district in Valenza and the furniture district in Brianza discussed in this volume are emblematic of this, as both regional economies are experiencing a 'generational vacuum'. Since both entrepreneurs and the skilled labour force are ageing, various attempts to revive vocational training and apprenticeship have been made. Yet, the responsiveness of local institutional and private actors has been sporadic and uneven in its effects due to a lack of collective and synergic actions between the local/regional and the national levels. The crisis of apprenticeship also inhibits the potential long-term beneficial effects of subsidies and tax exemptions introduced as incentives to stimulate entrepreneurial activities and start-ups; these merely become palliative measures, given that craft production can hardly survive without the transfer of craftsmanship to the younger generations of workers and artisans. In conclusion, what the ethnographic accounts in this volume have documented is that Italian industrial districts, despite having gained wide currency among scholars who saw them a decisive remedy to the crisis of Fordist mass production, have become themselves a source of instability. As a result of the pressure of recurrent economic crises, they show vulnerabilities and contradictions that we interpret as warning signs of a systemic crisis.

Interpreting the Crisis and Its Effects: Crisis of Presence and 'Horizons of Redemption'

Italian anthropological studies on work and enterprise (c.f. *anthropologie de l'entreprise* in France) have arrived much later than their European counterparts, due to the prevalent folkloric orientation recalled and analysed by Italian studies on the history of anthropology (Fabietti 2001; Signorelli 2011). However, even within the line of folkloristic study, we must remember that there is a tradition of research that has analysed not only the craft trades, but also the objects and artefacts of the popular farming world: this is the perspective of the studies of so-called 'material culture', which constituted a specific feature of Italian folklore compared to other European countries (Cirese 1973). However, this perspective has privileged material work tools, and therefore products, in their material and symbolic functions, rather than the production processes, and is far from being a perspective on the specific dynamics of the work itself. Other studies have focused specifically on farming and artisanal work, examining material, social and symbolic aspects in specific historical-cultural contexts, such as Sardinia (Angioni 1986, 2003) and, in a more dynamic perspective oriented towards processes of transformation, there are those of Papa (1985) on the production of bread and olive oil in the Umbria region.

In Italy at the end of the 1990s, Papa's *Anthropology of the Enterprise* (*Antropologia dell'impresa*, 1999) introduced a different perspective that tried to define, through the criticism but also the synthesis of different international theoretical perspectives, an approach to enterprise as an anthropological object of study. From this viewpoint, the company has been considered above all as a point of intersection of more complex convergent dynamics. This perspective, inspired by authors such as Miller (1997) and Strating (1998) and following their research at the end of the 1990s on the island of Trinidad and on the flower industry in Rijnsburg in the Netherlands respectively, tried to overcome the idea of studying the local variations of a supposed model of global capitalism – fruit, in Papa's view, of an ethnocentric vision of the homogenous spread of Western capitalism.

In recent decades, anthropological research aimed at industrial work has multiplied in Italy, aided by the contribution of foreign scholars in various sectors: crafts and big industry (Blim 1990; Yanagisako 2002; D'Aloisio 2003, 2014, 2017; Ghezzi 2007; Carosso and Ghezzi 2015; India 2017), but also in sectors of Italian labour that expatriate in the new global productive chain (Redini 2008), and also in relation to the work of migrants, who, conversely, arrive in Italy, placing themselves in various sectors of production of goods and services (Miranda 2008; Ceschi 2007; Ceschi and Giangaspero 2009; Riccio 2007). Italian studies focused on work in extra-national contexts should also be mentioned (Viti 2007; Vignato 2010). In all these studies, from different theoretical perspectives, the outflow from merely local contexts prevails, and so does the search for underlying global logics, with much attention being paid to intersections, syncretisms and global dynamics.

The ethnographies that make up this volume analyse the transformations resulting from the economic crisis, and all transcend local contexts, linking to the global scenarios in which the processes of production and work are inserted, and in which the locally developed strategies make it possible to trace similarities and differences. The transversal and underlying focus, even within the different theoretical perspectives adopted by the authors in different geographical and productive areas, relates to some fundamental points:

- the change in the anthropological meaning of work, that is, the meaning and value that work takes on in the experience and the daily life of the subjects, following the changed conditions of the companies in the global framework; the effects of this change on the tasks, the contents of work, the job role, the status connected to work and the perception/self-representation elaborated by the workers, but also on social contexts, often identified or strongly connoted by local industrial productions (e.g. the so-called gold city of Valenza);
- the conditions of cultural and existential crisis, which result from the economic crisis of 2007/2008; the transformation of work related to its reduction, disappearance or precariousness, which are read from the anthropological point of view using the concept of the 'crisis of presence', elaborated upon by Ernesto de Martino in his research in southern Italy in the 1940s; connected to this, the construction of a possible 'horizon of redemption', a concept also elaborated upon by de Martino, which indicates a strategy for the search for new values capable of overcoming a distressing present and transcending the contingent situation, fiercely maintaining one's own position in history and at the same time prefiguring oneself in future projects. In the case of the economic crisis, the 'crisis of presence' is generated by the weakening or loss of job positions in the face of economic constraints, in the impossibility of main-

taining companies handed down from generation to generation; as a consequence, the 'horizons of redemption' indicate the effort by social actors to find ways out and a new position from which to restore their presence in history;

- subsistence strategies, or strategies that the subjects are able to make use of in order to resist the crisis, both in material and in relational terms, with explicit reference to the notion outlined by Narotzky (1997);
- finally, all the research contained in the volume reiterates the role of ethnographic methodology, particularly to analyse the different configurations that the capitalist model and its transformations take on in local contexts. Ethnography also helps us in capturing minute and daily aspects of the changes induced by the crisis in the lives of the subjects, and the problematic local/global connections, both in the sense of the repercussions of global processes on everyday existence and, in the opposite direction, the elaboration of responses and reactions – that is, as we have said, the activation of possible strategies of resistance, reorganization and overcoming, which brings us back to the problem of the construction of new horizons of redemption.

In relation to the last point in this list, the ethnographic methodology allows us to analyse in depth and bring to light the new meanings of work, which correspond to profound transformations of the living conditions of workers (and also entrepreneurs), of their identity and of the cultural horizons of present and future life. Contemporary ethnography, which is at the centre of a great debate that is beyond the scope of this discussion given here, is increasingly oriented towards multilocated collocations, critical and self-critical positions, and dialogic and self-reflective perspectives, which have moved away from a holistic and objectifying perspective which is by now completely impractical given the fluid and diffused situations of contemporary conditions. [5]

In the chapters presented in this volume, the economic crisis is analysed in its various aspects: the reduction or disappearance of work (Ghezzi and D'Aloisio), the exacerbation towards increasingly oppressive and exhausting working conditions (Bogani) and the loss and transformation of entrepreneurial activities (Fontefrancesco, Blim and Zanotelli). Within the various situations, the discussion can be linked to a common category: a new, general appearance of the crisis of presence. This conceptual expression was coined by Ernesto de Martino (1948, 1959, 2002; de Martino and Zinn 2005), during his research in southern Italy during the 1950s. It was a historical condition lived and experienced by agricultural workers in southern Italy (which can be extended to the populations of the various 'Souths' of the world studied by ethnologists), who lived on the margins of national socioeconomic development after the Second World War, when modernization entered the Italian peninsula at different speeds and with different results in its various areas. The crisis of presence is conceived by de Martino as a historical condition, which was collective and never individual in its nature, and was generated by the material and psychological misery that narrowed the possibility for people to act on negative events and to maintain their own presence. In this regard, Crapanzano explains: 'The crisis of presence refers to a sense of not being there (*esserci, daisen* in Heidegger's sense), yes, of death but also of loss, loss of subjectivity, vulnerability, alienation, dissociation, being out of control – overwhelmed if you will, to the point of extinction. Individuals in crisis lose their sense of dynamic relationship with the world around them and therefore of themselves and their intentional capacity, with their place in history' (Crapanzano 2005: ix).[6]

The protagonists of the crisis of presence in the studies conducted here are social subjects who have experienced a new condition of precarity and insecurity, which affects work starting with the impossibility of maintaining an occupation and of taking home a steady income; thus, the crisis strikes at the certainty of one's identity throughout, from one's working life to one's larger existence, as well as across generations, through the transmission of entrepreneurial activities and skills from parents to children. This represents a new condition of the impossibility of being in the world and therefore of producing contrasting actions; a new risk of cultural chaos, linked not only to the ongoing economic crisis, but also to the increasingly difficulty of subjects to understand the causes and how to control them.

In the first paragraph of this chapter we discussed the crisis and its consequences in the current neoliberal scenario, but two aspects are worth mentioning again briefly: the increasingly elusive and uncontrollable character of productive and working dynamics in the global scenario, and the breaking of the so-called 'Fordist pact' in terms of its characteristics of protection and labour guarantees. The current phase of the industrial revolution, according to Peter Marsh (2012), leads to shorter production cycles, fragmented and dislocated in various areas of the globe, to supply increasingly narrow and specialized groups of consumers. In this scenario, it becomes ever more difficult for manufacturing companies to establish not only the different locations where it is most appropriate to produce, but also, as pointed out by other authors, which new indicators will be attractors for businesses locations. This takes place alongside a passage from mere territorial and labour resources to new resources such as new skills, localization of financial companies and spin-offs (Dore 2004; Moretti 2013). In this scenario, the ability to control and even to know one's working destiny is reduced for many categories of workers, while the continuous exposure to contingent and uncontrollable situations makes workers vulnerable to increasing risks and precariousness. On these bases, a condition of the crisis of presence takes root in the fragmentation of work processes at the global level, in their more rapid and intense delocalization and relocation, in the reduction of trade union protections and in the intervention of the state in limiting or mitigating these processes, as some studies on the global dislocation of capital and labour have demonstrated (Harvey and Krohn-Hansen 2018).

This crisis of presence is then articulated in situations such as the inability to assert one's own rights or to establish one's skills, work commitment and hard work; even in the difficulty of keeping a job and in the loss of social capital and skills. Among family businesses, the crisis of presence manifests itself in the loss of the intergenerational transmission of companies, which makes continuation no longer possible in the case of the small craft industries described in the book.

In addition, another factor contributes to determining a widespread crisis of presence in contemporary workers: the end of what the economist Andrea Fumagalli has effectively described as the golden rule of the Fordist social compromise (Fumagalli 2013, 2015; Fumagalli and Morini 2013). In other words, the core of the Fordist era had introduced a new, different view of wages, not as a mere cost to be reduced and therefore to increase profits, but as one of the main components of final consumption demand. The simultaneous growth of profits and wages, typical of the Fordist phase, also represented the substantial regulatory model, so that the permanent employment contract entailed the submission of the worker to the needs of production and technology, but in exchange guaranteed stability, putting an end to the precarity of income which was typical of the pre-Fordist phase. It is not difficult to deduce that, starting from so-called post-Fordism, this mutual link has failed, instead triggering the phase that Fumagalli defines as 'cognitive biocapitalism', connoted by two main processes. The first is characterized by the fact that the social relationship of capital moves away from the relationship between the labour force and machines to that between mind and body, in which the whole life of individuals, their cognitive-relational capacity, becomes capitalizable. The second process consists of the increasingly mobile and dispersed nature of work, which increases precariousness to the point where it becomes a pervasive and generalized condition of life (Fumagalli 2011). Starting from these characteristics of precariousness, coupled with the increasing absorption of the lifetimes and of the intellectual and relational faculties of workers, we can speak of a crisis of presence, corroborated by the fact that this growing submission of the worker to the new rules of production is no longer accompanied by the certainties of the Fordist era.

As is typical of a crisis of presence, it becomes necessary to search for new horizons of values, designed to outline a possibility of overcoming the criticality of the present and opening up new avenues towards existential redemption. According to de Martino, and as noted by Signorelli, the horizon of redemption is not to be found only in the use of magical-religious rituals, such as among the Australian Aborigines or the agricultural workers of southern Italy: 'at its highest level of abstraction the scheme can be applied to study the dynamics of crisis and redemption in practically any society' (Signorelli 2015: 84). According to Signorelli, although the symbolic universes produced so far have been mostly magical-religious in form, and in any case metahistorical, this does not exclude the notion that in today's societies, which are predominantly secularized, it could be different. The overcoming of negative events and the need to find new cultural instruments to tackle the crisis can be achieved using other means, such as political engagement, economic resources and leisure distractions. According to de Martino, Signorelli remarks, 'the control of the negative is achieved by using even symbolic constructions based, however, on the immanence of values and not on the transcendence of powers' (ibid.: 88).[7]

A final reflection regards subsistence strategies, a concept borrowed from Susana Narotzky and identified as a useful category that summarizes and explains the actions and reactions put in place to deal with the crisis at various levels and in different situations by the protagonists of the ethnographies presented here. It is indeed the daily subsistence strategies, alongside and mixed with the search for new points of reference, which seek to reintegrate the presence shaken by the crisis. Narotzky has remarked that the boundary between productive and reproductive work is permeable. As voluntary organizations or leisure activities contribute to social welfare activities, the category of work must also be extended outside the narrow field of employment (Narotzky 1997). Moreover, 'the "means of livelihood" thesis points out how people manage to get the necessities of life. Formal, market-mediated economic relations such as employment and informal, non-market systems for getting hold of resources are considered on an equal methodological standing' (ibid.: 39), and 'by focusing on how people manage to earn a living, in fact, "production" has become an epiphenomenon of "reproduction" processes ... The "means of livelihoods" framework enriches our understanding of economic processes and focuses on human agents and their everyday social relations in a daily struggle for livelihood' (ibid.: 40).

More recently, with explicit reference to the political-institutional crisis that has accompanied the current economic crisis, Narotzky observes the new moral value of the demands of disadvantaged groups (above all the unemployed), starting from the Spanish case, but usefully applicable in other contexts. In substance, the classic demand by workers for a different economic policy seems to have been replaced by the demand for a new 'moral economy' (e.g. the demand for dignity in the collective Spanish protest movements), which protects citizens from corruption and speculation on a global scale, which in the general public opinion has been responsible for the current situation of increasing precarity and insecurity (Narotzky 2016). Although organized in different forms and still far from reaching a fully organized form, these demands are directed towards a new form of solidarity, in which the author sees new principles of global cohesion and aggregation.

From the perspective traced by Narotzky, it is evident how relationships of kinship, neighbourhood, forms of exchange and solidarity, generational transmissions and also informal relationships with institutions are instruments that act, moment by moment, to tackle, mitigate and manage the crisis. These strategies can reasonably be included in the progressive construction of a 'horizon of redemption', in de Martino's terms, just as the search for a new ethical cohesion and the appeal to dignity would seem to open new possibilities. Therefore, even these could be configured, in the terminology of de Martino used here, as the 'horizon of redemption', which evokes a system of culturally generated values, able to guarantee the possibility of going beyond the threatening condition of the present, and the possibility of transcending a critical phase, of overcoming negativity, of reconstructing a solidity of presence in real life. This means encountering a scenario in which companies, which are increasingly globalized, distribute their processes in different and distant contexts which increasingly escape the control of national policies, while at the same time becoming more difficult for scholars to analyse. However, this process increasingly conditions the lives of millions of people around the world.

The studies contained in this volume analyse some enterprises and the work processes within them, but also look at local contexts, conflicts and institutional synergies, which are sometimes lacking or absent, and at the social relations that the actors build inside and outside the companies. They also analyse the practices of transformation and adjustment, the systems of relationships and the values (both old and new) put in place by male and female workers, which clash with the economic and organizational transformations located within each context, the effects of which are felt in their daily lives.

The chapter by the economist Andrea Fumagalli in this book serves to add a different perspective beyond the anthropological one to explain the Italian situation, inasmuch as, according to the cases described, Italy seems to have weakened, or reduced, and almost squandered much of its industrial structure (Berta 2001; Bianco 2003; Gallino 2003). Fumagalli traces this balance and indicates the causes, using the skills of an expert on the transformation of contemporary capitalism and precarious work, and with the sensitivity that makes him willing to enter into a dialogue with other social sciences. This chapter therefore represents a useful analysis that summarizes the characteristics of precarious work in contemporary Italy and the lack of economic policies (but not investment, it is worth noting) intended to support businesses, and also clarifies the confusing and perhaps mystifying principle that has represented the flexibility of work as a sort of solution to all current industrial problems. Especially in Italy, this perspective has translated into a further thinning of the propulsive drive of the industrial sector and therefore into a vicious circle that flexibility produces in the overall economic system, reducing skills, technological change and innovation. All these characteristics, in addition to political instability, contributed to the delay with which Italy has faced the crisis. In line with the ethnographic research presented, Fumagalli's analysis also clarifies that behind these difficulties there are more remote issues, systemic aspects of Italian economy, which contribute to explaining why the Italian industrial apparatus has shown itself to be so clearly inadequate in terms of dealing with the current crisis.

In concluding this introduction, the anthropological viewpoint allows us to go deeper and to highlight some problematic aspects: the disappearance of tasks and competences, the redefinition of roles and new job duties, the breakdown of the generational transmission of knowledge and activities, the narrowing of the material horizons of life, and even more, the restriction of future expectations. Even the cases showing a more dynamic reaction to the crisis raise questions about the future of these areas and of the workers engaged in new tertiary activities. Subsistence strategies include the efforts of technological modernization, extending commercialization and the use of 'traditional' systems, such as parental support, but at the same time they show a distancing from familiar enterprise, encouraged by older generations, that leads towards the advanced tertiary sector described by Fumagalli: this new sector seems to be more dynamic and in greater expansion compared to manufacturing activities, which are now in a state of crisis that seems inexorable. Regarding the construction of horizons of redemption, the issue has become more complicated, more viscous and more uncertain. The protagonists of the ethnographies show the disappearance of values, the shortcomings of institutions, industrial policies and supranational bodies, the weakening of the trade unions and the increasing inaccessibility of the centres of power and decision-making to which they can seek recourse. Furthermore, the sense of work has radically changed, transforming an ethical system of commitment, sacrifice and skill (typical of the artisanal categories described here) into a new tertiary and cognitive form of work, with new and different characteristics.

So where are the horizons of redemption? Colin Crouch (2011) clearly indicates the importance of values and civil society as the only intermediaries against the neoliberal power of a few elitist groups (in his words, the power of the giants). This power has weakened the opposition between the state and the market, and the latter tends to increasingly coincide with companies. In this scenario, Crouch contends, the triangular confrontation between corporations, the state and the market no longer takes the form of a dialectically comparative triad, but leads to an overall loss of democracy that results in greater instability and insecurity: 'One consequence is that democracy is joined by the market as a kind of victim… One might talk of a triangular confrontation among state, market and the corporation, but I prefer "comfortable accommodation"' (Crouch 2011: ix, x). As such, loneliness, uncertainty and poor intervention possibilities often characterize the lives of workers and entrepreneurs.

'Caught in a situation defined by a distant economy power structure and pedagogic political technologies that advocate less social protection for the market's invisible hand, vulnerable people, being de-unionized and unable to forge a "class in itself" solidarity, become powerless to defend themselves and are unwittingly led to a grey area regarding their work identity and life trajectories' (Spyridakis 2018: 3). These traits characterize the protagonists of the changes in companies and work, and their attempts to face the crisis, which are analysed in this volume.

Fulvia D'Aloisio is Associate Professor of Cultural Anthropology at the University of Campania 'Luigi Vanvitelli'. Her research activities range from the anthropology of the enterprise and work to the processes of economic and cultural change, with a focus on the north-south gap. Her most important publications include *Donne in tuta amaranto. Trasformazioni del lavoro e mutamento culturale alla FIAT-SATA di Melfi* (Guerini & Associati, 2003) and *Vita di fabbrica. Cristina racconta il decollo e la crisi della FIAT-SATA di Melfi* (Franco Angeli, 2014).

Simone Ghezzi is Associate Professor of Economic Anthropology and Social/Cultural Anthropology at the University of Milano-Bicocca. He has carried out research on the informal economy, family businesses, urban kinship and more recently on Italian wood-carvers and artisan furniture. He is the author of *Etnografia storica dell'imprenditorialità in Brianza* (Franco Angeli, 2007) and recently co-authored *Antropologia della crisi. Prospettive etnografiche sulle trasformazioni del lavoro e dell'impresa in Italia* (L'Harmattan Italia 2016) with Fulvia D'Aloisio.

Notes

This introduction is the result of scientific dialogue between the two authors. Specifically, the first and third sections were written by Fulvia D'Aloisio; the second was written by Simone Ghezzi.

1. The data were reported by the daily newspaper *Repubblica – Economia e Finanza*, retrieved 14 February 2020 from www.repubblica.it/economia/2016/09/23/news/investimenti_produzione_industriale_crisi-148365722.
2. This is how the ILO expresses itself in its brief presentation of the results: 'The report shows that average incomes for workers in non-standard forms of work tend to be lower than is the case with stable jobs. Furthermore, the rise in informal employment, undeclared and temporary work arrangements, as well as involuntary part-time work, has contributed to the widening of income inequalities, which have been recorded in the majority of countries over the past two decades' (ILO 2015: 5).
3. The seven indicators identified by Standing are: job security (understood as the opportunity to receive adequate income), job safety (i.e. protection against dismissal), safety of the professional role, safety at work (from the risk of accidents or illness), the safety

of training at work, security of income (as a fixed or adequate income) and finally the security of representation (Standing 2011).

4. According to data provided by the European Commission in 2014, 9.3 per cent of 18–64 year-olds in the EU were living below the relative poverty level in 2012 (up from 8.5 per cent in 2008). The distribution of these employees in EU countries is as follows: about 4 per cent in Finland and Belgium, about 5 per cent in Austria, the Czech Republic and the Netherlands, about 13 per cent in Spain and Italy, 15 per cent in Greece and 19 per cent in Romania (Saraceno 2015: 51). The book *Nickel and Dimed: On (Not) Getting by America*, by American journalist Barbara Ehrenreich (2001), is a report of the direct experience of exploited workers and low-paid jobs that the author undertook for about two years, providing an acute and detailed account.
5. After the well-known fracture made by the Santa Fe seminar, only some contributions to the recent debate on ethnography (such as Piasere 2002) are mentioned here: Robben and Sluka 2006; Gallini and Satta 2007; De Lauri and Achilli 2008; Faubion and Marcus 2009; Hannerz 2010; Matera 2015.
6. We are referring to the introduction by Vincent Crapanzano in the English edition of de Martino's masterpiece *The Land of Remorse*, translated by Dorothy Zinn (2005).
7. Colin Crouch identifies five types of groups that in civil society are inspired by values able to hypothetically counteract the dominance of the company and the market: first, political parties, then religions, opinion groups (which direct opinion campaigns, not always and not only against large companies), volunteering groups and finally the professions, with their respective professional ethics often opposed to the logic of profit maximization. Organized in a civil society as a whole alternative to the market, the author sees in these groups a useful bulwark that, notwithstanding conflicts of interests, can contribute to act in the interstices of power, mitigating 'the power of the giants' (Crouch 2011: 144–61).

References

Accornero, A. 2000. *Era il secolo del lavoro. Come era e come cambia il grande protagonista del '900*. Bologna: Il Mulino.

Amin, A. 1989. 'Flexible Specialisation and Small Firms in Italy: Myths and Realities', *Antipode* 21(1): 13–34.

Angioni, G. 1986. *Il sapere della mano: Saggi di Antropologia del lavoro*. Palermo: Sellerio.

———. 2003. *Sa laurera. Il lavoro contadino in Sardegna*. Nuoro: Il Maestrale.

Bagnasco, A. 1977. *Tre Italie. La problematica territoriale dello sviluppo italiano*. Bologna: Il Mulino.

Becattini, G. 1978. 'The Development of Light Industry in Tuscany: An Interpretation', *Economic Notes* 7(1): 107–23.

———. 1986. 'Small Firms and Industrial Districts: The Experience of Italy', *Economia Internazionale* 39(2–4): 98–103.

———. 1990. 'The Marshallian Industrial District as a Socio-economic Notion', in F. Pyke, G. Becattini and W. Sengenberger (eds), *Industrial Districts and Inter-firm Co-operation in Italy*. Geneva: ILO, pp. 37–51.

Beck, U. 1999. *The Brave New World of Work*. Cambridge: Polity Press.

———. 2000. *Il lavoro nell'epoca della fine del lavoro. Tramonto delle sicurezze e nuovo impegno civile*. Turin: Einaudi.

Berta, G. 2001. *L'Italia delle fabbriche. La parabola dell'industrialismo nel Novecento*. Bologna: Il Mulino.

Bianco, M. 2003. *L'industria italiana. Numeri, peculiarità, politiche della nostra economia industriale*. Bologna: Il Mulino.
Blim, M. 1990. *Made in Italy: Small-Scale Industrialization and Its Consequences*. New York: Praeger.
Brusco, S. 1986. 'Small Firms and Industrial Districts: The Experience of Italy', *Economia Internazionale* 39(2–4): 85–97.
———. 1989. *Piccole imprese e distretti industriali. Una raccolta di saggi*. Turin: Rosenberg & Sellier.
Carrier J.G., and D. Kalb (eds). 2015. *Anthropologies of Class: Power, Practice, and Inequality*. Cambridge: Cambridge University Press.
Carosso, M., and S. Ghezzi. 2015. 'Introduzione. Artigiani fra bottega e artigianato industriale', *Antropologia* 2(2): 7–17.
Ceschi, S. 2007. 'Esistenze multisituate. Lavoro, condizione transnazionale e traiettorie di vita migrante', *Mondi Migranti* 2: 129–49.
———. 2014. 'Lavoro', in B. Riccio (ed), *Antropologia e migrazioni*. Rome: CISU, pp. 105–16.
Ceschi, S., and G. Giangaspero. 2009. 'I comportamenti socio-economici e finanziari dei migranti nella sfera transnazionale', in J.L. Rhi Sausi and M. Zupi (eds), *Banche e nuovi italiani. I comportamenti finanziari degli immigrati*. Rome: Bancaria Editrice, pp. 171–194.
Cirese, A.M. 1973. *Cultura egemonica e culture subalterne*. Rome: Palumbo Editore.
Clifford, J., and G.E. Marcus (eds). 1986. *Writing Culture: Poetics and Politics of Ethnography*. Oakland: University of California Press.
Crapanzano, V. 2005. 'Foreword', in E. de Martino and D. Zinn, *The Land of Remorse: A Study of Southern Italian Tarantism*. London: Free Association Books, pp. vii–xiv.
Crouch, C. 2011. *The Strange Non-death of Neoliberalism*. Cambridge: Polity Press.
D'Aloisio, F. 2003. *Donne in tuta amaranto. Trasformazione del lavoro e mutamento culturale alla Fiat Sata di Melfi*. Milan: Guerini & Associati.
———. 2014. *Vita di fabbrica. Cristina racconta il decollo e la crisi della Fiat Sata di Melfi*. Milan: Franco Angeli.
———. 2016. 'Work Inequalities between Global Transformation and Local Embedment: The Case of FIAT-Chrysler and the New Course at Melfi's Factory', *Antropologia* 3(1): 53–68.
———. 2017. 'Post-Fordist Work Organization and Daily Life from a Gender Perspective: The Case of FIAT-SATA in Melfi', in S. Narotzky and V. Goddard (eds), *Work and Livelihoods: History, Ethnography and Models in Times of Crisis*. New York: Routledge, pp. 77–92.
De Lauri, A., and L. Achilli (eds). 2008. *Pratiche e politiche dell'etnografia*. Rome: Meltemi.
De Martino, E. 1948. *Il mondo magico*. Turin: Einaudi.
———. 1959. *Sud e magia*. Milan: Feltrinelli.
———. 1961. *La terra del rimorso*. Milan: Il Saggiatore.
———. 2002 *La fine del mondo. Contributo all'analisi delle apocalissi culturali*, ed. by C. Gallini and M. Massenzio. Turin: Einaudi.
———. 2015. *Magic: A Theory from the South*. Chicago: Hau Books.
De Martino, E., and Zinn, D. 2005. *The Land of Remorse: A Study of Southern Italian Tarantism*. London: Free Association Books.
Desai, M. 2010. 'Hope in Hard Times: Women's Empowerment and Human Development', in *Human Development Research*, Paper 14. New York: United Nations, pp.1–75.
Dore, R. 2004. *New Forms and Meanings of Work in an Increasingly Globalized World*. Geneva: International Institute for Labour Studies.
Ehrenreich, B. 2001. *Nickel and Dimed: On (Not) Getting by America*. New York: Henry Holt and Company.
Fabietti, U. 2001. *Storia dell'Antropologia*. Milan: Zanichelli.

Faubion, J.D., and G.E. Marcus (eds). 2009. *Fieldwork is Not What It Used to Be: Learning Anthropology in a Time of Transition*. Ithaca, NY: Cornell University Press.
Fumagalli, A. 2011. 'La condizione precaria come paradigma biopolitico', in F. Chicchi and E. Leonardi (eds), *Lavoro in frantumi. Condizione precaria, nuovi conflitti e regime neoliberista*. Verona: Ombre Corte, pp.63–78.
———. 2013. *Lavoro male comune*. Milan: Bruno Mondadori – Pearson Italia.
———. 2015 *La vie mise au travail. Nouvelles formes du capitalisme cognitive*. Paris: Etherotopie France.
Fumagalli, A., and C. Morini 2013. 'Cognitive Bio-capitalism, Social Reproduction and the Precarity Trap: Why Not Basic Income?', *Knowledge Cultures* 1(4): 106–26.
Gallini, C., and G. Satta (eds). 2007. *Incontri etnografici. Processi cognitive e relazionali nella ricerca sul campo*. Rome: Meltemi.
Gallino, L. 2003. *La scomparsa dell'Italia industriale*. Turin: Einaudi.
———. 2007. *Il lavoro non è una merce. Contro la flessibilità*. Rome-Bari: Laterza.
———. 2012. *La lotta di classe dopo la lotta di classe*. Rome-Bari: Laterza.
———. 2014. *Vite precarie. Lo scandalo del lavoro precario*. Rome-Bari: Laterza.
Ghezzi, S. 2003. 'Local Discourses and Global Economy: Production Experiences of Small Family Workshops in the Brianza', *International Journal of Urban and Regional Research (IJURR)* 27(4): 781–92.
———. 2007. *Etnografia storica dell'imprenditorialità in Brianza. Antropologia di un'economia regionale*. Milan: Franco Angeli.
———. 2015. 'Familism as a Context for Entrepreneurship in Northern Italy', *Human Affairs* 25 (1): 58–70.
———. 2016. 'Familism in the Firm: An Ethnographic Approach to Italian Family Capitalism', *Ethnologie française* 162(2): 241–54.
Ghezzi, S., and E. Mingione. 2003. 'Beyond the Informal Economy: New Trends in Post-Fordist Transition', in J. Friedman (ed.), *Globalization, the State, and Violence*. Walnut Creek, CA: Altamira Press, pp. 87–106.
Gibson-Graham, J.K. 2006. *The End of Capitalism As We Knew It: A Feminist Critique of Political Economy*. Minneapolis: University of Minnesota Press.
Goddard, V. 2017. 'Work and Livelihood: An Introduction', in S. Narotzky S. and V. Goddard (eds), *Work and Livelihoods: History, Ethnography and Models in Times of Crisis*. New York: Routledge, pp. 1–27.
Gorz, A. 1964. *Stratégie ouvrière et néocapitalisme*. Paris: Edition di Seuil.
Hadjimichalis, C. 2006. 'The End of Third Italy as We Knew It?', *Antipode* 38(1): 82–106.
Hannerz, U. 2010. *Anthropology's World: Life in a Twenty-First-Century Discipline*. London: Pluto press.
Harvey, D. 1989. *The Condition of Postmodernity: An Enquiry into the Origins of Cultural Change*. Oxford: Blackwell.
———. 1991. 'Flexibility: Threat or Opportunity?', *Socialist Review*, 21(1): 65–77.
———. 2005. *A Brief History of Neoliberalism*. Oxford: Oxford University Press.
———. 2010. *The Enigma of Capital and the Crises of Capitalism*. London: Profile Books.
Harvey, P., and C. Krohn-Hansen. 2018. *Dislocating Labour: Anthropological Reconfiguration*, Special Issue of the *Journal of Royal Anthropological Institute*, 24(S1).
Herzfeld, M. 2014. 'Serendipitous Sculpture: Ethnography Does as Ethnography Goes', *Anthropology and Humanism* 39(1): 3–9.
Hobsbawm, E. 1994. *Age of Extrems: The Short Twentieth Century 1914–1991*. New York: Vintage.
ILO. 2015. *World Employment and Social Outlook: The Changing Nature of Jobs*. Geneva: International Labour Office.
India, T. 2017. *Antropologia della deindustrializzazione*. Florence: Editpress.

Jessop, B. 1992. 'Fordism and Post-Fordism: Critique and Reformulation', in M. Storper and A.J. Scott (eds), *Pathways to Industrialization and Regional Development*. London: Routledge, pp. 42–62.

———. 2003. *The Future of the Capitalist State*. Cambridge: Polity Press.

Kalb, D. 2009. 'Conversation with a Polish Populist: Tracing Hidden Histories of Globalization, Class, and Dispossesion in Postsocialism (and Beyond)', *American Ethnologist* 36(2): 2017–223.

Kasmir, S. 2014. 'The Saturn Automobile Plant and the Long Dispossession of US Autoworkers', in S. Kasmir and A. Carbonella (eds), *Blood and Fire: Toward a Global Anthropology of Labor*. New York: Berghahn Books, pp. 203–49.

Kasmir, S., and A. Carbonella (eds). 2014. *Blood and Fire: Toward a Global Anthropology of Labor*. New York: Berghahn Books.

Lash, S., and J. Urry. 1987. *The End of Organized Capitalism*. Madison: University of Wisconsin Press.

Latouche, S. 2006. *Le pari de la décroissance*. Paris: Librairie Arthéme Fayard.

Lipietz, A. 1988. 'Accumulation, Crises, and the Ways Out: Some Methodological Reflections on the Concept of "Regulation"', *International Journal of Political Economy* 18(2): 10–43.

———. 1992. *Towards a New Economic Order: Post-Fordism, Ecology and Democracy*. Oxford: Oxford University Press.

Marsh, P. 2012. *The New Industrial Revolution: Consumers, Globalization and the End of Mass Production*. New Haven: Yale University Press.

Marshall, A. 1919. *Industry and Trade*. London: Macmillan.

———. 1920. *Principles of Economics*. London: Macmillan.

Matera, V. 2015. *La scrittura etnografica. Esperienza e rappresentazione nella produzione di ricerche antropologiche*. Milan: Elèuthera.

Miller, D. (ed.). 1997. *Capitalism: An Ethnographic Approach*. Oxford: Oxford University Press.

Miranda, A. 2008. *Migrare al femminile. Appartenenza di genere e situazioni migratorie al femminile*. Milan: McGraw-Hill.

Mollona, M. 2009. 'General Introduction', in M. Mollona, G. de Neve and J. Parry (eds). *Industrial Work and Life: An Anthropological Reader*. New York: Berg, pp. xi–xxviii.

Mollona, M., G. de Neve and J. Parry (eds). 2009 *Industrial Work and Life: An Anthropological Reader*. New York: Berg.

Moretti, E. 2013. *The New Geography of Jobs*. New York: Mariner Books.

Narotzky, S. 1997. *New Directions in Economic Anthropology*. London: Pluto Press.

———. 2016. 'Between Inequality and Injustice: Dignity as a Motive for Mobilization during the Crisis', *History and Anthropology* 27(1): 74–92.

Narotzky S., and V. Goddard (eds). 2017. *Work and Livelihoods: History, Ethnography and Models in Times of Crisis*. New York: Routledge.

Negrelli, S. 2013. *Le trasformazioni del lavoro*. Rome-Bari: Laterza.

Papa, C. 1985. *Dove sono molte braccia è molto pane*. Perugia: Editore Umbra.

———. 1999. *Antropologia dell'impresa*. Milan: Guerini.

Papa, C., G. Pizza and F.M. Zerilli (eds). 1998. *Incontri di etnologia europea/Euopean Ethnology Meetings*. Naples: ESI.

Piasere, L. 2002. *L'etnografo imperfetto. Esperienza e cognizione in antropologia*. Rome-Bari: Laterza.

Piore, M., and C. Sabel 1984. *The Second Industrial Divide: Possibilities for Prosperities*. New York: Basic Books.

Pollert, A. 1988. 'The "Flexible Firm": Fixation or Fact?', *Work, Employment and Society* 2(3): 281–316.

——— (ed.). 1991. *Farewell to Flexibility?* Oxford: Basil Blackwell.
Redini, V. 2008. *Frontiere del 'made in Italy'. Delocalizzazione produttiva e identità delle merci.* Verona: Ombre Corte.
Riccio, B. 2007. *Tubab e Vu cumprà. Transnazionalità e rappresentazioni nelle migrazioni senegalesi in Italia.* Padua: Cleup.
——— (ed.). 2014. *Antropologia e migrazioni.* Rome: CISU.
Rifkin, J. 1994. *The End of Work.* New York: Tarcher Cornerstone.
Robben, A.C.G., and J.A. Sluka (eds). 2006. *Ethnographic Fieldwork: An Anthropological Reader.* Oxford: Blackwell.
Saraceno, C. 2015. *Il lavoro non basta. La povertà in Europa negli anni della crisi.* Milan: Feltrinelli.
Sennett, R. 1998. *The Corrosion of Character: The Personal Consequences of Work in the New Capitalism.* New York: W.W. Norton & Company.
Sherif Trask, B. 2014. *Women, Work and Globalization: Challenges and Opportunities.* New York: Routledge.
Signorelli, A. 2011. *Antropologia culturale.* Milan: McGraw-Hill.
———. 2015. *Ernesto de Martino. Teoria Antropologica e metodologia della ricerca.* Rome: L'Asino d'oro.
———. 2016. *La vita al tempo della crisi.* Turin: Einaudi.
Spyridakis, M. 2018. *Market versus Society: Anthropological Insights.* New York: Palgrave Macmillan.
Standing, G. 2011. *The Precariat: The New Dangerous Class.* New York: Bloomsbury Academic.
Strating, A. 1998. 'Misleading Concepts: Localization and Globalization', in C. Papa, G. Pizza and F.M. Zerilli (eds), *Incontri di etnologia europea/European Ethnology Meetings.* Naples: ESI, pp. 23–31.
Vignato, S. (ed.). 2010. *Soggetti al lavoro. Un'etnografia della vita attiva nel mondo globalizzato.* Novara: UTET.
Viti, F. (ed.) 2007. *Lavoro, dipendenza personale e rapporti familiari.* Modena: Edizioni Il Fiorino.
Whitford, J. 2001. 'The Decline of a Model? Challenge and Response in Italian Industrial Districts', *Economy and Society* 30(1): 38–65.
Yanagisako, S. 2002. *Producing Culture and Capital. Family Firms in Italy.* Princeton: Princeton University Press.

— Chapter 1 —

BREAKING THE CHAIN, MENDING THE CHAIN

A Decade of Socioeconomic Transformation in the Jewellery District of Valenza, Italy

Michele Filippo Fontefrancesco

Introduction

'The real problem in this city is not that there are no jobs. Rather, it's that there is no one who can do those jobs.' In this way, in an interview[1] in February 2018, Mario, a goldsmith and owner of a small jewellery enterprise in Valenza, a city in northwest Italy internationally known for its jewellery production, described the recent change in the job market in the city: a novel and unexpected situation that contrasted starkly with the economic history of the decade that began after the economic crisis erupted at the end of 2008 as a consequence of the Credit Crunch (Spyridakis 2018; Tooze 2018):

> The crisis of ten years ago deeply affected the city. We lost thousands of jobs and good workers. Now, the market is growing again, and we lack new goldsmiths, newly trained people ready to be employed for a decade. All the enterprises of Valenza have only considered how to keep down the costs of production, how to cut useless expenses. We did not think about what we would have needed in case of a new boom of the market. Now it risks being too late ... We do not have new blood and with no new trained workers, the very question is whether we are able to maintain and pass over our knowledge, the arts that made Valenza great in the world.

The words of Mario summarize the experiences shared by many other jewellery entrepreneurs I encountered during my fieldwork in Valenza in 2018. All of them expressed a common understanding of the Valenza jewellery industry. It is a vision in which the sense of fragility and lack of trust in the market trends entail a rekindled hope and where the recognition of the impact of the 2008 economic crisis went far beyond the figures concerning job losses or firms' closures; it eroded the social and cultural capital that Valenza's industry was built on.

The case of Valenza is a special case study that enables us to examine and understand the impact of the 2008 crisis on the Italian manufacturing sector because the city is a representative case of the 'Made in Italy' brand (Paulicelli 2014) and of the inherent dynamics of industrial districts that have characterized the manufacturing growth of the country since the post-Second World War period (Bianchi 2009; Rabellotti, Carabelli and Hirsh 2009). In particular, while Castells et al. (2012) have pointed out that the social meaning of an economic crisis is expressed by its aftermath, the ethnographic study of the city and its changes between 2008 and 2018 offers elements to complete the analysis proposed by these scholars about the 2008 Credit Crunch, and to address the anthropological question concerning the impact of an economic crisis upon local production knowledge. To this end, this chapter highlights the theme of the maintenance of production know-how in the Valenza district after the 2008 crisis. If it is true that this know-how is one of the main elements that contribute to the success and the strength of the district, then its current slow decrease may lead us to consider what the chances are of this industrial district (and others like it) surviving. Indeed, following the 2008 crisis, the importance of developing methods to maintain know-how and to ensure its intergenerational transmission has come to the forefront in Valenza.

This chapter begins by presenting the main features of the anthropological debate related to the impact of the 2008 crisis. It continues by investigating from an ethnographic point of view the case of Valenza, presenting the main features of this anthropological and economic field. As such, it proposes a periodization of the last decade of the socioeconomic history of industry in Valenza in order to better define the specific evolution of the aftermath of the crisis in this city. It also explores the bond between the city of Valenza and the jewellery manufacturing industry to which its identity has been closely linked, describing the main events and initiatives that have been employed to boost the district in the recent past.

The Aftermath of the Crisis in an Industrial District

Italian economic history over the last decade has experienced the effects of one of the worst periods of uncertainty since the Great Depression of the 1930s. It started with the Credit Crunch in September 2008 (Langley 2014; Tett 2009; Tooze 2018). Iceland was among the first European nations to pay the price of market disruption (Loftsdóttir 2010), and in subsequent years the countries of Southern Europe suffered its consequences too, experiencing a long period of recession and austerity, which has become the topic of a thorough ethnographic analysis (e.g. Knight and Stewart 2016; Muehlebach 2016; Spyridakis 2018). In this context, Italy has experienced the very same cycle of crisis, recession, austerity and democratic crisis that Walby (2015) described as the main trend experienced by all Western countries in this decade.

By analysing at a global level the trajectories of socioeconomic transformation since the collapse of Lehman Brothers, Castells et al. (2012: 12) identified four main transformations in the aftermath, during the postcrisis period:

1. A revamped informational capitalist economy for a much smaller segment of the population – probably the sector dominated by the professional class. There is a new wave of technological and organizational innovation; a kind of new economy unfolding, with new products and new processes in the field such as energy, nanotechnology and bioinformatics. However, because there is a reduced pool of venture capital, this new round of innovation does not have the potential for increasing the consumption of the majority of the population, thus hampering overall economic recovery.

2. The public and semi-public sector is in crisis, increasingly unable to generate employment and demand as the fiscal crisis deepens.

3. Survival-oriented, traditional economic activities, with low productivity and high employment potential for low-skill jobs, with an important component of informal economy.

4. An alternative economy sector (not necessarily excluding for-profit production) based on a different set of values about the meaning of life.

Therefore, this analysis, considering the decline of Tayloristic and state-controlled industries, interprets the postcrisis period as an opportunity to develop new alternative economic models to the traditional ones – for example, the rise of cryptocurrencies (Dodd 2017), the growth of *fair trade* (Fretel Cotera and Ortiz Roca 2010), as well as the expansion of the *sharing economy* (Sundararajan 2016). The recent history of the Italian economy confirms the presence of these trajectories in the country. However, there has been little detail available that allows us to interpret the transformations within one of the main sectors of the Italian economy – the industrial districts, whose work relies mainly on local networks of small and medium-sized enterprises (SMEs) that have made the application and production of artisanal knowledge (Sennett 2008) the basis of their success.

The economic model of industrial districts was originally investigated by Marshall (1920) at the beginning of the twentieth century and it was relaunched on an international level in the 1970s by Becattini (1978) and Piore and Sable (1984). Becattini et al. refer to specific local production agglomerations:

> characterised by a certain degree of local economic dominance of an industry ('local specialisation'). This main industry includes a mix of horizontal (competitive), vertical (input-output), and diagonal (related services and instruments) specialised activities. Together with the main industry, other secondary industrial activities may be localised in the district, more or less related to the main one, as a result of various evolutionary adjustments and developments. (Becattini, Bellandi and De Propris 2009: xviii)

These production areas are also characterized by:

> the nature and quality of the local labour market, which is internal to the district and highly flexible. Individuals move from firm to firm, and owners as well as workers live in the same community, where they benefit from the fact that 'the secrets of industry are in the air'. (Markusen 1996: 199)

Therefore, as Becattini suggests (2006: 347), an industrial district is a local system; that is, an area where a community of people live and work, with a great deal of persistently overlapping experiences. Anthropology has been interested in the study of these production systems (Blim 1990, 1993; D'Aloisio and Ghezzi 2016; Ghezzi 2007; Narotzky 1997, 2006; Yanagisako 1991), having pointed out not only the importance of the connection between social structures on a local level and forms of development in industrial and entrepreneurial districts, but also, and most importantly, the crucial topic of building production know-how within both firms and the community.

Taking this into consideration, the exploration of the aftermath of the 2008 crisis in a district represents an open discussion related not only to the transformation of economic systems, but also to social and cultural structures that reproduce the production know-how linked to a particular production and to a particular product. In fact, Miyazaki and Riles (2005) have already highlighted how an economic crisis can potentially act as a moment that causes individuals to reconsider their participation in a system of enterprises and to think deeply about their own visions of the world, so much so, in fact, that the crisis can be a turning point in personal biographies. Taking into consideration the sociocultural consequences of the 2008 crisis in Italy, of which D'Aloisio and Ghezzi (2016) have offered a first glimpse which this volume extends and deepens, the economic sudden downturn resulted in an overall sense of disorientation, which was followed by substantial social and economic immobility (Kleist and Jansen 2016: 374–77). The field research in the districts was an instrument to sample how the crisis has affected the bond that united a community to a particular industry, the extent of the damage to that bond and possible strategies employed to rejuvenate the industry and increase local trust in the workplace (Miyazaki 2004), thus giving local people a chance to envision a new possible future.

The Case Study and the Field Research

In the light of these considerations, this chapter explores the production reality of Valenza, in the province of Alessandria. The Piedmont city of Valenza is a representative case of an Italian industrial district (Carcano, Catalans and Vaccara Capello 2007; Carcano et al. 2002; De Marchi, Lee and Gereffi 2013; Gaggio 2007; Gaibisso 1995; Garofoli 2004; Magni 1999), based on jewellery production. Valenza is indeed one of the most popular international centres of jewellery production in the world and one of the three main Italian centres of jewellery production. Collections of important international brands are produced in Valenza, brands that have their production factories in the city (e.g. Bulgari and Damiani) or operate through a wide network of supplier companies (e.g. Boucheron and Cartier). Jewellery production is bound to a large network of firms. There were about 1,200 companies in 2008 (and 7,000 employees over a population of about 20,250), while in 2019 there were only 650 (and fewer than 3,500 employees over a population of about 18,750 people) according to the data released by the Chamber of Commerce of Alessandria. These firms are mostly SMEs that create a network that 'includes a mix of horizontal (competitive), vertical (input-output), and diagonal (related services and instruments) specialized activities' (Becattini et al. 2009: xviii).

The comparison between these data concerning 2008 and 2019 reveals the key role that the jewellery industry plays and has played for the city. Moreover, these statistics reveal the importance of the 2008 crisis in terms of redefining the face of the city and its relationship with the jewellery industry.

This chapter draws from ongoing ethnographic research conducted in Valenza since 2008. This work aimed to study the actual origins of the transformation of the jewellery industry and of the city itself. The study was carried out using different methodologies: archival research, ethnographic analysis and historical research concerning the economic and social development of the town and its industry, in particular from the 1940s to the present day. The fieldwork has been developed through different survey campaigns conducted during the decade (2008–12, 2013–14, 2015–16, 2017–18 and 2019). The results of these pieces of research have already been published in other studies and, for a more detailed study of the history of the district, its articulation and ethnographic insights on the experience of the crisis, it is necessary to refer to those publications (e.g. Fontefrancesco 2012, 2013, 2015a, 2015b, 2016b).

This chapter builds on the results shown in previous research and expands upon them with new data, collected in the years 2017–19 in a fieldwork campaign based on the analysis of the role played by the Foundation Mani Intelligenti (http://www.maniintelligenti.it) after its inception in 2015. The activities involved interviews based on the 'life history method' (Bertaux 1999) conducted with entrepreneurs, Valenza town council officials and professionals involved in the constitution of the Foundation, as well as participant observation of jewellery making in Valenza district, in accordance with the extended case method (Burawoy 1998).

The tale of the field (van Maanen 1988) that this chapter presents elaborates the ethnographic, statistical and archival materials and develops in a historical perspective (Schmitt 2008; Viazzo 2012) to present a clear account of the transformation that has occurred in the Valenza jewellery industry since 2008. In so doing, while the use of ethnographic vignettes is limited, the words of the informants are included in the text as evocative (textual) objects (Turkle 2007) to better appreciate the ordinary affects (Stewart 2007) of the recent history of the city. For the sake of clarity, the original text in Piedmontese or Italian has been translated into English.

A Periodization of the Decade

The figures presented above offer a first estimate of the changes that have emerged in Valenza since 2008. Moreover, by reading daily online comments posted by the inhabitants of the city on major social media sites, as well as the comments and the articles that have been published in main local newspapers, one can see that after ten years, citizens are still discussing the crisis that began in 2008. Slowly, however, comments that suggest an economic recovery and the rise of a new positive season for the city are gaining ground.

> It would seem we see the light at the end of the tunnel, but it might be a train … To see people begin to ask [for] extra hours is a good sign … I do not know why they are not hiring someone again.

In these terms, Pietro, a sixty-year-old goldsmith, expressed his opinion on the local economy during an interview conducted in April 2018. Over the last decade, notwithstanding many difficulties, he succeeded in staying on the labour market, even though that meant working for several different companies before being recruited by his current employer (a medium-sized Bulgari supplier company). In a similar way, in the spring of 2018, taking into account a sample of one hundred entrepreneurs and goldsmiths' employees, selected for gender and age so as to match with the demographic profile of the city, the perception of the economic situation of the town appeared to be on the whole not a negative one. For less than 20 per cent of these people, the city was still perceived as in a recession phase, while for 35 per cent, the 2008 crisis was 'completely over'. These ambivalent and partially optimistic views may provide us with some insights in order to better understand the 'human dimension' of economic trends (Hart, Laville, and Cattani 2010). Some interesting data on the current situation are reported below. The figures are annually delivered by the Banca Intesa–San Paolo Research Centre, which provides an outlook of the economy in its 'Districts Monitor'.

Table 1.1 shows export performance of Valenza in parallel with Valenza's demographic data. In this way, it offers a socioeconomic insight into the city and its transformation during the last decade. It looks like an apparently contradictory period. After an initial clear downturn (2008–11), the economy of Valenza went through a relatively long and steady recovery (2012–16) that fostered a new expansion of the trade (2017–18). By contrast, the sociodemographic data show a period of noticeable demographic decrease and ageing of the

Table 1.1. Resident population, average age and the export sales in the goldsmith sector in Valenza, 2007–17.

Year	Total of the resident population	Average age	Export sales of goldsmith sector (€ millions)
2006	20,329	45.2	400
2007	20,268	45.5	498
2008	20,282	45.7	650
2009	20,163	46	541
2010	20,169	46.2	372
2011	19,680	46.6	562
2012	19,434	46.9	864
2013	19,492	47.2	1,007
2014	19,341	47.5	1,287
2015	19,178	47.9	1,681
2016	19,054	48.1	1,549
2017	18,250	48.5	2,073
2018	18,634	48.3	2,102

Source: Banca Intesa–San Paolo Research Centre.

population during the 2008 crisis that has continued in spite of the recent market growth. This contrasting picture can be understood only by considering the transformation of the forms of entrepreneurship and labour that took place during the 2008 crisis.

The Impact of the 2008 Crisis on the Industrial District

'The crisis came at the end of October and swept us away.' Anna made this comment about her experience of the 2008 crisis. The interview was conducted in the summer of 2010. Anna was a professional jewellery designer; she experienced the crisis from the privileged point of view of a professional who was in daily contact with several companies, listening to their stories, vicissitudes and the different problems experienced by each of them. To Anna, the period 2008–11 was characterized by a progressive loss of orders and customers. This was a concrete result of the change in Italian and foreign markets that within a few months almost completely halted the purchase of jewellery.

Starting with the Credit Crunch, Western countries quickly reduced their spending, especially on nonessential goods. Among these, luxury goods and above all the jewellery market were the most heavily hit (de Marchi et al. 2013). Attali (2009) commented that the Credit Crunch 'brought the world to the edge of catastrophe'. Jewellery entrepreneurs met during my fieldwork at that time did not share this analysis; they thought it was more than a catastrophe. To them, the Credit Crunch brought the district *over* that edge, setting off the phenomenon of city *desertification.* Following the closing of over a third of the local goldsmith enterprises, the perception of Valenza among the local population had altered: from being 'the city of goldsmiths' to being a city in search of a new economic vocation (Fontefrancesco 2015). As a matter of fact, although exports represented an important market for Valenza's jewellery products, the Italian market accounted for a large proportion of sales (Garofoli 1981; Paradiso 2008a), a market that plummeted from the last months of 2008 and started off a recessionary period that only ended in 2015 (ISTAT 2016). The slump in the home market together with the foreign market epitomized the crisis that affected Valenza from 2008 to 2011.

While in October 2008 jewellery entrepreneurs still seemed confident of a fast upturn, in the days before Christmas – which was as a rule the period of maximum peak in sales for the annual production – this confidence ceased and the foreshadowing of an epochal change characterized by a great recession emerged. The following statements by a goldsmith entrepreneur of a medium-sized company in the city described the phenomenon thus: 'The crisis came as a Tsunami ... it is a catastrophe that will change the face of Valenza.'

The crisis in the jewellery sector struck Valenza very heavily in comparison to the other Italian districts (Gereffi and de Marchi 2010): while Italian jewellery in general lost −28.1 per cent of its sales in the period 2007–9, Valenza underwent a reduction of its exports totalling a massive €274 million, that is, −31.3% (Gereffi and de Marchi 2010; de Marchi et al. 2013). To withstand the effects of the crisis, there were attempts (both individual and collective) to find better promotional tools and increase customer awareness of the history and quality of items made in Valenza (Fontefrancesco 2012). However, enterprises faced the new emerging market scenario mainly by focusing on cutting production costs. In a production system where the human factor rather than the technological factor prevails in price formation (Carcano et al. 2007), entrepreneurs therefore adopted an approach based on a policy mainly linked to the renegotiation of the contracts of employment (formal and informal), the use of social shock absorbers and staff mobility (Fontefrancesco 2016a; Garavaglia and Perrone 2010; Gereffi and de Marchi 2010). The impact of the crisis, as reported by the professional associations of the goldsmiths, became public when the number of employed workers halved and the recruitment of apprentices and young people in the field almost completely ceased (Fontefrancesco 2016b).

The loss of available jobs was accompanied by the closure of a large number of smaller companies. The production milieu of the city in 2008 appeared effectively unchanged compared to the observations of Garofoli in 2004: there was a wide network of about 1,200 enterprises, for the most part of very modest size, with on average six workers in every company. This particular production milieu was the outcome of a historical process developed during the course of the twentieth century, starting at the end of the First World War. In 1911, when the goldsmiths' art spread through the city, there were 674 employees (Gaggio 2007: 59). The First World War then reset the number of employees to almost zero because of the compulsory enlistment of male workers and the slump in the demand for jewellery (Gaggio 2007: 58–64). In the immediate postwar period, the prompt and strong demand for jewellery gave new life to the sector and expanded it, thanks to a few enterprises that had remained active during the war. They met the demand for labour by outsourcing the work to the many goldsmiths who, returning from the front, found they had lost their jobs during the war and were seeking new employment. These craftsmen seized the opportunity to open new workshops, often in interstitial spaces. Valenza's specific set-up has its origins here. It is characterized by the presence of a limited number of big enterprises (mostly with over sixty employees), with direct access to the market, able to complete the production cycle inside the enterprise and outsource to lots of small enterprises and workshops. These are specialized in the completion of specific phases of production (modelling, fusion and metal-cutting, stonework, setting and polishing – see also Lenti 1994; Lenti and Pugnetti 1974; Molina and Manenti 1994), whose economies are based entirely on orders from other companies in Valenza, in particular the bigger ones. From the 1920s, Valenza developed its jewellery industry by extensively resorting to outsourcing some production processes. Outsourcing allowed many craftsmen to easily pursue business opportunities by setting up small firms, whereas for the biggest enterprises, it meant substantially lowering economic and social costs linked to the expansion of the production system and externalizing the impact of an economic recession, as demonstrated by the events after 2008. This production context, then, is based on a strong imbalance in bargaining power: the supplier firms are 'held captive' by the production structure and are unable to find alternative solutions in the face of a crisis.

Where Gereffi (2007) used a pyramid model to illustrate this situation, the goldsmiths I interviewed normally used the metaphor of a tree that distributes its lymph (labour and capital) from its roots (the largest firms) to its various branches, eventually reaching the smaller twigs (the smaller companies). When referring to the 2008 crisis, the tree in the metaphor underwent some adaptation: 'the great tree of jewellery of Valenza is reduced to its trunk, letting fall almost all its leaves'. Indeed, the prolonged contraction of demand led to a progressive reduction of the flow of outsourcing contracts for smaller companies. Where these companies were first forced to reduce their staff and then to shut down, the more structured enterprises enforced strategies aimed at integrating their own production processes by internalizing the different stages of production, also through the recruitment of new workers, who were generally experienced goldsmiths and entrepreneurs who had lost their jobs during the onset of the crisis. Therefore, the 2008 crisis began a process of redefinition of the structure of the enterprises. It also spurred a new internationalization of business. Indeed, because of the progressively difficult Italian market, companies increasingly turned to the international market, in particular in Europe, by intensifying their presence, their sales and trading networks, and gave impulse to the development of exports, as Figure 1.1 shows.

The events following the 2008 crisis not only affected the industrial structure of the district; it also changed the way in which its inhabitants perceived Valenza and the jewellery sector. Since the Second World War, although some downturns in the jewellery market had occurred (e.g. 1973–75, 1996, 2001–2 and 2004–5 – see Gaggio 2007; Paradiso 2008b), the city itself developed its own self-representation linking its name to jewellery production (Fontefrancesco 2011). Valenza was, in fact, known as 'the city of gold'. This fact is bound to the progressive transformation of the city as a 'jewellery monoculture'; in other words, jewellery production had been the first and most important economic and employment sector in the city since the end of the 1960s (Fontefrancesco 2013). This identification between the image of the city and the jewellery sector is clearly seen in the urban planning of the town that, starting from the end of the 1970s, was reshaped according to the needs of the sector: from the desire to allow an improvement in hygienic and sanitary conditions for the enterprises to the creation of a better road system and appropriate exhibition spaces (Bovero 1992; Gaggio 2007). As the early years of the 2000s were characterized by a slowdown in the economic performance of the district, the 2008 crisis began a strong public debate about the future of the jewellery industry in Valenza. Since 2009, strong rumours, coming from politicians and businessmen in the area, began circulating, foretelling the 'end of the city of gold' (Fontefrancesco 2013). This situation gave shape and made intelligible to the public the crisis that this sector was experiencing, but at the same time, it turned the crisis into a moment of suspension, an eternal present without perception of a future. As highlighted by commentators on the public use of the concept of 'crisis' in the American political debate (Masco 2017), a crisis can be a proactive moment for a community when it binds to a precise idea and ideology connected with the future; alternatively, when it is not bound to a precise idea of the future, as in the case of this city, it mostly causes the community to focus on conservative and nostalgic views and to idealize the past rather than create a new image of the future. The public debate in the city, as attested to by newspapers and blogs, focused on the memory of former glories, underlining the distance between the *chronotope* (Bakhtin and Holquist 1981) of the past and that of the present. The rhetoric of the past as opposed to the present was based on and supported by memories, but also by direct experience of life in the city, and was underlined by the increasing emptiness of urban space, as people moved away from the area. This was often characterized as a 'plague' that had affected the district (Fontefrancesco 2015b). Indeed, despite political directives since the end of the 1960s aimed at relocating the jewellery workshops outside the urban fabric of the city, in 2008 only 20 per cent of firms were located within the artisan area; the remaining firms were located in the city, inside buildings and houses, often on the ground floor. This particular background turned the urban context of Valenza into a production-residential continuum, which is considered by many people to be one of the distinctive features that characterized 'the city of gold' (Bovero 1992; Gaggio 2007; Fontefrancesco 2011). With the progressive closure of companies since 2009, this situation quickly began to disappear. The increasing number of vacant production spaces and the growing number of 'for sale' and 'factory to rent' signs enhanced, in everyday life, the perception of living in a moment of no return for the city and its main economy – an experience that was felt even more strongly by those goldsmiths who were still working and saw the factories progressively becoming silent, with no employees and customers.

This awareness increasingly fuelled a sense of distrust towards the future of the jewellery sector, causing a break in the general climate of confidence that bound the population of Valenza to the industry, which since the Second World War had represented a thriving field of work and business and was able to also provide quick profits and business opportunities to people with a low level of education (Bovero 1992; Gaggio 2007; Magni 1999). As Luca, a jewellery trader also involved in the political life of the city, commented in 2010: 'After this crisis, after these years, we've arrived at an endpoint. The crisis cut the legs off this city ... Our legs ... In the last year, above all, it has changed this city ... Its jewellery industry ... The dream of gold now appears to have ended' (Fontefrancesco 2013: 194). These words bring to the fore a more common way of understanding the transformations the city was going through. This also emerged in the increasing number of public and private debates on possible alternatives available for the city. In particular, it was made clear by the discussions within families about which studies their school-age and teenage children should undertake and whether it would be better for them to learn the goldsmiths' art or to find a different job. Even those families with a successful history of work in the jewellery sector considered the trade as 'difficult' or, even worse, 'dying' (Fontefrancesco 2015). This search for a new job could not be read as the willingness of craftsmen's families to reach a social distinction through the education of new generations (Bourdieu 1984), considering that this phenomenon had already happened in previous decades (Fontefrancesco 2013). The choice was experienced and described as an 'escape' and an 'abandonment'. This departure was seen in the progressive and rapid decrease in the number of enrolments in the two jewellery schools of the city: the Art Institute Benvenuto Cellini and the Professional School For.Al. A further sign was the eventual closure of the Art Institute Benvenuto Cellini and its transformation into the Liceo Artistico in 2011, which shifted the focus of the high school from the training of newly skilled jewellery workers to the creation of students potentially able to follow university studies that focused on art and design. In this way, jewellery training was limited to a basic offer of short advanced courses or biennial courses for 14–16-year-olds, provided by the Professional School For.Al. This was a limited offer as regards the effective possibility of placing new professional goldsmiths in the labour market, which was limited to a hundred graduate students every year. In the context of an evident market downturn, the possible impact that this figure would have on the city was only marginally discussed in the public debate, but within a few years, it emerged in all its consequential complexity.

Despite the constant growth in exports that started in 2011, mistrust towards the jewellery sector characterized the subsequent years (2012–15). The daily routine appeared marked by a sense of expectation and impatience, by the succession of closures of business cycles and the loss of jobs. In particular, the horizon also appeared to be marked symbolically by events that suggested a continuous erosion of the jewellery district. The most controversial of these was the crisis and therefore the end of the Valenza Gioielli, the jewellery fair organized by the AOV, the business association of Valenza goldsmiths, which had been held annually since 1977 (Gaggio 2007). The event represented an important showcase for the companies of the city, hosting more than 200 exhibitors. Because of the success of the event, a new building, called Expo Piemonte, was designed, constructed and financed by the Piedmont regional council. It was placed outside the city and was supposed to become the second trade-fair centre in the region. Expo Piemonte was created to replace the old spaces of Palazzo Mostre, which was inaugurated in 1983 in the city centre and turned out to be insufficient to host events. The construction of the new building lasted for almost a decade and was opened for the 31st fair on 21 October 2008, about one month after the bankruptcy of Lehman Brothers. During the previous decade, the exhibition had lost its importance in the Italian context in comparison to the exhibition in Vicenza, which was preferred by the same entrepreneurs of Valenza. In the following years, also due to the effect of the district crisis, the number of exhibitors decreased, making the event economically unsustainable. In 2014 the Expo Piedmont complex was used for the event for the last time and then the building was abandoned, as an entrepreneur of the city ironically commented:

> It already seemed a cathedral in the desert [because of the underuse that characterized the whole life of the structure]. Now it seems the house of ghosts.

The following year, an attempt to transform the event into a traveling exhibition did not bring about the desired results, and the Valenza association of goldsmiths (which meanwhile officially became part of Confindustria, the largest national entrepreneur association) brought it to an end in 2016.

Even if the decline of the Valenza Gioielli exhibition was for the city a further confirmation of the district crisis, in 2016 there was a positive change, a new beginning, as proposed by Castells et al. (2012), for the local situation: the opening of the new Bulgari factory, directly in front of the Expo Piemonte building. The company, which today is owned by the French group LVMH, had produced its collections in the city since the Second World War, through a wide network of suppliers run by the firm Crova Spa. Between 2002 and 2006, Bulgari had acquired the majority of shares in the company, with over 300 employees, and thus had started to be directly active in the district. In 2014, the company started the process for the creation of a new factory, aiming at the creation of its most important production in the city centre, with over 700 employees. The factory of 1,400 square metres was inaugurated on 17 March 2016, becoming the largest jewellery production centre in Valenza. A large number of craftsmen criticized this new presence, considering it a distortion of the artisan reality of the town and calling the new factory 'Bulgatraz', with reference to its form, but especially to the assumed detention of goldsmiths inside the factory, evoking in the collective imagination the idea of the US prison Alcatraz. However, the new consolidated presence of Bulgari strengthened the district in both export and labour. Contrary to the expectations of many local entrepreneurs, the opening of the new factory did not stop the flow of externalization that bound the previous set-up to the city, but strengthened economic relations with suppliers and gave new impetus to the network economy.

However, the opening of the new factory highlighted the problem of estrangement between the city and the jewellery sector, a problem that had developed in the years following the Credit Crunch. In fact, the opening was accompanied by a precise plan of recruitment aimed at the selection of 300 new workers over a period of three years. Bulgari launched its plan of recruitment in 2015. The selection aimed at workers under the age of fifty, but with experience. One could expect the recruitment to have easily satisfied the need for personnel. However, the result was the selection of only twenty-three employees who were resident in the district, forcing the company to widen its search to a national level, employing people from other parts of Italy. Apparently, this situation may seem paradoxical considering that the crisis of 2009–11 left thousands of workers out of work. Yet, during these years, many of these workers found new jobs in other sectors or in other parts of the country. In addition, most of the unemployed

Table 1.2. Distribution of the number of companies in the sample for range of personnel (end of year 2014).

Range of employees	Number of enterprises
50+	3
25–50	5
15–24	3
10–14	8
5–9	7
1–4	32
Total number of companies	58

Source: Mani Intelligenti Foundation.

goldsmiths were over fifty years old or had abandoned the craft for over three years; as a result, these workers could hardly be employed in a workplace based on skilled labour, and flexible enough to be easily integrated within the working environment of a new factory. As a matter of fact, the company's recruitment fell victim to another problem: the lack of skilled and young labour. As a consequence, the recruitment process did not find any candidates under the age of thirty, so the problem of the lack of a generation ready to replace older people in production was clearly apparent, and common across the entire district. In 2016, a preparatory study of what would become the Foundation Mani Intelligenti explored the economic and employment potential of a representative sample for size and sales of fifty-eight companies in Valenza (see Figure 1.2) able to generally develop a turnover of over €1 billion (€1,067,048,243 to be exact) in 2014. As can be seen in Figure 1.3, out of a total of 409 employees, companies generally had twenty workers under the age of thirty, of whom only three were under the age of twenty-five.

The age of the staff in the companies above highlights the impact of a decade of blocked recruitment and, above all, the lack of younger generations capable of maintaining continuity in the transmission of knowledge in the goldsmith sector. In addition, the training courses planned locally were unable to fill the gap that was created after the 2008 crisis. Bulgari's attempt to finance the creation of annual courses for fifteen students and a training course for thirteen people beginning in 2015 at the Professional School For.Al was clearly insufficient.

Table 1.3. Age and number of workers in the fifty-eight companies used as a sample (end of year 2014).

Age classes	Number of employees	Percentage
20–25	3	0.73
25–30	17	4.16
30–35	41	10.02
35–40	77	18.83
40–45	76	18.58
45–50	80	19.56
50–55	73	17.85
55–60	31	7.58
60–65	8	1.96
65–70	2	0.49
70+	1	0.24

Source: Mani Intelligenti Foundation.

This project was not adequate to meet the needs of the company itself, let alone that of a whole sector that had slowly started to search for new employees to renew its factories.

Considering this resulting framework, since 2016, the municipality of Valenza has become the promoter of initiatives to effectively and systematically broaden local training opportunities. In 2017, the municipality of Valenza, together with fourteen companies which were among the most important in the city (BMC, Bulgari, Costanzo and Rizzetto, Sieves, Damiani, Filostil, Gioj, Giorgio Visconti, Greco F.lli, Palmiero, Leo Pizzo, Pasquale Bruni, Vendorafa Lombardi and VPA) began the procedure for the constitution of a foundation focused on the planning and the support of new educational paths aimed at staff with a diploma or a university degree. These courses were to teach the art of jewellery manufacturing by directly involving the best employees from different firms, as well as offering two internship periods in two of the member companies. In this way, on 24 June 2018, the Foundation Mani Intelligenti was created, and its aim was to train, in a three-year period (2018–21), 1,000 new goldsmiths to enter the goldsmith sector, thus strengthening the chain broken in 2008 and involving key businesses in the training process.

Analysis

Overall, considering these new developments from an economic and cultural point of view, a precise outline emerges of the transformations the district has undergone. The 2008 crisis has weighed on the production network. The crisis has particularly affected the smaller companies, based on outsourced workflows and with limited direct access to the market. Today, these firms still represent the largest number of Valenza jewellery businesses and, in particular, they represented the main instrument for social mobility for many goldsmiths in the period between 1970 and 2000. As highlighted by Gaggio (2007), the low initial capital that they required for the start-up as well as the equally limited needs related to maintaining a warehouse and to creating and managing a wide commercial network had in fact allowed many specialized goldsmiths to set up their own businesses, allowing for more profits and an obvious social upgrade. The 2008 crisis has led to the crisis in this business model, which had represented the main instrument for many young people who entered the jewellery industry to realize their own dreams for the future.

If the possibility of getting 'easy money' (as was the reputation of work in the jewellery sector) was the basis of local prestige related to the profession, the disappearance of this perspective seems to have undermined the bond and the confidence that linked the city to the jewellery business, on the one hand by starting a public debate about economic alternatives for Valenza and on the other hand by deeply affecting the attractiveness of this sector for younger generations. While in 2015, the resulting distance still appeared difficult to bridge (Fontefrancesco 2015), the opening of the new Bulgari factory, the progressive and stable growth in exports, the increasingly pressing need for labour and the increase of the economic possibilities for employees involved in the sector have all created fertile ground for reconsidering the topic of workforce training in public debate, almost fifty years after the creation of the first goldsmith school (Gaggio 2007). In addition, many young Italians have been attracted to work in Valenza thanks to Bulgari: research conducted by the town council of Valenza and shown during the public presentation of the Foundation Mani Intelligenti has highlighted that since 2016, there have been at least 150 new employees in the sector who were recruited by that company alone and who have come to live in the city.

The creation of the new Bulgari factory also began a new process of structuring of enterprises that to all intents can be read as a progressive move away from the reality of artisanal and family businesses towards that of more structured industries, considering the administrative point of view and industrial relations. In particular, the public debate has repeatedly highlighted the progressive transformation of the role of the goldsmith from craftsman to labourer, perhaps also due to a loss of skills, technical and practical ability related to the job and the greater structure of a company when it is not following the family-artisanal model. This concern is symptomatic of a greater problem as regards the transmission of knowledge and the forms of knowledge related to the art of the goldsmith. Beyond the institutionalized processes of training, the goldsmith's job has been primarily learned directly in the companies, whilst working on the production line. As in the case of Rethemnos that was analysed by Herzfeld (2004), in many cases learning depended not only on daily manual practice, but also on observation of the most expert craftsmen, 'stealing the work with the eyes', to use an expression employed several times by the same goldsmiths. This method of learning followed the model of legitimate peripheral participation (Lave and Wenger 1991) and involved young boys being gradually recognized as master craftsmen. It was based, first of all, on the presence and participation of several generations of artisans in the same environment. This generational chain was broken in 2008, leading to a generational vacuum that today the institutions and companies are trying to fill, focusing on relaunching formal education. In addition, the training of the goldsmith's art was related to labour mobility among recruitment companies, based on a labour market in expansion and in search of the most highly qualified personnel. As such, different companies knew the methods of other firms and used them to expand their production possibilities. In this way, in a system where a lack of company loyalty was an element of collective cultural and production growth, the district had increased for more than thirty years. However, the decade 2008–18 mostly saw a shrinking market that limited the passage of workers between companies and therefore led to a weakening of this important vector of knowledge. Today, the recovery of the labour market is qualitatively expressed by increasingly frequent stories of people who have changed companies, a sign of a possible revitalization of this model of knowledge.

The goldsmiths' concern about their transformation into factory workers also depends on another factor. Over the last decade, the profession has experienced a rapid expansion of the production possibilities and technologies used in everyday activities. If the 1950s marked a fundamental production revolution, allowing the serialization of the individual pieces with the introduction of precision casting processes, the last decade has seen the introduction of techniques of CAD-CAM digital modelling, as well as the introduction of equipment such as the microscope and pneumatic onglets for settings, seeing a paradigm shift in the field of production. But like all sudden cultural changes, this has also caused fear and uncertainty. The senior goldsmiths are worried that these new technologies will cause craftsmen of the district to lose their ability. If, as suggested by Sennett (2008), craftsmanship is based not on both the presence and use of instruments and tools, but on the proactive and creative use of the same tools, a serious reconsideration of the forms of goldsmiths' knowledge and how it grows and develops is required.

More generally, the 2008 crisis appears to have opened up a new phase in the life of the city, questioning those elements of identity that for more than forty years had led Valenza to be dubbed the 'city of gold' and an artisanal city – a community that had founded its hierarchy of value (Herzfeld 2004) on the primacy of jewellery, the confidence of quick profits and the possibility of entrepreneurial autonomy. Today, these assumptions appear to have been called into question. Undoubtedly, in the last decade, the community has had to consider a possible future 'without' or at least with 'less' jewellery production for the city, marking a fissure in the solid identity of the 'city of gold'. Nevertheless, the initiatives put forward in the past three years suggest a positive attempt to mend the damage suffered following the 2008 crisis.

Conclusion

This chapter has tried to reconstruct from an economic and ethnographic point of view the transformations that have occurred recently in the goldsmith district in Valenza. Highlighting how the jewellery sector was affected and is currently experiencing a fundamental reconfiguration, it has focused on how economic changes were also characterized by a change of attitude towards the work of goldsmiths by the local population, and more broadly a fast erosion of the cultural and social capital which the district relied upon.

Industrial districts are the most common examples of flexible industries, making the entrepreneurial dynamism of their production and commercial networks the basis of their success. In the face of an economic crisis, the research suggests that it should not be company closures or job losses that should worry observers; rather, they should be concerned about the impact on the link that binds a community with a profession and a field of enterprise. This is because it is local attitudes to work that form the basis of conservation of local know-how. The heavy contraction after the 2008 crisis actually affected Valenza not only by ejecting hundreds of craftsmen from the labour market, but, above all, by almost stopping the generational succession, leading to a potential failure of the generational turnover in the district. The consequence is a failure in the sustainability of knowledge as well as the dynamic of the labour market that are prerequisites for the successful running of a district. Facing this necessity, since 2017 Valenza entrepreneurs have started focusing on coping with this future emergency, training skilled workers in the industry and rejuvenating the image of the profession.

The Valenza case also highlights a further aspect, which was somewhat overlooked by Castells et al. (2012) in the aftermath of the 2008 crisis, i.e., not only the problem of the dynamics of economic sectors, but also the strong impact of the crisis on knowledge and the transmission of knowledge. This topic is particularly important if we consider countries such as those of Southern Europe, which have experienced the consequences of the recession more dramatically than their northern counterparts. The goldsmith sector of Valenza will only have a future if it is able to fill the generational vacuum. The Foundation Mani Intelligenti is one solution, but today there is a lack of collective action at the national, European and international levels, leading to a failure to ensure the continuity of knowledge, in particular in those sectors where artisanal awareness and skills are the basis for growth and success. However, recognizing the importance of supporting the transmission of knowledge, the urgency of filling this gap is clear.

'Without firms there is no district, but without artisans not only are there no more firms but there is not industry at all.' In this synthetic manner, a goldsmith summarized the challenge the city was experiencing and the concern many entrepreneurs share facing the near future. Through the Foundation Mani Intelligenti, goldsmiths together with the town council are trying to create a solution to this silent emergency, and the next few years will show whether this initiative will be able to contribute to reconnecting a new generation to jewellery craftsmanship.

In conclusion, the research opens up new questions, first of all linked to the future of the city. In fact, whether or not a further implementation of methods and technologies linked to Industry 4.0 (Fontefrancesco 2016b) may reduce the need for a new workforce, it is mistaken to entrust the future of the local jewellery production merely to further mechanization and automatization of production, because this solution does not answer the real question the goldsmith community is posing, which is how to preserve and transfer artisan knowledge once the generational chain is broken. The acceleration programmes designed by the Foundation may also be a model useful for other professional communities and social contexts that are facing the same conundrum as Valenza.

Moreover, the case of Valenza informs the anthropological debate on the meaning of an economic crisis. In fact, it suggests moving from the tangible aspect of the change of life conditions experienced by entrepreneurs, workers and the community at large, and exploring further the symbolic and emotional dynamics that bond a community and specific production practices and knowledge. The crisis of Valenza can be described as the crisis of this intangible link that mainstream economic categories fail to describe and estimate. Thus, the anthropological lens shows an economic crisis as an upset of the tangible and intangible aspects of the ordinary, and suggests that the long-term sustainability of a form of economy depends mainly on intangible aspects, as the ethnography of Valenza has shown.

Michele Filippo Fontefrancesco is Assistant Professor at the University of Gastronomic Sciences (Bra, Cuneo). His research focuses on local development in Italy and Eastern Africa. His recent publications include *The End of the City of Gold? Industry and Economic Crisis in an Italian Jewellery Town* (Cambridge Scolars, 2013) and *Food Festivals and Local Development in Italy: An Economic Anthropology Approach* (Palgrave, 2020).

Note

1. My thanks here go to those numerous enterprises that have contributed to my research in the last ten years, to the Town Council of Valenza and to the Foundation Mani Intelligenti and their representatives, for the support and the data provided.

References

Attali, J. 2009. *La Crisi e Poi?* Rome: Fazi Editore.

Bakhtin, M.M., and M. Holquist. 1981. *The Dialogic Imagination: Four Essays*. Austin: University of Texas Press.

Becattini, G. 1978. 'The Development of Light Industry in Tuscany: An Interpretation', *Economic Notes* 7: 107–23.

———. 2006. 'Industrial District', in J. Beckert and M. Zafirovski (eds), *International Encyclopaedia of Economic Sociology*. London: Routledge.
Becattini, G., M. Bellandi and L. De Propris. 2009. 'Critical Nodes and Contemporary Reflections on Industrial Districts', in G. Becattini, M. Bellandi and L. de Propris (eds), *A Handbook of Industrial Districts*. Cheltenham: Edward Elgar, pp. xv–xxxv.
Bertaux, D. 1999. *Racconti di Vita. La Prospettiva Etnosociologica*. Milan: Franco Angeli.
Bianchi, R. 2009. 'The Italian Revival of Industrial Districts and the Foundations of Political Economy', in G. Becattini, M. Bellandi and L. de Propris (eds), *A Handbook of Industrial Districts*. Cheltenham: Edward Elgar, pp. 103–110.
Blim, M. 1990. *Made in Italy: Small-Scale Industrialization and Its Consequences*. New York: Praeger.
———. 1993. 'The Third Italian Economies at Middle Age: Problems and Prospects for Industrial Renewal', *Anthropology of Work Review* 14: 20–28.
Bovero, S. 1992. *Vivere a Valenza: Mondo Orafo e Disagio Urbano*. Valenza: Unità Socio-Sanitaria Locale N.71.
Bourdieu, P. 1984. *Distinction: A Social Critique of the Judgement of Taste*. London: Routledge & Kegan Paul.
Burawoy, M. 1998. 'The Extended Case Method', *Sociological Theory* 16: 4–33.
Carcano, L., A. Catalani and P. Vaccara Capello. 2007. *Miti da Sfatare nel Gioiello. Le Relazioni Industria Distribuzione in Italia e nel Mondo*. Milan: Egea.
Carcano, L. et al. 2002. *Il Mondo Orafo tra Tradizione e Innovazione*. Milan: Etas.
Castells, M., J.M.G. Caraça and G. Cardoso (eds). 2012. *Aftermath: The Cultures of the Economic Crisis*. Oxford: Oxford University Press.
Cotera Fretel, A., and H. Ortiz Roca. 2010. 'Fair Trade', in K. Hart, J.-L. Laville and A.D. Cattani (eds), *The Human Economy*. Cambridge: Polity, pp. 107–18.
D'Aloisio, F., and S. Ghezzi (eds). 2016. *Antropologia della Crisi. Prospettive Etnografiche sulle Trasformazioni del Lavoro e dell'Impresa in Italia*. Turin: L'Harmattan Italia.
De Marchi, V., J. Lee and G. Gereffi. 2013. 'Globalization, Recession and the Internationalization of Industrial Districts: Experiences from the Italian Jewellery Industry', *European Planning Studies* 22(4): 866–84.
Dodd, N. 2017. 'The Social Life of Bitcoin', *Theory, Culture and Society* 35(1): 35–56.
Fontefrancesco, M.F. 2011. 'City of Goldsmiths: Economy, Local Identity and Rhetoric in Valenza', *Anthropological Notebook*, 17(1): 29–51.
———. 2012. 'Crafting the Local: GIs, Jewelry and Transformations in Valenza, Italy', *Social Analysis* 56(3): 89–107.
———. 2013. *The End of the City of Gold? Industry and Economic Crisis in an Italian Jewellery Town*. Newcastle upon Tyne: Cambridge Scholars Publishing.
———. 2015a. 'Artigianalità Valenzana: Retorica e Manifattura in un Distretto Industriale italiano', *Antropologia* 2: 105–21.
———. 2015b. 'Invisible Presences and Visible Absences', *Journal of Cultural Economy* 8(5): 597–612.
———. 2016a. 'Exploring Limbo: The Experience of Job-Loss and Unemployment in a Jewellery City in Italy', *Issues in Ethnology and Anthropology* 11(4): 519–37.
———. 2016b. 'La Fine della Città dell'Oro? La Crisi dell'industria Orafa Valenzana', in F. d'Aloisio and S. Ghezzi (eds). *Antropologia della Crisi. Prospettive Etnografiche sulle Trasformazioni del Lavoro e dell'Impresa in Italia*. Turin: L'Harmattan Italia, pp. 60–82.
Gaggio, D. 2007. *In Gold We Trust: Social Capital and Economic Change in the Italian Jewelry Towns*. Princeton: Princeton University Press.
Gaibisso, A.M. 1995. *L'industria Orafa Italiana: Struttura e Strategie di Settore*. Milan: Franco Angeli.
Garavaglia, L., and E. Perrone. 2010. 'Il Distretto Orafo Valenzano tra Crisi Globale e Spinte Innovative', *Newsletter dell'Osservatorio di Distretto di Valenza* 3: 2–9.

Garofoli, G. 1981. 'Lo Sviluppo delle Aree Periferiche nell'Economia Italiana degli Anni Settanta', *L'Industria* 2: 391–404.
———. (ed.). 2004. *Il Distretto Orafo di Valenza: Tendenze Evolutive e Prospettive.* Milan: Franco Angeli.
Gereffi, G., and V. de Marchi. 2010. 'Gli Effetti della Recessione Economica sulle Catene del Valore del Gioiello in Oro: le Tendenze in Atto nei Mercati Globali e nei Distretti Orafi Italiani', *Newsletter dell'Osservatorio di Distretto di Valenza* 3: 2–9.
Ghezzi, S. 2007. *Etnografia Storica dell'Imprenditorialità in Brianza. Antropologia di un'economia regionale.* Milan: Franco Angeli.
Hart, K., J.-L. Laville, and A.D. Cattani (eds). 2010. *The Human Economy.* Cambridge: Polity.
Herzfeld, M. 2004. *The Body Impolitic: Artisans and Artifice in the Global Hierarchy of Value.* Chicago: University of Chicago Press.
ISTAT. 2016. *Spese per Consumi delle Famiglie.* Rome: ISTAT.
Kleist, N., and S. Jansen. 2016. 'Introduction: Hope over Time: Crisis, Immobility and Future-Making', *History and Anthropology* 27(4): 373–92.
Knight, D.M., and C. Stewart. 2016. 'Ethnographies of Austerity: Temporality, Crisis and Affect in Southern Europe', *History and Anthropology* 27(1): 1–18.
Langley, P. 2014. *Liquidity Lost: The Governance of the Global Financial Crisis.* Oxford: Oxford University Press.
Lave, J., and E. Wenger. 1991. *Situated Learning: Legitimate Peripheral Participation.* Cambridge: Cambridge University Press.
Lenti, L. 1994. *Gioielli e Gioiellieri di Valenza: Arte e Storia Orafa: 1825–1975.* Turin: Allemandi.
Lenti, L., and G. Pugnetti. 1974. *Arte Orafa Valenzana.* Alessandria: Cassa di Risparmio di Alessandria.
Loftsdóttir, K. 2010. 'The Loss of Innocence: The Icelandic Financial Crisis and Colonial Past', *Anthropology Today* 26(1): 9–13.
Magni, C. 1999. *Modelli di Sviluppo a Macchia d'Olio: Ipotesi di Lettura dell'Evoluzione di Sistemi Locali.* Milan: Franco Angeli.
Markusen, A. 1996. 'Sticky Places in Slippery Space: A Typology of Industrial Districts', *Economic Geography* 72(3): 293–313.
Marshall, A. 1920. *Principles of Economics: An Introductory Volume*, 8th edition. London: Macmillan.
Masco, J. 2017. 'The Crisis in Crisis', *Current Anthropology* 58(S15): S65–S76.
Miyazaki, H. 2004. *The Method of Hope: Anthropology, Philosophy, and Fijian Knowledge.* Stanford: Stanford University Press.
Miyazaki, H., and A. Riles. 2005. 'Failure as an Endpoint', in A. Ong and S.J. Collier (eds), *Global Assemblages.* Oxford: Blackwell , pp. 320–31.
Molina, M.G., and M.C. Manenti. 1994. *Oro e Lavoro, Cento Anni Oreficeria in Valenza 1840–1940.* Turin: Lindau.
Muehlebach, A.K. 2016. 'Anthropologies of Austerity', *History and Anthropology* 27(3): 359–72.
Narotzky, S. 1997. *New Directions in Economic Anthropology.* London: Pluto Press.
———. 2006. 'Binding Labour and Capital: Moral Obligation and Forms of Regulation in a Regional Economy', *Etnografica* 10(2): 337–54.
Paradiso, R. 2008a. 'L'industria Alessandrina della Gioielleria: I Principali Indicatori', *Newsletter dell'Osservatorio di Distretto di Valenza* 1: 32–33.
———. 2008b. 'L'industria Alessandrina della Gioielleria: Il Commercio Internazionale', *Newsletter dell'Osservatorio di Distretto di Valenza* 1: 1–11.
Paulicelli, E. 2014. 'Fashion: The Cultural Economy of Made in Italy', *Fashion Practice* 6(2): 155–74.
Piore, M., and C.F. Sable. 1984. *The Second Industrial Divide.* New York: Basic Books.

Rabellotti, R., A. Carabelli and G. Hirsh. 2009. 'Italian Industrial Districts on the Move: Where Are They Going?', *European Planning Studies* 17(1): 19–41.
Sennett, R. 2008. *The Craftman*. London: Penguin.
Schmitt, J. 2008. 'Anthropologie Historique', *Bulletin du Centre d'Études* Médiévales d'Auxerre 2(23): 1–9.
Spyridakis, M. (ed.). 2018. *Market versus Society*. London: Palgrave Macmillan.
Stewart, K. 2007. *Ordinary Affects*. Durham, NC: Duke University Press.
Sundararajan, A. 2016. *The Sharing Economy: The End of Employment and the Rise of Crowd-Based Capitalism*. Boston: MIT Press.
Tett, G. 2009. *Fool's Gold: How Unrestrained Greed Corrupted a Dream, Shattered Global Market and Unleashed a Catastrophe*. London: Little Brown.
Tooze, A. 2018. *Crashed: How a Decade of Financial Crises Changed the World*. London: Allen Lane.
Turkle, S. (ed.). 2007. *Evocative Objects: Things We Think with*. Cambridge, MA: MIT Press.
Van Maanen, J. 1988. *Tales of the Field: On Writing Ethnography*. Chicago: University of Chicago Press.
Viazzo, P. 2012. *Introduzione all'Antropologia Storica*. Bari: Laterza.
Walby, S. 2015. *Crisis*. Cambridge: Polity.
Yanagisako, S.J. 1991. 'Capital and Gendered Interest in Italian Family Firms', in D.I. Kertzer and R.P. Saller (eds), *The Family in Italy*. New Haven: Yale University Press, pp. 321–39.

— Chapter 2 —

Crisis of Production and Crisis of Reproduction

The Disappearance of Woodcarvers in the Furniture-Making District of the Brianza, Lombardy

Simone Ghezzi

Introduction

'We are like pandas: we are disappearing from the Brianza.' These words by Carlo Crippa, a local seventy-year-old woodcarver, were the first he said to me by way of welcome in his tiny workshop, in a small town where once upon a time virtually each resident could boast at least one woodcarver as a relative. The same metaphor may also apply to other highly skilled artisans, such as wood inlayers, gilders and ébénistes, who were equally popular in this area not so long ago. Behind this light-hearted metaphor, there thus lies an indisputable and troubling concern towards the demise of several skilled occupations, which have always been the pride of the whole furniture industry in the Brianza. The drop in these vocations has brought these artisans to the verge of 'extinction', for neither the local youth nor migrant workers are available to fill in upcoming vacancies.

I began to study the production system of antique-style furniture in 2010,[1] in the midst of the Global Financial Crisis.[2] At that time, the enterprises of furniture, upholstery and woodworking were just recovering from the recession that had hit the sector in 2002 and had caused a reduction in terms of both firms and employment. By driving through the towns where the majority of these highly skilled artisans work and reside, I periodically visited their workshops, observed their activities and mapped their network within the production chain in order to better understand the flows of material goods, information, knowledge and labour circulating in the industrial district (Becattini and Rullani 1996; Becattini 2004). The core of the antique-style furniture production extends over two provinces, including the towns of Barlassina, Lentate sul Seveso and Meda in the provincial district of Monza, and the towns of Cantù, Cabiate, Mariano Comense and Figino in the district of Como. These are renowned locations for the excellence of their production and are also those in which I have carried out my ethnographic fieldwork. While most of the production takes place within the borders of the industrial district, the end-product is mostly export-oriented.

As I became more familiar with the social and economic history of the area, it seemed clear to me that the rampant economic crisis of recent years could not account for all the problems this industry was (and still is) facing. The concerns regarding the de-skilling of woodworkers, the decline of fine craftsmanship, the ambiguous value and quality of the products and the shrinking earnings were already a matter of fact and were only being aggravated by the economic and financial crisis. Most of my interlocutors have a clear idea about what is to blame for the situation, be it the unpredictability of the market, the unresponsiveness of the state or the exploitative power of the client firms, but they have no clue as to how to tackle it through proactive and collegial mobilization. There is a sense of inevitability about the whole situation: the acceptance of the ill-fated destiny of craftsmanship and artisanry, and the impotence before a constellation of hegemonic powers over which they have no control, but cannot do without.

The demise of these occupations may still be far off in the future, but nonetheless significant changes are occurring. Indeed, prior to their extinction, there is currently a more pressing reality to cope with: the link between deteriorating craftsmanship – articulated through discourses regarding the pervasive decline of artistic quality – and the shift in the culture of work. The transformation of work practices, institutional arrangements and family obligations that were to secure the continuation of kin-based artisan specialization are affecting the ongoing circulation and renewal of contextual knowledge in the process of value creation. Central to my notion of culture of work is thus the interplay of two specific but intertwined dimensions: culture as know-how or artisan skill and culture as socialization to artisan activity and its symbolic construction (such as work ethics and the meanings of material production). In the long run, the crisis in these two dimensions will also have a significant impact on the reproduction of the whole system. As for reproduction, I make reference to the analytical framework given in Willis (1981), which provides a critical review of this key concept in feminist and neo-Marxist theories. Willis helps to clarify that different meanings are conflated into one single term: biological reproduction and production of gendered persons; reproduction of the labour force (daily reproduction of labour power as well as generational replacement of labour power); the reproduction of the circuit of capital; and finally the reproduction of the social relations necessary for capitalist accumulation to occur (Willis 1981: 48). The problem with these multiple meanings is that they convey a 'very abstractedly conceived notion of "structure"' and an 'undialectical transmission' (1981: 49), namely a static and therefore a mistaken dimension of what social reproduction should account for. Thus, the workplace, the household and everyday life constitute different landscapes in which one can notice both the maintenance of cultural models and their interpretations – or 'reworkings' in Willis' words – leading to cultural change. But there are also inherent tensions and contradictions in the development and transmission of knowledge and cultural practices, as I will argue later; therefore, 'we need a version of social reproduction that can expose these tensions in all sites where they occur', as Gavin A. Smith has recently put it (2018: 67).

This chapter aims to explore the current crisis of this local district through the sector that has always been reputed to be the feather in the cap of the Brianza, producing the highest-quality furniture, according to my interlocutors. Such aesthetic prowess was continuously affirmed during our conversations, yet time and again was also questioned when current commercial production was compared to the handmade items manufactured for sale just a few decades earlier. The core of my discussion is thus based on such ambivalences and the split between public prowess and private concerns. It develops along two lines of discussion that may provide insights into the complexity of the crisis in the Brianza furniture industry as well as possibly providing a comparative lens to widen the ethnographic investigation in other industrial districts. The first is the contradictory opinions that circulate among those working in the furniture sector in relation to their labour experiences and material productions, especially their concern with the value and quality of the products they produced and their responses (or lack thereof) to the alleged artistic decline of woodcarving. In examining this, I acknowledge William H. Sewell's 'language of labour' approach – that is, language is 'not only about workers' utterances or about theoretical discourse on labour, but about the whole range of institutional arrangements, ritual gestures, work practices, methods of struggle, customs and actions that gave the workers' world a comprehensive shape' (Sewell 1980: 12). The second line of discussion will centre on the transformation of work ethics and the changes that are under way among artisan households, and which are jeopardizing the reproduction of craftsmanship in the antique style and luxury furniture production. My general argument is that the crisis in the Brianza local economy is cultural prior to being economic: it has much to do with cultural change towards labour that occurred prior to the 2007 economic recession. Hence, I will elaborate on the idea of crisis concerning not only the *production* of commodified items, but also the *reproduction* of a specific culture of work and production. Such a culture is no longer reproducible in practice, but it still appears to be sound as a public discourse.

The Reproduction of the Local Economy through the Crises

Marxist scholars of capitalism, such as Arrighi (2009), Harvey (2014), Streeck (2014) and Wallerstein (Wallerstein et al. 2013) have argued that crises are unavoidable events in the cyclical logic of capital accumulation. As a matter of fact, 'they are essential to the reproduction of capitalism. It is in the course of crises that the instabilities of capitalism are confronted, reshaped and re-engineered to create a new version of what capitalism is about' (Harvey 2014: ix). However, this new configuration does not occur without a social cost. The decline and disappearance of regional specializations and their know-how is often one of the effects of these cyclical crises; the inevitable trajectory of succumbing economic systems unable to withstand the emergence of new and more competitive regions. The result is almost always the demise of the specialized local production and/or its relocation to more competitive regions with variable and at times unpredictable consequences for the local economy as a whole. The Brianza is no exception. Since the Second World War, this area had already experienced several economic crises, but these were short-term phenomena with positive long-term effects, as they sparked the beginning of a virtuous circle. For example, the downsizing of the textile and clothing sector that peaked in the 1950s did not produce long-term unemployment. The male workforce that was laid off from the firms producing power looms, knitting machines and various accessories for textile companies could redirect their know-how to the rising mechanic sector, which, in turn, supplied metallic components and accessories to the pre-existing furniture industry that was booming following the rising domestic demand for furniture. For the female workforce, the implications of the restructuring were not so positive, for their know-how was not an expendable resource for the booming manufacturing sectors. As a result, some withdrew from the labour market, while others were hired as unskilled workers in the mechanic industry. Later, in the 1970s, unemployment caused by the gradual disappearance of large companies, due to closures or relocations, was rapidly reabsorbed by the growing number of mainly family-run micro-enterprises, which thrived through subcontracting activities (Ghezzi 2007). Each time that the restructuring and/or the closure of leading local factories took place, a redundant but highly specialized labour force would be hired in small firms or would find its own way into entrepreneurship, which in turn would create more jobs. Paradoxically, it produced redistributive effects. The thick networks of firms in different sectors constituted the mainstay of flexible specialization that this area is widely known for and allowed medium-sized firms to use the local supply chain in order to be highly competitive in the globalized market.

However, starting from the second half of the 1990s, the district as a whole had to face new challenges. As a player in the open market of the global economy, it had to confront an economic setting with new international competitors, especially Chinese companies that were able to manufacture a wide range of cheap products that were accessible to a large number of consumers. Ironically, during the postwar economic boom, it was the very Brianza along with other Italian industrial districts that played the role of aggressive newcomers. 'We were the Chinese of Europe', I was frequently told by older local entrepreneurs. Their competitive advantage only partially stemmed from their exceptionally flexible technical skills and hard work; in fact, they could also benefit from the devaluation effects of the lira, the informal economy, tax evasion, public funded incentives and a networked system of production characterized by a myriad of small family-run artisan enterprises (Ghezzi 2016).[3] But in the 1990s, these institutional and informal mechanisms were no longer viable or sufficient solutions to remain competitive in the global market, so the woodworking sector of the Brianza shifted to high-end production, completing a transformation that had already been initiated as early as the 1970s by a few forward-looking firms, and by the early 2000s was entirely accomplished. Since then, antique-style furniture – mostly custom-made – has constituted an important component of the so-called luxurious interiors, a niche for which the Brianza is widely known in the world. This notwithstanding, high-end production and tailor-made furniture to please the wealthiest in the population did not shield the local economy from economic crises and market turbulence. The first Gulf War, between 1990 and 1991, almost wiped out the demand for luxury furniture coming from the Middle East as a retaliation for Italian involvement in the conflict, demand that was only partially offset by the lucrative emerging markets in some post-Soviet states. In the early 2000s, another recession hit the Italian economy and the furniture sector went through another restructuring process, before being crushed again in 2010 in the aftermath of the Global Financial Crisis. The niche managed to survive only thanks to the fact that the exports of luxurious made-to-measure furniture held up well, as it is still one of the most coveted Made in Italy goods by the upper classes worldwide.

The three charts reported below (Figures 2.1–2.3) provide a contrasting picture of the current situation and seem to suggest two different courses of events. Local newspapers and business reports issued from various local agencies have repeatedly announced that the furniture sector is finally getting out of the economic downturn – in line with the rest of the local economy – as if to reinforce the myth of a short-term economic crisis. As shown in Figure 2.1, it would be hard to argue that the crisis is still lingering, for the growth has been

Figure 2.1. Index of industrial and artisan furniture production in Lombardy, 2010–19 (index 2010=100). Source: Unioncamere, Milan.

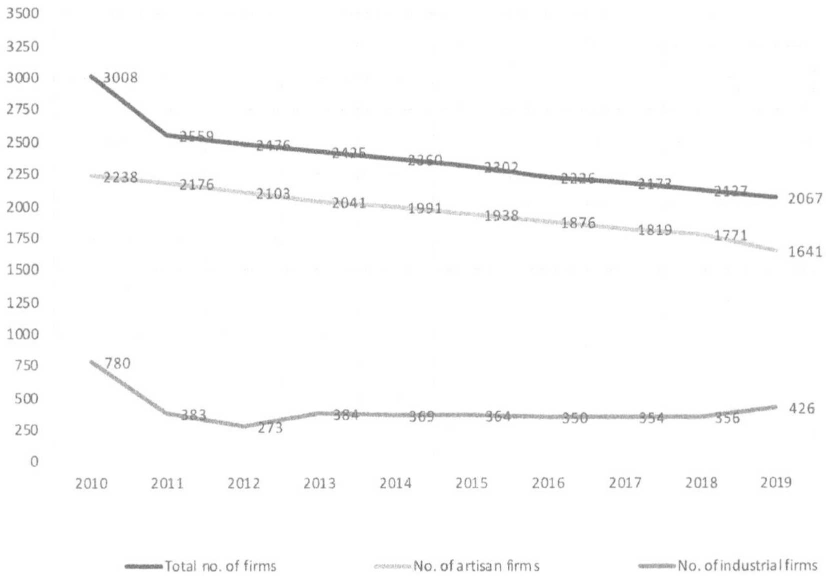

Figure 2.2. Number of firms in the Monza-Brianza and Como furniture district, 2010–19. Source: Chamber of Commerce of Como and Lecco.

constant since 2013 (not only in the woodworking sector but also in the other manufacturing sectors), albeit that it is still a far cry from the peak of 2010. By contrast, Figures 2.2. and 2.3 seem to suggest a much gloomier picture for the furniture industry. This is especially true of the artisan sector: the data show that firms and employment have been shrinking for several years now and the negative trend is continuing, despite the buffering measures of state intervention through the extension of temporary lay-offs indemnity to artisan firms (see note 3) and despite the alleged end of the economic crisis.

Figures 2.2 and 2.3 also show that unlike in the previous crises, the unemployment caused by the recent recession was the consequence of lay-offs arising from the restructuring of the thick network of small firms, precisely those that in previous cyclical crises contributed to absorbing the labour force made redundant by industrial firms during the transition to neoliberal flexible specialization. Now it looks like the tables have turned: the industrial firms are absorbing a portion of that labour force. This role has also recently been taken on by shopping mall centres, supermarkets and firms in the tertiary sector. However, these employers are only partially able to do so:

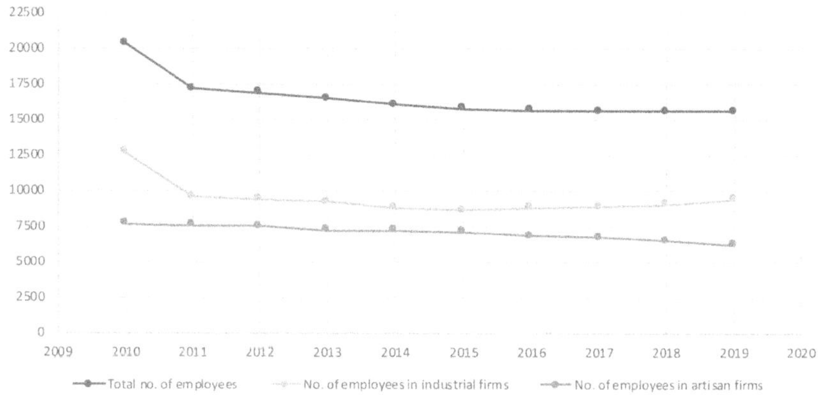

Figure 2.3. Number of employees in artisan and industrial firms in the Monza-Brianza and Como furniture district, 2010–19. Source: Chamber of Commerce of Como and Lecco.

first, they employed only a fraction of the skilled workers made redundant by the manufacturing sector; second, they would prefer to hire a younger labour force; and, third, the job contracts are mainly short-term and precarious.

From Classic-Style to Luxury Furniture Production

'Until forty years ago we were all woodcarvers here.' Ambrogio Belotti (b. 1939), whose family have been in the woodcarving business for three generations, remembers that in the 1950s in the towns of Barlassina, Meda and Lentate and the surrounding area, thousands of woodcarvers were active in the classic-style furniture industry. Since there are no historical statistics that differentiate between the different specializations (gilders, inlayers, woodcarvers, etc.) in the furniture trade, it is hard to corroborate his statement. Such estimates were also shared and backed up by the oral histories of other informants of his generation, who also lamented that the presence of so many craftsmen competing with one another kept remuneration fairly low.

The production of classic-style furniture was already one of the most important artisan activities of its kind in the Brianza from the mid-nineteenth century onwards. It is likely that it started off following the construction of numerous estates by the Milanese aristocracy who used to holiday in the region in the summertime. These villas required artisans specialized in the manufacture and maintenance of doors, frames and furniture; initially, they came from the city of Milan, but eventually this craft spread and consolidated among the rural population of the region. By the late nineteenth century, local artisan craftsmanship had already outclassed Milanese craftsmanship, and by the turn of the twentieth century, it had already made a name for itself beyond Lombardy to compete with the much more expensive artistry of French ébénisterie. The qualitative leap in furniture production could be achieved thanks to the local arts and crafts schools that were established by Catholic as well as nonreligious institutions in the towns that are still known nowadays as centres of classic-style furniture production. Their goal was twofold: providing education and practical training to children without means, and allowing those already working to improve or expand their skills (drawing, ornamentation, etc.).[4]

According to an investigation conducted by the Società Umanitaria[5] of Milan in 1904 on wood workers of the Brianza (Schiavi 1904), in the early twentieth century, some 91 per cent of the whole workforce in the furniture sector was employed in about 3,000 home workshops (with an average of four to five workers each), and the rest (9 per cent) was occupied in what we might call 'small factories'. This activity required good manual skills and very low technology, and therefore could be generally carried out at home – usually in the kitchen of the house, the only room equipped with a table, transformed for the occasion into a workbench – by a male master-artisan helped by his children and other family members, and by a few low-paid young apprentices who, eventually, would leave the workshop to pursue an independent artisan profession. At the time, the increasing demand for furniture was dealt with based on the principle of a division of labour among artisans. The final output of one single item, whether a cabinet, a sofa or a bed, would require the effort of several workers, most of which were highly skilled craftsmen in their own field: lacquerers, decorative painters (including those applying silver and gold gilt), veneerers, inlaid wood workers and, obviously, woodcarvers. As woodcarving was an essential component of this cottage industry, carvers must have been quite numerous, but being peasant-artisans who were probably not used to keeping accounting books and files of their activity, very little documentation has been preserved to trace them (Guenzi and Marelli 1965). To prove their existence in this area of the Brianza, apart from the oral testimonies I have been collecting, there are a very few records that can be retrieved from the historical archives of the Chamber of Commerce of Milan; these are requests to activate companies bearing the name of the applicants, which probably represent only the tip of the iceberg. Many micro-shops could in fact be known in the municipality in which they carried out their activities, but their notification was never reported to the Chamber of Commerce. In addition, many carvers worked alone at home and therefore had no incentive to comply with the rules.

Among the whole phases of production, woodcarving is still the cornerstone of classic-style furniture, the one that set the value of the piece and the type of style (see note 1). The basic tools of the woodcarver have not changed; mallets, clamps, rasps, V-shape and U-shape gouges are used today as they were at the time of the Società Umanitaria's investigation. The workplace is often carved out from the family home: the basement, the garage, an empty room or the first floor of a two-storey house. The production was entirely handmade until the 1950s, but during the economic boom, the need for greater productivity brought about significant transformations in artisan production. While in previous generations the rising demand for furniture was met with the intensification of the cottage industry and artisan specialization, this time that same pressure led to more standardized styles through the partial mechanization of the carving or even its substitution in a few cases (using, for example, wood pulp casts or polyurethane resin for the reproduction of specific details in less valuable pieces of furniture). The first machinery to be introduced was the mechanical carving machine with variable milling heads that is operated by one person, the *abbozzatore* (sketcher). This machine – which nowadays is available in numerically controlled models – is able to grossly reproduce various floral motifs and other kinds of decorations on several wooden pieces (as many as there are milling heads) at the same time, utilizing the prototype placed in the central head of the machine as a master copy. These pieces will then be worked on by a woodcarver, who will simply have to do the finishing, allowing him to quickly deliver the pieces with the friezes identical to that of the prototype. The introduction of this machinery has undoubtedly speeded up the carving phase, not through the substitution of the woodcarver with a mechanic tool, but through its reconfiguration within the supply chain, giving him less control over the production process, and introducing greater routinization and standardization.

By looking at these transformations in the supply chain, it is possible to see the similarity of what I describe to the process of skill dispossession suggested by Harry Braverman (1974), whereby the logic of capitalism forces the artisan to share his craftsmanship and accumulated knowledge with machinery that has been devised to virtually replace his skill. While the introduction of the carving machine and the use of wood pulp and of artificial resins increased productivity when the market demand for classic-style furniture was on the rise, woodcarving turned into a routine labour of finishing, retouching and adjusting the rough grooves left by the machine. The only exception is the creation of the prototype that, even today, must be made manually from a block of rough wood and therefore requires fine craftsmanship.

The technological innovations to increase the productivity of woodcarving have contributed to creating three different statuses of woodcarvers with specific skill requirements: the highly prized prototype makers who speak of themselves not just as craftsmen, but as artist-craftsmen; the finishers who modify the rough grooves by imprinting their artistic hand on the piece; and the so-called polishers who limit themselves to grinding, sanding and polishing the piece previously machined by the mechanic carver, without using a gouge, the defining tool of the woodcarver.

In the 1970s, the massive diffusion of modern designed furniture and modular furniture, free from decoration and more functional, met the new tastes of both working-class and middle-class households. Production was more industrial-oriented and this element triggered relevant structural changes in the artisanal component of the supply chain. The use of mass-produced wood-based material, such as plywood, fibreboard and chipboard, with plastic laminate as finishing instead of solid wood, and artificial wood veneers pushed many woodcarvers and several other types of skilled artisans either out of business or towards other trades.

Following the early warning signals of weakness in the sector, Aldo Boffi (b. 1946), woodcarver and son of a woodcarver, made choices that were followed by others. Trained in the 1950s and the 1960s, he experienced the maximum expansion of woodcarving and its incipient decline. Although he receives a retirement pension, he continues to work in his own individually owned firm as a carpenter and cabinet-maker:

> Let's say … from 1965 to 1976, if I remember well, I both carved and used wood pulp, then from 1977 to 1990 I made ordinary chairs and classic-style chairs, with light carving. Then I stopped because I was making very little money. All those people who produce industrial stuff have decimated us all … So I turned into a carpenter and made furniture to measure. I have a business of my own.

> I have a retired worker who helps me out a few hours. Work comes and goes, but I go on because it's what I do.

Conversely, Luigi Falconieri (b. 1940) had to give up woodcarving due to health problems, even though he has continued to practise it on occasion as a second job:

> The carving is a drudgery: I had to stay bent over on the workbench all day, so I began to get stomach problems and could no longer digest food well. I just had to stop. I found a job at Pirelli's … and then when it closed I got another job and became a warehouse manager in a small company in Pessano. I was recommended, because you know, it would have been hard to find a job at fifty. But I always did a little bit of carving. For example, when I lost my job at Pirelli's, I made all the furniture that we have in the house; my wife liked it. I was lucky, because nowadays women don't want this stuff, because it's difficult to dust. I never stopped [doing carving]. So many times they called me to make prototypes! Because the generation that came after mine, is no longer capable of doing 'em. Lately I do some work only for C., because we are friends. I made some models a few years ago, and now they are going into production; there is some more little work to do, though. It's been a while since I got my tools out again … because this is a time of crisis and some firms have closed.

For Falconieri, the decision to quit woodcarving as his main activity was determined by health reasons, but in the mid-1980s, the crisis in the sector had prompted many craftsmen to follow a similar path, that is, to seek a better paid and steadier job and to practise woodcarving as a moonlighting activity, fully exploiting the opportunity of working in shifts.

Luigino Binelli (b. 1954), still a full-time woodcarver and son of a woodcarver, recounts having been tempted to quit woodcarving and get a new job:

> In 1984 woodcarving work orders were scanty, there was a serious crisis. I was already married and had a small child. I recall that through a relative of mine employed at the local bank I managed to get a job interview. To cut a long story short, I could have gotten the job, but I got cold feet. Gee! I started thinking about the troubles my father and my brother were going through … but I know that at the time many woodcarvers were getting jobs in factories, working in shifts so that they could arrange to do woodcarving at home.

Carlo Crippa's work history is quite revealing in explaining the ups and downs of woodcarving. He started off as a young trained woodcarver in the early 1970s, but due to the low income he was earning from his activity, he begrudgingly had to quit and take up a new career as a truck driver. After retirement just a few years ago, he has resumed his old passion for woodcarving and now basically works full time as woodcarver-polisher. He does not consider himself a skilful craftsman. He claims that he did not have enough training and although his work as truck driver had always allowed him to do some woodcarving for small workshops in his spare time, he never achieved enough proficiency, nor has he the talent that this trade requires.

Most elderly people like Carlo continue to work as woodcarvers after retirement for extra cash. In order to respect the status of his late brother, who was known locally as a remarkable woodcarver and decorator, Ambrogio Belotti, a self-declared woodcarver-polisher, still works in the same premises where he, his brother and their old father used to run their family business. He laments that woodcarving is not highly valued by furniture factories: 'We underwent so many humiliations. I can say that because I was in the middle of all that.' He raises the issue of outsourcing and the low remuneration by client firms due to the relatively weak position of woodcarvers. Most of them are either self-employed artisans or business partners in micro-family firms without much bargaining power. Therefore, as subcontractors of client firms, they are always confronted with potential tensions. They must rely on the client firms because these are their most important work providers; nonetheless, they fear them because they may turn into exploitative parties by reducing the price of subcontracting work and by exerting control over their work process. Indeed, one of the main complaints from small artisans is that 'the big ones' do not redistribute their profits fairly: 'Sono una potenza' – i.e. they are powerful for better and for worse – is how the artisans usually refer to them. They also take advantage of the fact that many woodcarvers work in the informal economy or are retired and already have an income.

These short excerpts of woodcarvers' work histories confirm that the changes in middle-class tastes created a severe crisis for this sector; its precarious survival conjured up an agonizing niche. Yet, by the end of the 1990s, the scenario would change completely. The emergence of new elite groups in various developing countries (Russian and Kazakh oligarchs, Qatar billionaires, rich residents of Dubai and so forth) opened up new market opportunities. The craze for old-style furniture that would recall the pomp and grandeur of the *ancien-régime* European aristocracy boosted the demand for luxurious made-to-measure furniture.

The new economic conjuncture prompted some artisans to get back to their trade full time. Giuseppe Cattaneo's (b. 1954) work history is illustrative of this new situation. Giuseppe started woodcarving in his teens as an apprentice at the Belottis' workshop and took evening classes in decoration and in the art of gilding at two different arts and trades schools that coincidentally discontinued these courses while he was still studying them, due to a lack of students. In his early twenties, he was already a self-employed woodcarver, but in the early 1990s, he had to give up his craft because: 'The payment I was given was ludicrous and not negotiable by the client firm. I could barely make enough money to pay taxes. So I gave up.' First he got a job in a thermoplastic polyurethane factory, and when production was moved to China, he worked in one of the client firms. In the meantime, however, demand for woodcarving increased and he was asked to get back into full-time woodcarving by some of his clients for whom he occasionally worked off the books. He was unsure of what to do, given his previous discouraging experience. Eventually, what convinced him to resume the trade of his youth was a family problem. His elderly mother broke her femur and his octogenarian father was unable to take care of her. Therefore, he decided to work as a self-employed woodcarver in his parents' home. This time, though, in order to make a living, he only works for the high-end furniture sector.

The excerpts of these work biographies depict a group of craftsmen that has become more fragmented during the diverse crises not only in relation to their threefold skill requirements (as mentioned above), but also in relation to their work trajectories. These are the escapers (those who have left the craft indefinitely), the moonlighters (those who practice the trade as a second job or after retirement), the homecomers (those who came back after several years) and, finally, the regulars (those who formally never stopped). Newcomers are basically absent, as I will explain below. Yet, there is also a silver thread among them: income loss, technological innovation, de-skilling and exploitation have produced a deep contradiction between production exigencies and the exigencies of reproduction, both in terms of living conditions and of transmission of the trade.

Braverman has written that 'the capitalist mode of production systematically destroys all-around skills where they exist, and brings into being skills and occupations that correspond to its needs' (1974: 82). This is the kind of hubris that has characterized classic-style furniture in the Brianza. And yet, the current situation signals another contradiction: the high demand for luxurious interiors seems to favour the return of these traditional skills, the accumulated knowledge of materials and processes that were demeaned. A failure to address this issue is going to turn the luxurious furniture sector into an agonizing niche.

Apprenticeship and the Crisis of Reproduction

In *The Craftsman*, Richard Sennett describes the artisan workshop in this way:

> Peering through a window into a carpenter's shop, you see inside an elderly man surrounded by his apprentices and his tools. Order reigns within, parts of chairs are clamped neatly together, the fresh smell of wood shavings fills the room, the carpenter bends over his bench to make a fine incision for marquetry. The shop is menaced by a furniture factory down the road. (Sennett 2008: 19)

In imagining the carpenter's shop, Sennett does not make any reference to a specific location, but if I peeked into a small cabinet-making or woodcarving workshop in the Brianza, some remarkable incongruences with Sennett's image might arise. An artisan workshop is usually anything but a neat place: it is stuffed, dusty and messy. Moreover, there is always a furniture factory in close proximity to an artisan workshop. The coexistence of artisan and industrial firms is a structural feature of most industrial furniture and interiors districts, particularly in the Brianza. Artisan and industry productions do coexist in a symbiotic way, although with strong asymmetries of power, inasmuch as together they constitute the backbone of the production chain.

What is furthest from Sennett's ideal-typical description is the presence of apprentices. So far in my fieldwork research, I have not met a single one, not even off the books. In some workshops, apprentices have never been hired; in others, especially in those that are in their second or third generation, the presence of apprentices is rarely documented, and when it is, it took place only in the early period of their activity, some thirty years ago. The youngest generation of woodcarvers are already in their fifties, but the majority of those still in business are in their mid-sixties or early seventies.

The apprenticeship system that enabled the transmission of craftsmanship and the various skills of cabinet-making to the younger generations collapsed quite rapidly in the 1980s. The intergenerational transfer of know-how came to a halt and the generational turnover of the labour force is now visibly in jeopardy. All lament the lack of new apprentices, but many disagree on the causes and on the action to take.

The anthropological literature on apprenticeship has pointed out that this mix of informal and formal training is not just a 'method of passing on acquired trade skills and of maintaining supply of craftsmen' (*Encyclopaedia of the Social Sciences*, cited in Goody 1989: 237).

Rather, it is a complex system in which the trainees begin to assimilate confident attitudes and behaviours towards work in a specific sociocultural context (Lave and Wenger 1991; Herzfeld 2004). Therefore, the disappearance of apprentices from the classic-style furniture district hints as much at the transformation of the cultural milieu that enabled the social reproduction of craftsmanship in the Brianza as at the discontinuity of skill. By reporting some excerpts from my conversations with people working in this sector, I will offer a glimpse of the different explanations that circulate. However diverse such explanations may be – diversity stemming from my informants' different positions within the production chain – they seem to relate to cultural aspects, at times disguised by economic aspects. Giuseppe Elli (b. 1953) acknowledged that in his workshop:

> In forty years of work I have never seen one apprentice here … Actually, I had one for a short time … It looks like a comfortable job, but it's a drudgery, a position full of renunciations: eight, nine hours standing still … The early years are deadly for a beginner. If you are seventeen, eighteen or even twelve years old, and you are going to do a job like this, I do not know how many would be able to keep up.

Luigino Binelli (b. 1947) confessed something that few would openly admit:

> I have to tell you the truth: I did not like being a carver. But my father was a carver … I went to school in the morning and in the afternoon I had to work in his workshop [in the family house]. I was not like my fellow schoolmates. They could have fun after class. Not me. I would stay in to learn how to polish, to sand and then I would clean up woodchips that piled up on the floor. It is a culture that you begin to like slowly and slowly.

Fulvio (b. 1954), Luigino's brother and business partner, is even more explicit: 'let's just say it: that [culture] was somewhat imposed upon us'. Luigino nodded and went on:

> I wanted to be a draftsman … but since the carving was the main activity at home, I studied ornamental design for two years, always in the evening, because during the day I would work in my dad's workshop … Had I chosen anything else, it would have been trauma for my father … I do not regret it because … because it turned out like this. But kids nowadays … to think to place them here working, it's hard … Do you know that once parents would pay the master artisan to make him keep their kid in his workshop? The artisan would teach him the trade, and the parents would pay him to do that.

Ambrogio's work history is remarkably similar to that of the Binelli brothers:

> This job is over, because today the youngsters no longer have the humility to knuckle down. They live a different life. And maybe that's the right thing to do. I did it too with my children. I began by working in an electrical engineering company and in the evening I attended electronic engineering classes. Then it turned out that that school was used to sending many students to work in the Navy. But my father told me: 'you'd better stay home and help your brother'. And it was not a bad choice, after all. So I stayed home, but I had to betray my personality, because I had no talent for this job [woodcarving] but I had to submit to it. I poured my heart and soul into it, though. It cost me dearly, you know?

From these excerpts, I draw two points that seem relevant to my argument: the importance of kin-based apprenticeship and the upbringing of apprentices into a patriarchal culture of work. In the Brianza, woodcarving work and training preferably took place in one's own family context and in a male structure of production. With very few exceptions, all of the artisans I have met are second- or third-generation woodcarvers who were trained by fathers and grandfathers without fellow apprentices. It is likely that exclusive apprenticeship in the family was practised to limit the privileges of transmitting knowledge outside the domestic group and ensure its economic resources for the next generation. In case of market expansion the need to increase production may also favour the hiring of non-kin apprentices, but as every artisan is very well aware, apprentices are always potential competitors and therefore may constitute a threat, particularly in a highly competitive arena. Hence, when skill lost its labour power and revenues weakened among woodcarving, apprenticeship began to diminish and was practised solely among kin.

These excerpts of conversations dealing with the retrospective reflection on their own work experience provide some insights about the social and cultural environment in which these artisans had grown up. The tight discipline they were subjected to, the intergenerational conflict that was solved by 'knuckling down' and finally by making themselves like what they initially did not constituted relevant aspects that characterized their socialization to work and shaped their work ethics. But such social construction of work is no longer shared and therefore is neither viable nor sustainable nowadays. These too are cultural elements seriously affecting apprenticeship in the long run. As the range of work opportunities in the local labour market increased, the only way to have children follow in their fathers' footsteps was through the exerting of patriarchal authority. Yet, it is evident that those who suffered from it have not imposed it upon their children; as a consequence, they have greater freedom of choice around their work experiences. With reference to this point, there is the pervasive conviction among woodcarvers that today's young generations could hardly handle the fatigue of this trade, but they never hired apprentices to test their attitude towards disciplined training. Perhaps the alleged unbearable working conditions in their own workshops relate to what they had endured as children under their fathers' authority, an experience they would rather not impose upon their own children. Thus, the perspective of seeing their children go through their same drudgery has had the effect of alienating the latter from the family trade and, in the end, of disrupting apprenticeship as a form of reproduction of both skill and work ethics. Why should an artisan invest his time and money in training a non-kin apprentice who will eventually end up setting up an activity on his own, given the low cost of the equipment required to start up? Indeed, some artisans have been very explicit in addressing the prohibitive economic cost of hiring apprentices. There are no grounds for keeping apprentices due to the high cost of training, as explained below by Giuseppe Elli and Giuseppe Cattaneo:

> It takes at least four to five years to decently train an apprentice woodcarver. I may teach the basics for two to three years, but then he needs two or three more years to perfect himself. Who is going to help me out? As I work by myself, my day will no longer be productive for a long time. Either someone helps me financially, or nothing can be done. And what if he then goes away? Yes, I may have trained a young worker and turned him in a skilled worker. But that's about it. What did I get in return? I don't think I'm being selfish by saying that … We all have a majority shareholder to deal with. It's worse than signing a sharecropping contract. I work at home, I put my money in my job, and yet I have to give back at least 50 per cent of what I make to the state! [Giuseppe Elli]

> In the past it was much easier because the state was not so greedy and taxes not so exorbitant. Artisans could resort to trickery to have low-cost apprentices. Because when teaching you have to stop working … and the apprentice does not produce either … We [apprentices] were satisfied with little and learned a lot. I basically started fiddling around with tools in the afternoon during middle school. If you do that now, you [the artisan] go to jail. Turning a blind eye made training practicable and successful. I learned so much this way! But that's all gone and those people are gone too. I'm really scared that we are not as good as those who preceded us and that there will be no one after us. [Giuseppe Cattaneo]

The training to be a highly qualified woodcarver is very long when compared to other activities in the supply chain of the furniture district. It is deemed that five years is the minimum time necessary to master the various techniques of carving in relation to the types of wood and the decorative styles. This span of time has never been entirely subsidized by the various national laws that have been enforced in recent years in order to stimulate apprenticeships. Some fee waivers concerning taxes and social security contributions are applicable to firms that hire apprentices; in addition, the hourly pay of an apprentice has been further reduced, and yet these measures are not regarded as sufficient to make apprenticeship economically sustainable in the small workshops. The main issue is that such incentives are conditional. The artisan-employer must abide by strict procedures regarding the tasks of the apprentice and reporting them to the school where his young employee is enrolled. Hence, apprenticeship is no longer a private matter between the master artisan and the apprentice's parents. Yet, if the artisan's apprentice were his own offspring, perhaps the state incentives would not be disregarded. Moreover, the negative effects on productivity would be taken into account and accepted as the price to pay in order to guarantee the continuity of the trade within the family. Thus, the inadequacy of state incentives, the insatiable appetite of the state for the artisans' dividends, and its policing role seem to constitute a collective and all-purpose rhetoric that in this specific context is called upon to rationalize the choice of foregoing apprenticeship – a choice that causes emotional distress stemming from the failure to pass on to their young children the craftsmanship they have so painstakingly acquired.

However, there are some dissenting voices that are not so lenient towards the artisans regarding the crisis of apprenticeship. Sergio Albertini (b. 1952), for example, is the principal of a local vocational school that has graduated many students working in the furniture sector. He is himself the son and the brother of woodcarvers. When I mentioned these complaints to him, he immediately began by criticizing his fellow artisans' short-sightedness:

> It's really easy to talk like that after a certain age and with a fat belly … to come and say that the best school is the workshop [*la bottega*] and then blame others because they never hired apprentices. What did they do? They did not transmit any knowledge. It is obvious that the apprentice makes you waste time, especially in a job like this, where there is little routine. But I know of very serious workshops that for love, for passion of this trade have employed apprentices, even if that meant losing some money.

The crisis of apprenticeship is unquestionably having an impact on the general level of craftsmanship, but it is also an explicit manifestation of a wider and more profound crisis in relation to the meaning of artisan work. There is no longer a shared notion of what artisan work means between those whose apprenticeship was regarded as an opportunity to emerge out of poverty – and where abuse and exploitation could be tolerated and actually perceived as a necessary step towards upward mobility – and those who clearly never experienced that social condition. Indeed, the latter are also institutionally fully protected from such potential forms of exploitation. The increasing disaffection towards woodcarving is triggering a short circuit in the traditional training system. As I have illustrated above, the high standard of craftsmanship was originally achieved through the founding of local arts and crafts schools that were widespread in the area where the furniture sector was developing. They became the main source of formal training for the working class and the foundation for youths' transition into skilled artisans. In reviewing the biographies of the craftsmen who are regarded as being among the best based on the precision of their carving, their artistic talent and their creative inspiration, the fundamental role played by the formal training of these schools clearly emerges. Among those who were regarded as the best woodcarvers and cabinet-makers, such training paralleled and enriched their apprenticeships. By the mid-1990s, all the surviving local schools had shut down evening classes on ornamentation and woodcarving due to a lack of applicants. Currently, a few short-term evening classes are occasionally held for adult students who apply for fun or to expand their practical knowledge, hoping that they may help out in their respective professions (as architects and interior designers). None of the applicants is looking for a career in woodcarving. In the meantime, the artist-woodcarvers who used to teach the evening classes are ageing and disappearing.

Conclusion: The Epilogue of the Local Culture of Production

The luxury-furniture industry of the Brianza has responded to the recent economic crises by building on the idea of the 'production of beauty'. This kind of production continues to be one of the cornerstones of the Brianza furniture district, but on the whole, it presents a series of critical issues that the last economic crisis has amplified. Employment in artisan workshops is unrelentingly falling, along with the number of artisan firms; apprenticeship is virtually disappearing in several artisan trades; the household is no longer the customary place to pass down skills, crafts, knowledge and specific approaches to work. The global market has contributed to saving many jobs, but has not provided means for the social reproduction of local craftsmanship. It has created an apparently successful niche, but it is then incapable of providing the necessary resources to secure the survival of this very niche. Tackling this issue would require a collective effort and a holistic approach that should include policy-makers as well as entrepreneurs and trade unions, particularly in a highly competitive system, but I do not see this on the horizon. Instead, what I see are more practical, albeit patchy, solutions to paper over the cracks. For example, the idea of beauty applied to furniture is highly dynamic and undergoes stylistic changes in accordance with the tastes and preferences of global customers. In practice, these changes are accomplished through simpler variations of what is already available. Woodcarvers in particular have to scale up or create more lavish and ornate versions of prototypes and ornaments from their own artistic repertoire in order to furnish mansions and luxurious hotels that require much larger furniture than the original models. They come to devalue this kind of work because they see it as an expression of tackiness and bad taste. These simply represent commodities, set against the products of high culture, which embody a rich cultural heritage that is captured by their 'Italian-ness', even though they evoke craft traditions that are not necessarily Italian. But being Made in Italy justifies their high price value.

The aesthetic-prowess rhetoric of Made in Italy production also disguises a local secret that represents another 'shortcut', locally devised to bypass the problem concerning the social reproduction of craftsmanship. This is a local secret that I was timidly made aware of during my fieldwork research: the outsourcing of woodcarving outside Italy to countries such as Bulgaria and Egypt. Very few firms openly admit to outsourcing in locations outside Italy. Such secrecy should not be exclusively seen as a competitive strategy among firms. Indeed, I detected discomfort among those who mentioned it. First, they were explicitly contradicting the adage that 'the best crafts are still produced in the Brianza' and, secondly, they were blatantly admitting that craftsmanship may be available and, above all, easily purchasable elsewhere, with possible negative consequences on the local economy. One entrepreneur said to me that he is perfectly aware that by outsourcing across borders, he is impoverishing his own region, 'but I have no alternative choice other than to close down my firm'. As a matter of fact, the savings in labour costs are substantial, up to 50 per cent. And what about the whole issue of so-called Made in Italy? 'Would you consider this a Made in Italy piece of furniture?', I asked the same entrepreneur as I pointed to a carved piece. He replied with another question: 'Would you have considered this a Made in Italy piece if the same Bulgarian woodcarver had worked in my workshop here in the Brianza?' In other words, what counts more: the hand of the woodcarver or the physical workplace? We are still debating this. What is clear, though, is that even if the economic crisis may seem to be behind us in the district, the crisis of social reproduction, as well as the crisis of the local culture of production, are not.

Simone Ghezzi is Associate Professor of Economic Anthropology and Social/Cultural Anthropology at the University of Milano-Bicocca. He has carried out research on the informal economy, family businesses, urban kinship and more recently on Italian woodcarvers and artisan furniture. He is the author of *Etnografia storica dell'imprenditorialità in Brianza* (Franco Angeli, 2007) and recently coauthored, with Fulvia D'Aloisio, *Antropologia della crisi: Prospettive etnografiche sulle trasformazioni del lavoro e dell'impresa in Italia* (L'Harmattan, 2016).

Notes

1. By antique-style or classic-style furniture, I mean the reproduction and imitation of *ancien régime* styles, or a pastiche thereof, such as Louis XIV, XV and XVI, and later styles such as the Empire style, the Rococo, the neoclassical, the Chippendale, the Liberty, the Venetian and so forth. Each style comes with specific ornaments, undulating scrolls, floral themes and Greek symbols in high relief (or in-laid), sometimes enriched with gold leaf (or imitation gold leaf) gilding (Auslander 1996).
2. This research was initially funded by an AESS-REIL grant (Archivio di Etnografia e Storia Sociale – Registro delle Eredità Immateriali of Regione Lombardia) in 2010, which has continued intermittently up to now thanks to annual research grants provided by the University of Milano-Bicocca.
3. In Italy, 'artisan firm' encompasses a wide range of activities, as stated by Law n. 443/1985 (*legge-quadro per l'artigianato*). In the case of manufacturing enterprises, the aforementioned law may apply to plants with: 1) a maximum of ten employees, when the work involves mass assembly, namely standardized production, provided that this is not completely automated; 2) a maximum of eighteen employees in firms not involving mass assembly; and 3) a maximum of thirty-two employees in workshops of traditional productions such as tailoring, artistic productions, luxury classic style furniture and so forth. The recruitment of apprentices may raise the number of employees up to twelve, twenty-two and forty, respectively. Artisan and industrial enterprises differ in terms of tax regimes, labour contracts and job protection. Before the recent economic recession, in case of economic downturns, only industrial workers were eligible to receive a government temporary lay-offs indemnity (CIG – Cassa Integrazione Guadagni) to subsidize their temporary redundancy. In early 2009, due

to the critical economic situation in the manufacturing sectors, the government temporary lay-offs indemnity was extended to artisan firms as well. This form of institutional aid came to an end in 2016, but it was immediately replaced by a new solidary fund especially created for artisan firms. The term 'artisan' comprises a wide range of activities. Basically, most professions fall into such a category – bakers, barbers, truck drivers, electricians, masons and plumbers, if self-employed, are artisans, have to register with the Chamber of Commerce, Industry, Artisanship and Agriculture (CCIAA) and are subject to specific tax regulations. Thus, a self-employed woodcarver would fall in this category, whereas a woodcarver employed in an artisan firm is formally a worker-employee, not an artisan.

4. Originally these arts and crafts schools only provided evening classes, to allow pupils and teachers to work during the day.
5. The Società Umanitaria is a charitable trust. It was founded in 1893 in Milan in accordance with the will of Prospero Moisé Loira, a wealthy Jewish merchant, who bequeathed his entire estate to the constitution of a philanthropic association under the aegis of the Municipality of Milan. Thanks to the contribution of the Società Umanitaria, it was possible to open several arts and crafts schools in the Brianza.

References

Arrighi, G. 2009. *The Long Twentieth Century: Money, Power and the Origins of Our Time*. New York: Verso Books.

Auslander, L. 1996. *Taste and Power: Furnishing in Modern France*. Berkeley: University of California Press.

Becattini, G. 2004. *Industrial Districts: A New Approach to Industrial Change*. Cheltenham: Edward Elgar.

Becattini, G., and E. Rullani. 1996. 'Local Systems and Global Connections: The Role of Knowledge', in F. Cossentino, F. Pyke and W. Sengenberger (eds), *Local and Regional Response to Global Pressure: The Case of Italy and its Industrial Districts*. Geneva: ILO, pp. 159–74.

Braverman, H. 1974. *Labor and Monopoly Capital: The Degradation of Work in the Twentieth Century*. New York: Monthly Review Press

Ghezzi, S. 2007. *Etnografia storica dell'imprenditorialità in Brianza. Antropologia di un'economia regionale*. Milan: Franco Angeli

———. 2016. 'Familism in the Firm: An Ethnographic Approach to Italian Family Capitalism', *Ethnologie française* 162(2): 241–54.

Goody, E.N. 1989. 'Learning Apprenticeship and the Division of Labour', in M.W. Coy (ed.), *Apprenticeship: From Theory to Method and Back Again*. New York, SUNY Press, pp. 233–56.

Guenzi, F., and M. Marelli. 1965. *L'industria del mobile nella Brianza comasca*. Como: Camera del Commercio, industria e Agricoltura.

Harvey, D. 2014. *Seventeen Contradictions and the End of Capitalism*. Oxford: Oxford University Press.

Herzfeld, M. 2004. *The Body Impolitic: Artisans and Artifice in the Global Hierarchy of Value*. Chicago: University of Chicago Press.

Lave, J.M., and E. Wenger. 1991. *Situated Learning: Legitimate Peripheral Participation*. Cambridge: Cambridge University Press.

Schiavi, A. 1904. *L'industria dei mobili in Brianza e le condizioni dei lavoratori*. Milan: Editore l'Ufficio del Lavoro.

Sennett, R. 2008. *The Craftsman*. New Haven: Yale University Press.

Sewell Jr., W.H. 1980. *Work and Revolution in France: The Language of Labour from the Old Regime to 1848*. Cambridge: Cambridge University Press.
Smith, G. 2018. 'Rethinking Social Reproduction in an Era of the Dominance of Finance Capital', in A. Andreotti, D. Benassi and Y.Kazepov (eds), *Western Capitalism in Transition: Global Processes, Local Challenges*. Manchester: Manchester University Press, pp. 61–76.
Streeck, W. 2014. *Buying Time: The Delayed Crisis of Democratic Capitalism*. New York: Verso Books.
Wallerstein, I. et al. 2013. *Does Capitalism Have a Future?* New York: Oxford University Press.
Willis, P. 1981. 'Cultural Production is Different from Cultural Reproduction Is Different from Social Reproduction is Different from Reproduction', *Interchange* 12(2–3): 48–67.

– Chapter 3 –

Kin and Economic Crisis in an Italian Shoe District

Michael Blim

> Only a few years ago, when I outlined these arguments in a lecture, my prognosis of a long-term crisis made my audiences smile. To make forecasts like this in the name of history, and in the name of a long sequence of secular cycles in the past which we can only identify without being able to explain them, is of course a risky business. But today's economists, armed with all the data about the present experience, also seem to be reduced to hypotheses. Are they not just as incapable as the rest of us of predicting the *length* or even of explaining the nature of the crisis into which we are plunging a little further every day?
>
> —Fernand Braudel, *Civilization and Capitalism*

If the long lines of history, as Fernand Braudel understood them, offer little comfort and even fewer powers of economic prediction, then pity the rest of us, reduced to the odds of an office football betting pool in playing the paramount game of economic wellbeing. The vast operations of economies, when summarized statistically as so many rates and presented as the sum of so many individual outcomes, creates the impression that our fates are just so much Brownian motion. We are the pollen; the economy is the water in which we swim.

Statistical descriptions are indispensable to important purposes at hand. Economies require coordination, both in the long term and the short term, if they are to cut down the friction of unmet or competing needs. Firms allocate private goods, and states allocate public goods. A state cannot run a welfare system, an unemployment relief programme, power or transit systems without a continuous and reliable flow of data and their aggregate descriptions. For firms, the global economic picture is but a rolling average of transactions great and small in which only massive monopoly players possess the advantage of planning much beyond the upcoming business quarter.

Yet, we, the proverbial pollen whose movements in water enabled Albert Einstein to prove the botanist Robert Brown right, seek to control our caroms across the field of economic play. With interest and intentionality, we make our moves, often though not always in coordination with or for the mutual benefit of others. The highly regarded notion of 'embedding' disguises how tangled and often contradictory our social relationships are, as they typically involve commitments to significant others in households, kin groups, occupational orders and status groups. Our capacity to act can be both enabled and constrained by our affiliations, and the pull of each upon our loyalties can mitigate the pull of others. As Weber well noted, each relationship we acquire includes some while excluding others; the excluded, even if they can be denominated, become Simmel's strangers, deprived of the rights and devoid of the duties of insiders (Weber 1947: 139–43; Simmel 1950: 402–8).

The insiders, for the purposes of this chapter, are members of several local kin groups caught up in an economic climate marked by chronic crisis and the uncertain future of a shoe-producing industrial district located in the provinces of Macerata and Fermo in the Marche Region. These diverse sets of *parentela* have been heavily involved in the shoe industry since the mid-1950s. They are composed of kin groups and households stitched together with threads of consanguineal and affinal ties[1] binding each person at least in part with corporate obligations of members to one another and to the wellbeing of the group as a whole.[2] They have faced serious challenges to their collective wellbeing over the past decade, as have the individuals comprising these groups. The 'golden age' of the Marche regional shoe district has passed. Employment has declined from 48,000 in 1991 to 33,500 in 2012, production is 88 per cent of what it was in 2005, and a once widely dispersed popular artisanal mode of production has given way to a district dominated by Tod's (a multinational firm with a turnover of close to €1 billion a year) and three smaller firms, which together with Tod's account for two-thirds of the district's sales (Goffi 2013: 62–89; Balloni and Iacobucci 2011; Associazione Nazionale Calzaturifici Italiani and Banca Monte Paschi di Siena n.d.: 37–39). In brief, the once-Marshallian productive artisanal beehive of a district has become a more conventional set of a few company towns.

This shift in the character of the shoe district's economy, along with firm closures and the decline in employment opportunities, has generated a great deal of reflection and has triggered consideration of different employment options inside kin groups that a generation ago were fully committed to work and/or firm ownership in shoe manufacturing. Three issues have surfaced. First, given that one and sometimes two generations had already committed themselves to the shoe industry as artisans, industrialists or workers, many have found it necessary to manage the probability of their increased economic vulnerability in order that reduced or eliminated income streams do not have severe economic repercussions on their kin groups. Second, a new(er) generation has made job and career decisions mindful of the uncertainties of long-term employment in the shoe industry, for them as well as for older kin already engaged in shoe production. Third, the economic opportunity structure of the shoe district has shifted, as more new jobs are found in services rather than manufacturing, and educational preparation becomes more important for success in the labour market.

Surprisingly enough, as Ginsborg and Ramella (1999) point out in the introduction to their study of the Valdelsa in Tuscany, the family and the role of kin groups, which were once regarded as a crucial factor propelling the historical development of the economy of the Third Italy, have been neglected in recent studies seeking to understand how industrial district economies might recover:

> In the very extensive series of studies on the Third Italy, the family has mainly emerged as a causal factor. In other terms, scholars' attention has been essentially focused on the extent to which various resources, solidarity mechanisms and family capabilities, especially those available in the sharecropping family, have contributed to the formation of the industrial districts network. (Ginsborg and Ramella 1999: 9)[3]

In sympathy with Ginsborg and Ramella's concerns, I will show below that kin groups continue to play a significant role in the occupational choices of new(er) generations, but in this period by supporting the search of the new(er) generations for ways of living that are less vulnerable to the vicissitudes of an industrial district economy that is regarded as increasingly economically fragile and unreliable.

It should be stated from the outset that it cannot be assumed that members always or even strictly take actions to support the kin group or, conversely, undertake only actions that are self-serving. The notion that kin groups pursue collective strategies (both productive and reproductive) at the complete expense of individual interests and designs finds little support today among sociology's truisms. Durkheim's insistence on the supremacy of social solidarity in the governance of social life has found notable dissenters even in the French tradition, like the late Pierre Bourdieu, whose notions of strategy, which were shown to particular advantage in his discussion of matrimonial arrangements in his now canonical *Outline of a Theory of Practice* (1977: 35, 58–71), assume *a priori* an actor's interest in personal gain, albeit embedded in socially sanctioned competition over potential spouses. Moreover, the mix of motives that an actor carries, even in such a critical social reproductive task as making a marriage, lends an air of indeterminacy to the outcome that makes the reduction of a personal choice to the obedience to group norms unlikely, and for the investigator difficult to prove.[4] As Sylvia Yanagisako (2002: 83), writing about industrial capitalist families in northern Italy, notes, 'which norms should be followed, which kinship sentiments should have priority, how precisely legal rules should be obeyed, and what is considered fair and just, as well as practical and efficient, are constantly being rethought and renegotiated'.

In fact, individuals may manipulate kin group solidarity in order to advance their specific interests. In a sense, interested individuals can convert the corporate ties of the kin group into ego-centred networks, as was observed so acutely by Carol Stack in *All Our Kin* (1974). But perhaps Fortunata Piselli (1981: 164–70), in her classic study of migration and kin ties among households in the Cosentino zone of Calabria during the late 1970s, most explicitly and carefully demonstrates how the corporate ties of kinship are reconstructed by actors into networks for personal advantage. As Piselli shows, migration opened up, and effectively broke up, once-coercive kin group ties, allowing kin with varying degrees of power and authority to seek upward social mobility through advantageous alliances in Italy and abroad. A young man with poor career prospects, for instance, forsakes his fiancée in Italy for a marriage to a young Cosentino woman born and living in the United States whom he has never seen. A Cosentino couple seek to improve their social position by emigrating to Canada under the sponsorship of their son-in-law, who in return gains the hand of the couple's youngest daughter for an Italo-Canadian acquaintance of his. The daughter breaks her engagement to a Cosentino youth, who in desperation emigrates to Switzerland. The parents also obtain a good marriage for their youngest son, a dull, unpromising boy unlikely to make a good marriage match in the Cosentino. Piselli's remarkable investigation alerts us to treat the skeins of kin group solidarity sceptically and to appreciate that economic changes like emigration introduce ego-centred and dyadic network strategies as tools of actors bent on pursuing their own interests, even from within an ostensibly solidary kin group.

Thus, one cannot *a priori* assume, in the face of more than a decade of economic crisis and uncertainty in the Marche shoe district, that the occupational choices of new(er)-generation individuals are to support the kin group, the individuals in question or both. Yet surely it is the case that one can observe in their actions responses to the changing opportunity structure of the local economy under the stress of transition from shoe manufacturing to other forms of livelihood. And one can observe how kin groups, via discussion, dispute and reaction to individual actions, pull themselves forward, however uncertainly, in an uncertain economic world.

In this chapter, I propose to investigate some dimensions of this practical as well as theoretical problem by resorting to the analysis of occupational choices of three kin groups whose members I have known over the course of thirty-nine years of contact via fieldwork conducted in Monte San Giusto, one of the key shoe-producing towns (population of 7,700) in the shoe district of the Marche Region. I present the occupational histories (thus far) of two (and three where possible) generations of three kin groups, two formerly headed by small shoemaking artisans and one currently headed by former shoe workers. Save for representing the distinction between small business owners and workers, the three have not been chosen to stand as ideal-types; they happen to be the families with whom I have had the closest and most continuous contact over the years. Their small number is due to constraints of space. Whatever advantage I may be sacrificing by not constructing a typology and using paradigmatic cases will be compensated for by the close observations I can bring to this discussion of how individuals navigate the shifting seas of economic difficulty, albeit in the context of the salience of their membership in kin groups.

Finding Solidarity amidst Personal Choices: La Famiglia Bondi-Marchetti

Giorgio Bondi (b. 1940) and Barbara Marchetti (b. 1945) raised four boys, Riccardo (b. 1970), Roberto (b. 1973), Ruggiero (b. 1977) and Raimondo (b. 1983). Giorgio worked as a foreman for several shoe factories and Barbara as a shoe top-sole stitcher working illegally at home. Barbara's father was a fruit wholesaler, but her mother's kin were shoemakers whose lineage stretched back into Monte San Giusto's past as a centre of protoindustrial shoe production before the Risorgimento. Her five siblings were small artisans or workers in one of the town's shoe firms. Giorgio's kin on his father's side were sharecroppers in the countryside near Fermo and his father was a mason, while his mother's kin were shoemaking artisans in a nearby town. After Giorgio's mother died in 1956, he moved to Monte San Giusto to apprentice shoemaking with his mother's brother, an artisan who had a small shoe shop. He then went to work for one of Barbara's brothers making shoes, before moving on to work in a small factory in the early 1960s. By the mid-1970s, he was head foreman at a small firm that closed in the mid-1980s. After a period of working transiently and illegally in a friend's small workshop, he found work again as head foreman in a firm with a good-size production and something of a reputation in children's shoes.

Giorgio and Barbara raised four boys in a small three-bedroom cooperative apartment in a new district outside the old Monte San Giusto town centre. From first to last, none of the boys wanted to become shoemakers. Riccardo, the oldest, was in fact the only one to try shoe-factory work after finishing middle school, and his dislike of the work prompted his siblings to reject shoe-factory futures as well. He chose instead to take up the mechanical work of making shoe moulds, an activity that soon attracted his younger brother Ruggiero, with whom and he and three others founded their own firm. Roberto, the second son, shared with Riccardo a passion as well as an aptitude for mechanics, but as Riccardo settled into metalworking rather than automobile and motorcycle repair, Roberto cast about for a steady job. He had gotten a taste for motorcycles and engine repair during his compulsory stint in the army and followed his father Giorgio's advice to pursue employment with the state highway patrol. He succeeded and with Giorgio's help, through the husband of Barbara's cousin, was assigned to the state police barracks in the nearby provincial capital of Macerata.

Despite the success of the firm Riccardo and Roberto had founded with others, after half a dozen years, they no longer saw eye to eye about its future. Riccardo and one other partner were fascinated by the prospect of producing injection moulds, an advanced industrial process based upon revolutions in materials science, lasers and computer-directed manufacturing. They took their share of the accumulated capital of the firm and started a new one, betting heavily and very expensively on the future of injection moulds to fundamentally change shoe manufacturing – which it has. Roberto preferred to stay with metalworking mould-making, though he would later take his share of the firm's accumulated capital out, buy an apartment without a spouse on the horizon (an unusual step) and go to work as a factory foreman in the same field. Three years later, he married Samuela (b. 1985), a salesperson for a chic *pronta moda* womenswear chain who became unemployed following the 2012 recession.

Their youngest brother Raimondo proved a difficult character to place in the world of work. Like his brothers, he stopped his education after middle school and also rejected the idea of working in a shoe factory, something that could have been easily arranged by Giorgio. Instead, he worked for a while at the brothers' old firm, and did not cover himself with glory, with a diffident work attitude that incited bitter criticism from his brother Ruggiero. When the old firm ceased, Raimondo went to work at the new injection-moulding firm with his brother Riccardo. Within a year, he had gone from being a millstone around his older brother's neck to an instrumental part of the production team, developing a mastery of the computer-aided design process that a certified engineer would have had trouble acquiring in such a short time. He has joined Riccardo in expanding the firm's business to injection-mould production in Tunisia, while Riccardo's wife Tania (b. 1977), an accountant, handles the firm's finances in addition to her outside consulting for other firms.

Giorgio and Barbara managed their sons' transition to the world of work very carefully. Until their marriages, Barbara received and kept their wages, saving collectively for the successive marriages and first apartments of her sons. Though not all of their earnings were commingled as the brothers individually reached the age of twenty-one, enough was held aside as capital to finance each son's first apartment upon his marriage. In Roberto's case, the savings and his policeman's salary were not enough to rebuild a potentially beautiful apartment that was in a ruinous condition inside the old town walls. He and his wife Sabina (b. 1978), responsible for the inventory at Giorgio's factory with his sponsorship, lived after their marriage for an excruciatingly long (according to the couple) four years in Giorgio and Barbara's apartment, while Roberto and his cousin and Giorgio's brother's son Stefano, a mason, rebuilt the new flat from the ground up.[5]

Having grown up and prospered with the shoe boom, Giorgio and Barbara nonetheless did not insist that their sons stop their educations after middle school and go into the remaining nearby shoe factories. They could have continued their education if they had showed both interest and promise, but if not, their parents insisted that they go to work in a trade or occupation with a future. They did not interfere, for instance, when Riccardo and Roberto clashed over the direction of their firm, nor did they intervene to prevent its break-up, even though Riccardo was undertaking a financially risky new venture in injection moulding. However, suffice it to say that Giorgio was ideally positioned to steer work from his factory and the larger firm to his sons, as a result of which first the metalmaking and then the injection-moulding firms gained credibility and much-needed turnover.

Nor did their sons' dislike of a future in shoemaking dismay or offend them. Barbara never liked sewing shoe-tops, but it was work she had learned as a teenager, and working illegally at home had enabled her to make cash more quickly and still supervise her children. Giorgio, on the other hand, has been rewarded well as a factory foreman and has enjoyed travel opportunities to places as far away as China to support his firm's production. Privately he confesses to doubts about the future of employment in the shoemaking industry in the zone and is relieved that his sons have chosen factory leadership as a foreman in metalmaking (in the case of Ruggiero), a state police job (Roberto) and running a cutting-edge firm (Riccardo and Raimondo). He reasons that only a complete economic disaster would affect his sons. Both parents have strongly encouraged their sons to settle close to home, and succeeded in the cases of Ruggiero and Roberto, but have expressed great worry over Riccardo and Raimondo's residence in Tunisia.

Thus, it could be said that the Bondi-Marchetti household, now with the neolocality of their sons becoming a kin group in their own right, has skilfully sidestepped the declining economic opportunities that other worker families of their generations have suffered. All but one of their sons is still linked to the shoemaking industry, but they have advanced quickly in their preferred niches of metalmaking, some of the skills of which are indeed transferable to other areas of industrial fabrication, should they along with others succeed in generating new products in the shoe industry and the surrounding economic zones.

The Lifeboat Welfare Economy of the Grimaldi-Sarcetti

Husband and wife Costantino Grimaldi (1926–99) and Elia Sarcetti (b. 1935), along with Elia's unmarried sister, Giuseppa (1940–2012), created a formidable household from the mid-1950s and a viable firm as the principals of an artisanal shoe-parts-production firm from the mid-1960s until its demise in 2009. They provided work until retirement for two of Costantino's younger siblings, as well as a sister-in-law and a nephew of Elia and Giuseppa's. Though the three were born to artisanal shoemaking families, Costantino's father, overwhelmed by debt and business failure in 1929, committed suicide; Costantino was placed in *collegio* until he was sixteen, an experience he found difficult, though he did admit that it enabled him to get a diploma in agrarian studies. Elia and Giuseppa were two of ten children and the first-born of four to their father's second wife. They were quite poor, as their father laboured for another shoemaker doing piecework, and the town was visited by depression and war that made the lives of all but a few miserable and hard.

As such, the trio started from scratch, each first working for another before accruing the minimum necessary to start their own business. Though Costantino and Elia's two daughters, Viremma (b. 1957) and Marina (b. 1964), helped out in the firm as young people, both took up work outside the shoe sector, Viremma as a town clerk and Marina as a physical therapist and, for the past five years, as a state employee at a nearby rehabilitation hospital. Viremma helped her father with the invoices and, after his death in 1999, became the effective head of the firm.

By the time Viremma took over the firm, it was being kept alive only to forward pension payments for her husband, Enrico (b. 1957), who still needed, at the time of the firm's closure, almost four years of regular employment to become eligible for a pension. Indeed, the firm functioned as a kin group income and pension system (albeit a restricted one), in which decisions were made to accommodate each person's need for income and a pension. As the shoe business declined locally in the 1990s, shoe production, and shoe-parts production in particular, was shifted to the Balkans, and local producers like the Grimaldi-Sarcettis suffered badly. After a spate of kin retirements, the three partners along with Enrico carried on with the remains of their business. Even as the partners retired and started drawing their pensions (though Costantino and Giuseppa still worked full time), Enrico, the sole worker on the books, was being issued salary payments he never cashed because doing so would bankrupt the firm, while his pension payments were made regularly in the hope that the firm would last long enough to render him pensionable. They lived on Viremma's town-hall salary in a cooperative apartment less than 100 metres from the house of her parents and her aunt, originally purchased by the couple's parents. After the firms closed, Enrico worked irregularly and illegally as a leather cutter in his apartment garage until a space could be made for him at his maternal uncle's shoe factory, where his brother and sister-in-law had worked for over thirty years.[6] In 2019, thanks to the job at his uncle's, he reached pensionable age and retired.

Viremma's parents were keen that she should get a job in the town hall in the mid-1980s, even though the firm was doing very well at that time, and they importuned the mayor, a personal and political friend, to help out. She was intelligent and had completed some exams at university. More importantly, slight of build and rail thin, she was not considered suitable for labour in the household workshop, and as the single mother of two young girls (she and Enrico were separated for several years), her parents felt she needed the relatively easier workload and guaranteed employee benefits of state employment, to at least manage her children's lives in part.

Marina, the second daughter, struck out on her own early on, settling on physical therapy for an occupation and seeking training in France in a programme that was at the time not recognized as valid for an Italian professional license as a physical therapist. Her parents supported her studies in France, albeit reluctantly, while accurately foreseeing that this would lead to employment problems for her on her return to Italy. She became romantically involved with a man living on his parents' farm an hour's drive from Monte San Giusto and they undertook care of a foster child.

The children of Viremma and Enrico have broken with the shoe business altogether. Paola (b. 1977) completed a *laurea* degree with a specialization in recreational therapy for disabled children, moved to the provincial capital of Macerata and works as a partner in a cooperative providing services for children. For a time, she co-owned an apartment and lived with a young man from Monte San Giusto who worked for a firm wholesaling articles for shoemaking. They broke up after four years and she remained in Macerata, where she established a new romantic relationship and once more shares the cost of owning an apartment.

Elena (b. 1981), Viremma and Enrico's second daughter, helped out in her aunt and grandparents' shoe-parts firm as a teenager, and then moved on to work in several shoe factories, each time becoming unemployed after her time as an apprentice ended and a long-term contract was not offered. With shoe jobs being hard to come by, Elena received unemployment benefits and worked with her partner Stefano (b. 1981) at his parents' bread bakery, though once again it was not a good fit, as there was not enough work (or pay) for four adults. In 2011, she took a part-time job as a cashier in a supermarket and one year later took on a permanent part-time role. She decided that working less than full time would allow her to spend more time with her son, Marco (b. 2010) and daughter Maria (b. 2015). Along with her partner, she lives in an apartment across from Stefano's parents' bakery in the town centre.

Costantino Grimaldi, Elia and Giuseppa Sarcetti were born into Monte San Giusto households that had been active in shoemaking since the Risorgimento, but by the time that Costantino and Elia's children became young adults in the mid-1980s, work in the shoe industry was becoming more scarce, except (as we have seen above) for a son-in-law who narrowly missed out on losing his pension following the economic decline in the district that not only knocked out the household firm but scores of others like it. It was hard, back-breaking work creating shoe parts with shearing machines (*trance*), running the pieces through a dangerous folding machine, bending over glue tubs and coating each piece with thermoplastic resins, and wrapping the thousands of tiny shoe inserts in plastic for shipping to the factories. No one spoke pleasantly about it; pride was taken in the firm and, for the older generation, in possessing a skill (*mestiere*), but not in the work itself. Viremma and Marina were encouraged to pursue their education, as were Viremma's children. Viremma's daughter Paola was the first in her immediate kin group to have been awarded a university degree – and in fact remains the only one among all her first cousins.

However, this was not the only attempt to move the next generation(s) out of shoes: Elia and Giuseppa's younger brother Ennio, a leather-cutter who had worked illegally all of his working life and whose wife Emelda had worked in the shoe-parts firm of her in-laws for over twenty-five years, set his two sons up with a small pizza shop (which eventually became two – one for each son) in the provincial capital of Macerata. As he often expressed to me, there was no future in shoes and he wanted his sons, neither of whom was especially strong in school, to run a small business better suited to their habits of hard work and modest academic achievement.

In hindsight, it is evident that the family elders possessed foresight and displayed a great deal of altruism, given that they continued to do the dirty work while they offered their children (who in the case of Viremma and Enrico's children were the elders' grandchildren and nieces) the opportunity to study and to seek qualified work outside the shoe industry. Elia and Giuseppa's brother Ennio and his wife

Emelda virtually directed their sons out of the industry in which they had worked all of their lives and made the pizza shop a family business, as he and his wife spent hours in the early years gathering and preparing pizza ingredients for use by their sons. Leaving nothing to chance, in anticipation of his sons' marriages, Ennio supervised the construction of a two-apartment home for them in the countryside with his capital and the retained profits of the pizza shops.

Keeping the firm open to cover the pension needs of all the kin (including son-in-law Enrico) in the face of declining business and rising debts almost cost Elia and Giuseppa their home (Costantino had died in 1999), as it was used as security for a bank loan that was necessary to keep the firm afloat and make pension payments for Enrico. The firm was finally closed and the home was remortgaged. The two heirs, Viremma and Marina, contribute with their mother Elia (Giuseppa died in 2012) to making the monthly mortgage payments.

The Garzoni-Cecchi: The 'New' and 'Old' Economies under One Roof

The home of Michele Garzoni (1927–2006) and Graziella Cecchi (b. 1931) had stood like a great sentinel guarding the entrance to Monte San Giusto from two directions: the mountains and the provincial centre of Macerata. It was part of what remained of a great patriarchal kin group of coresident, multifamily households of former sharecroppers who by the turn of the twentieth century had become the principal mechanical grain-threshers for Monte San Giusto and nearby towns. They maintained several large farms in the adjacent town, processed local olive oil and lived well in a resident domestic kin group that at the end of the Second World War had twenty-four members.

Michele was bright, graduated from the *liceo classico* in Macerata, rode horses in the countryside and found friends among the sons of the town pharmacist and the farm managers (*fattori)* that supervised the sharecroppers for the local nobility. He wanted to be a veterinarian, but the only programme offering this was at a university that was too far from home. After a short, unpleasant stint in the faculty of law at the university in Macerata, Michele found himself, at the age of twenty-one in 1948, facing the declining economic prospects of his father's large residential kin group (his father was the third son and thus was far down the line of patriarchal succession as the household head. With several cousins, he moved to break up the kin group into autonomous extended households in 1950 and was forced to strike out on his own just as the Italian economy had bottomed out from the ruins of fascist autarky and foreign occupation. One of his paternal uncles ran an artisanal shoemaking firm, and Michele took consignments of his uncle's production and wholesaled the shoes in Belgium. Armed with his serviceable *liceo* French, his first foray went well, but on the second occasion, he was cheated out of the inventory and returned home empty-handed. He was lucky to find a job in the office of a shoe factory that proved to be a long-term business success – the same factory where sixty years later, Enrico, the son-in-law of the Grimaldi-Sarcettis discussed above, finally found work that would help him complete his pension contributions. After thirty years as a white-collar employee with the firm, Michele retired and with an assembly-line worker from the same plant opened a small artisan shoe-production firm that manufactured the same line of shoes that he and his partner had worked on for many years. They achieved some financial success producing shoes under their own label as well as for upscale chains of international boutiques owned by Swiss and English firms.

Michele's wife Graziella had trained as a teacher and was determined against the odds and the customs of the time to pursue a career. Starting at the bottom of the job ladder in the province, she spent ten years commuting six days a week to schools in the mountains before she obtained a role within a car ride of Monte San Giusto. Though her mother-in-law looked after her children Sara (b. 1957) and Ugo (b. 1964), Graziella still faced her share of the cooking, cleaning and childcare, as Michele, having been raised in a patriarchal household, had never considered these responsibilities to be part of his spousal duties.

Sara took a diploma in bookkeeping, worked part-time keeping the books for a shoebox maker nearby and married Davide (b. 1957), who partnered with his father in wholesaling leather for shoes; they had two children, Alessandro (b. 1985) and Lorena (b. 1992). After the death of Michele's mother in 1982, he and Graziella bought out Michele's sister's share of the house and remodelled it to create an apartment on the second floor for Davide and Sara. Their son Alessandro gained a diploma in information sciences, but found work in leather selling with his father more congenial, and after twelve years has definitely found his niche. Their daughter Lorena, on the other hand, has proved to be a talented and motivated student of languages, having completed the *liceo scientifico* with good grades and having finished an initial university degree in languages at the university in Macerata. As part of her courses, she has already studied in the United States and China.

Downstairs and living with his parents (and now alone with his mother Graziella since the passing of Michele in 2009) is Ugo, director and co-owner since 2011 of a centre for language and culture in Macerata, targeted at providing educated tourists with an intensive immersion in the Italian language and way of life. It has not been a straightforward path. Ugo graduated with good grades from the *liceo scientifico* and earned a university degree with honours at a local university in economic sociology. The faculty offered him admission and a fellowship to complete a Ph.D. in economic sociology, and he spent a year in the United States brushing up on his English and studying sociology. However, Ugo was not lucky in finding himself a mentor or, in effect, an academic sponsor, and did not complete his Ph.D. thesis. After teaching labour economics part-time for one of the national labour confederations for half a dozen years, he and his sister Sara pooled their resources and opened up an ice-cream shop in a nearby town, much to the disdain of many in Monte San Giusto, who considered it a waste of his studies. Ugo shrugged off this local disapproval and accepted the drudgery of scooping out ice cream because he wanted to learn how to manage a business. He had refused to work with his father in the shoe business, as much down to his lack of desire to work in shoes as to his discomfort working for his father, Michele, a man who had never strayed from the patriarchal norms instilled in him during his youth. Meanwhile, Michele gave up the firm to the last remaining partner in 2004 and it failed not long afterwards.

Ugo was a puzzle to his parents and to many in Monte San Giusto, even if he was well respected and equipped with a spotless, though circumspect and highly formal, character. After he and his sister sold off the ice-cream shop for a modest profit, following some searching and indecision, he accepted an offer to take over the business of a shoe-accessory wholesaler in Portugal who had begun to supply the shoe district that lay east of Porto. Ugo made good money in both salary and commissions over three years; he also received a living allowance that reduced his living expenses in Portugal to zero. His success enabled him to invest with a partner in the new Italian cultural centre for foreigners, which was targeted via a painstakingly wrought 'business model' at wealthier tourists able to spend more money in exchange for an 'authentic experience' of Italian life. The firm has achieved a modest success over the past eight years.

Ugo's failure to secure his Ph.D. was a real let-down for his parents, as it was for him. He withdrew from the university, taking with him a real sense of betrayal: an outsider from 'the provinces' initially encouraged and supported by his faculty, he felt discarded in a patronage game that was far more cunning than he was. His 'recovery' and relaunching of his career fulfilled his parents' hopes that he would find a job – indeed, a life – that would bring him happiness.

Michele and Graziella started with a family home in a town where at the end of the Second World War, only one in five households could say the same. With his *liceo classico* diploma, Michele was one of perhaps a dozen in the town who had progressed beyond middle-school education. Though his family's capital was depleted, he came from a respected family and found work as one of the few white-collar employees in town. Graziella had grown up in the provincial capital of Macerata and pursued a career as a teacher, which eventually brought her back to Monte San Giusto as one of the key teachers in the town's middle school. Neither had worked with their hands, and though Michele made a living after he retired as a shoemaking artisan, making a success of himself on his own rather than making shoes was his aim. Even Davide, Sara's husband, and her son Alessandro, though deeply connected to shoemaking, have begun to sell leather in Portugal and Spain and rely less on the Marche shoe district for their income.

Michele decided to quit his small firm just as the wholesalers from abroad who gave him product orders were shifting to lower-cost countries. To a lesser effect, his son-in-law has gone global too, seeking opportunities outside the district and trying to reduce his vulnerability to regional downturns. Davide began with the capital, contacts and business his father had built up. Sound, cautious and capable, he is now building a business with his son Alessandro that appears to be prosperous and durable.

One can observe in Ugo's career trajectory the desire to create economic activity outside the shoe industry – a desire, as well, of regional planners looking to renew the Marche Region's economy with more value created in services like tourism and culture, which is precisely the sort that Ugo and his business partner are seeking to provide. A close friend of Ugo's since *liceo* and comrade at university, Massimiliano Ceri (b. 1964) also had a strong desire to create a firm or economic activity that was modern and efficient, of the sort he had read about in American business magazines. Massimiliano grew up and still lives in an expansive palazzo composed of apartments in which he, his wife Carla (b. 1970), their two children, his parents, his maiden aunt and his two sisters live, which sits close to the walls of Corridonia, a town adjacent to Monte San Giusto, located at the beginning of a grand plot of land that his kin group has farmed independently for over a hundred years. Both Massimiliano and Carla, an elementary-school teacher hoping to take on more administrative responsibility for school improvement in the region, prefer to be an autonomous household within the remaining kin group setting, along with their children, twin boys (b. 1999); after Massimiliano's highly anxious and protective mother agreed to knock or call first, they settled happily into the kin group compound. After the death of Massimiliano's father in 2011, he assumed management of the estate, including the programming of the valuable agricultural land holdings for eventual commercial development.

The story thus far contains no hint of disillusion and struggle, but again, as in Ugo's case, there was plenty. Massimiliano also received a university degree with a concentration in economic sociology, but it provided him with little hint as to a possible future direction. For several years, he worked at odd jobs, such as clerking in the betting booths of the local race track, and he travelled abroad, particularly to the United States, which fostered his idea to create a well-run, 'modern' firm, either as a manager of someone else's or as an owner-operator.

Marriage generated a shift in Massimiliano's outlook. He went to work for a successful and expanding construction hardware firm and took a promotion that involved working full time in Bari, Puglia. For three years, he was in effect the manager of the firm in Puglia, commuting home most weekends. After his reassignment back to Corridonia, he left the hardware firm and invested in and managed a start-up firm that computer-manufactured prototypes for a variety of industrial projects, including yachts and other watercraft for shipbuilders in Ancona. The firm was small, including two other partners and three employees that manufactured state-of-the-art, three-dimensional models for complicated and expensive products. As with the injection-moulding business that Riccardo Bondi had entered, computer-aided prototype production uses expensive laser-guided machines and highly sophisticated software. Massimiliano has risked some of the family capital and his labour time to put himself at the cutting edge of an industrial sector in which, unlike for Riccardo, local demand is not yet sufficient to yield a good return on his investment and the need for national markets is keenly felt. After a dispute among the firm's partners, Massimiliano took the machines as part of the firm's dissolution and in 2017 re-created a small workshop in his basement where he alone manufactures the products and manages client contact. Thus far, he has been very successful.

The efforts undertaken by Ugo and Massimiliano are suggestive of economic development being generated by a generation for whom the shoe-district profits and the more generalized prosperity they brought about are being transformed into new industrial segments. Two questions remain: first, can the regional market provide the links and demand necessary to stimulate the growth of their ventures and, second, can they successfully reach clients in national and international markets?

The Region, the District and the Cases

The questions raised above beg the bigger question: what is the economic future of the Marche regional economy, built historically on the backs of industrial districts?[7] In the case of the shoe district, the growth of a local monopoly in Tod's that subcontracts its work to small firms fosters the illusion that the autonomous artisanal production of thirty and forty years ago is still characteristic of the district, even though, as noted above, Tod's and three other firms (each smaller than Tod's by a factor of twenty) produce or supervise the production of the lion's share of the region's shoes. Providing capital-intensive, high-tech products for very large producers as has been undertaken by the Bondi sons is one way to survive and perhaps thrive. Expanding a leather-wholesaling business to serve a greater European shoe-manufacturing sector as undertaken by the Garzoni-Cecchi son-in-law Davide and his son is another. But between the objections of the new generation(s) and the doubts of the older generation, working in the shoe district in factories and workshops is something young(er) people have been or are avoiding if they can help it. In a sense, we have seen that they are voting with their feet, exploring other options that are new to them and to their family histories.

The shoe-district labour market per se has been shrinking steadily for several decades (30 per cent since 1991) and the belief that the 'Wild West' times of the industry were over was widespread even as I began my fieldwork in the Marche Region in 1981. Yet, one must acknowledge the notable perspicacity with which the three kin groups analysed market trends and the needs of the new(er) generation for employment in the zone. While, as it turned out, it is clear that my informants were better placed than many to take up options other than artisanal shoemaking or factory work, the two occupational categories badly hit by the economic rationalization and economic decline of the shoe industry,[8] they nonetheless had no access to employment data or projections over the past thirty or so years. Their appraisals were based upon daily observations, conversations, passing local knowledge from a producer friend in the piazza or a client in the local bar, or a get-together of neighbourhood women at a kitchen table over a Coca-Cola. The decline in clients and in orders led to the most obvious of inferences: the industry would encounter conjunctural crises or one-off events like the imposition of protective tariffs by an important export-destination nation and then would recover, although never quite returning to its former state of robustness.

The broader Marche regional labour market communicates two seemingly discordant results. The first (and this is also true for other Third Italy regions) is that overall labour-participation rates are still far above national rates: 63 per cent for the Marche and 57 per cent for Italy. Women make the difference, as they are employed at much higher rates in the Marche than is the case nationally. A total of 60 per cent of women aged between twenty-five and thirty-four are employed; over 70 per cent of women between thirty-five and forty-four are employed; and the figure only declines slightly to 67 per cent for women aged forty-five to fifty-four (Osservatorio Regionale del Mercato del Lavoro 2013: 34–39). But, in addition, the Marche unemployment rate, which is historically much lower than the national rate, has decisively risen since the onset of the current financial crisis, such that in 2012, it was only 1.7 per cent lower than the 10.7 per cent national rate (Goffi 2013: 77–78). As Gianluca Goffi notes, the closer the Marche Region approaches the national unemployment mean, the less it has in common with the 'Third Italy' and the more it has in common with the ageing, deindustrializing regions of the Italian northeast (2013: 83).

If there is any consolation in the data aggregated annually by the Marche Region, it is that university degree holders are no longer penalized for their educational advancement. Adults who have been awarded a university degree or better are finding employment in greater numbers than less educated workers – an important reversal of a long-term trend in which better education credentials were not rewarded in the labour market (Osservatorio Regionale del Mercato di Lavoro 2013: 45). Though this is bad news for the vast majority of workers with lower levels of educational achievement, it may enable the region to retain workers who would otherwise move out of the Marche Region to secure employment.

If the first finding summarized is that people accumulate observations of important economic events typically without any recourse to information aggregated and interpreted for planning purposes and devise long-term strategies based upon these observations, the second major finding I would offer is that senior members of kin groups can exert significant influence on the economic courses of action that members of new(er) generations undertake. Taken in its most universal sense, such a finding would be as banal as it would be unnecessary, as kin interventions in the economic futures of the younger generation(s) are manifested historically via inheritance, dowries and other gifts, as well as employment in elders' professions and firms. However, too little credit is given to the seasoned insights of ordinary individuals, in this case nonexpert observers of the economy, and the impact of their influence, if macroeconomically slight, in the microeconomics of things, on the underlying long-term flow of the economy. A more restrictive and useful way of putting the argument is that ongoing conversations among kin generate something of an informed forecast of what might be a prudent course of economic action to take.[9]

As the cases discussed above suggest, people can be highly informed and yet make big errors. The Grimaldi-Sarcetti household played out the pension game too long, came close to losing their home and are now saddled with a long-term mortgage in order to pay off their debts. Yet, in moving his two sons into the pizza business, Ennio Sarcetti, Elia and Giuseppa's brother, showed remarkable good sense. Kin groups could provide no useful guidance at all for young people like Ugo Garzoni and his friend Massimiliano Ceri. Instead, and fortunately for them, their households could provide the minimal economic security necessary during the period of doubt and trial both experienced in pursuit of their 'new' economic alternatives.

These cases do not in any sense prove the continued viability of kin groups in the determination of economic action in the Marche Region, or anywhere else in Italy for that matter. Nevertheless, they illustrate in some detail how, as Italian population surveys indicate (Cioni 1997: 214–23),[10] kin groups, in some sense attenuated by individual interests and intents, are active sites of significant social interaction where meaningful judgements about life and labour are made.

Michael Blim is Professor of Anthropology at CUNY Graduate Center. He is former President of the Society for Anthropology of Work and has carried out research on the shoemaking district in the Marche Region. Among his main publications are *Made in Italy: Small-Scale Industrialization and Its Consequences* (Praeger, 1990) and

Equality and Economy: The Global Challenge (AltaMira Press, 2005). He has also coedited, with Frances Rothstein, *Anthropology and the Global Factory* (Bergin and Garvey, 1992).

Notes

1. Because I am focusing on cases produced by marriage and resulting consanguineal bonds between parents and children (and in two cases grandchildren), affinal bonds, though present in extending the kin groups in question, are not a focus of study here. In a formal sense, kin terms and the organization of the kindred, including extensional terms such as 'amici della famiglia' (friends of the family) remain the same as when Sydel Silverman in her classic study *Three Bells of Civilization* (1975: 202–9), described them for the Umbrian town Città di Castello in the early 1960s. A colloquial term, *mezzo-parente*, is used in Monte San Giusto to refer most often to affines whom one treats as a cousin.
2. Silvia Yanagisako (2002: 80–83) argues quite convincingly that the strong social-structuralist position anthropology inherited from the British tradition, as notably voiced by A.R. Radcliffe-Brown and dutifully followed by his important student Meyer Fortes, creates the distinct and unhelpful bias in contemporary practice that structures dictate a set of specific norms and resulting beliefs that are prescriptive and proscriptive of specific behaviours. While this chapter shows a significant amount of comity rather than conflict between and among the generations studied, my judgement is that this is the result of the times in which my informants live, wherein persons are expected to be able to enjoy an individual destiny which kin must strive to understand and, to at least some degree, respect (Taylor 1989). Also from the standpoint of those 'respecting their parents' wishes', something like Wittgenstein's following a rule applies (1958).
3. Their evocative opening description of the Valdelsa (Ginsborg and Ramella 1999: 9) as an exemplar of 'Italia minore' could well fit the industrial district straddling the provinces of Macerata and Fermo that is discussed here.
4. See also Tamara Hareven (1982) for the elaboration of the concept of family strategies, in which she skillfully shows normative patterns among households making adaptations to the rise of industrial labour in a New England factory town.
5. Daniela Del Boca (1997: 230) points out that two out of five Italian families obtain their house via a gift from their natal household.
6. Enrico's uncle's factory was operating under a labour management 'solidarity' compact, whereby job security would be guaranteed only to a fixed number of workers, and the owner was restricted from hiring any additional workers if those still on his books were without work. Thus, Enrico could not be taken on until one of the workers under the compact either quit or retired.
7. The native asset of the port of Ancona has proved increasingly important as a source of economic growth in the past thirty years, but I confine my comments to the more strictly industrial districts. For the best recent critical discussion of the invention and analysis of the concept and reality of the 'Third Italy', see Hadjimichalis (2006: 82–106).
8. Fortunata Piselli (2003: 65–75; 2006: 411–38) has effectively combined network analysis with a sophisticated appraisal of how families build and use social capital in new economic opportunities, including 'modern', high-tech artisanal firms.
9. In Stephen Gudeman's rich if restricted notion of 'the base', there is a strong implication of the development of a common outlook on the needs of the household as a community (Gudeman and Rivera 1990).

10. Martine Segalen (1984: 163–86) makes similar observations of heightened social interaction among networks of households in rural French domestic groups.

References

Associazione Nazionale Calzaturifici Italiani and Banca Monte Paschi di Siena. 2011. *Settori economici, distretti industriali: I distretti calzaturieri in Italia, realtà e prospettive*. Siena: Banca Monte Paschi of Siena.
Balloni, V., and D. Iacobucci (eds). 2011. *Classifica delle principali imprese marchigiane*. Ancona: Fondazione Aristide Merloni – ISTAO.
Bourdieu, P. 1977. *An Ouline of a Theory of Practice*. Cambridge: Cambridge University Press.
Braudel, F. 1984. *Civilization and Capitalism, 15th–18th Century*. Vol. 3: *The Perspective of the World*. New York: Harper and Row.
Cioni, E. 1997. 'Il sistema di parentela', in M. Barbagli and C. Saraceno (eds), *Lo stato delle famiglie in Italia*. Bologna: Il Mulino, pp. 214–23.
Del Boca, D. 1997. 'I trasferimenti di reddito nelle famiglie', in M. Barbagli and C. Saraceno (eds), *Lo stato delle famiglie in Italia*. Bologna: Il Mulino, pp. 224–331.
Ginsborg, P., and F. Ramella (eds). 1999. *Un'Italia minore: Famiglia, istruzione e tradizioni civiche in Valdelsa*. Florence: Regione Toscana.
Goffi, G. 2013. 'Il sistema economico delle Marche: Artigianato e mercato del lavoro dagli anni Novanta alla crisi attuale', *Economia Marche* 32(1): 62–89.
Gudeman, S., and A. Rivera. 1990. *Conversations in Columbia: The Domestic Economy in Life and Text*. Cambridge: Cambridge University Press.
Hadjimichalis, C. 2006. 'The End of Third Italy as We Knew It?' *Antipode*: 82–106.
Hareven, T. 1982. *Family Time and Industrial Time*. Cambridge: Cambridge University Press.
Osservatorio Regionale del Mercato di Lavoro. 2013. *Rapporto Annuale 2013*. Ancona.: Regione Marche
Piselli, F. 1981. *Parentela ed emigrazione: mutamenti e continuità in una comunità calabrese*. Turin: Einaudi.
———. 2003. 'Capitale sociale familiare: una indagine sulla piccola media impresa', *Inchiesta*, 139: 65–75.
———. 2006. 'Capitale sociale familiare fra "old" e "new economy"', *Rassegna Italiana di Sociologia* 47(3): 411–38.
Segalen, M. 1984. 'Nuclear Is Not Independent: Organization of the Household in the Pays Bigouden Sud in the Nineteenth and Twentieth Centuries', in R. Netting et al. (eds), *Households: Comparative and Historical Studies of the Domestic Group*. Berkeley: University of California Press, pp. 163–86.
Silverman, S. 1975. *Three Bells of Civilization: The Life of an Italian Hill Town*. New York: Columbia University Press.
Simmel, G. 1950. 'The Stranger', in K. Wolff (ed.), *The Sociology of Georg Simmel*. New York: Free Press, pp. 402–8.
Stack, C. 1974. *All Our Kin*. New York: Harper Colophon Books.
Taylor, Charles. 1989. *Sources of the Self: The Making of Modern Identity*. Cambridge, MA: Harvard University Press, pp. 3–24.
Weber, M. 1947. *The Theory of Social and Economic Organization*. New York: Free Press.
Wittgenstein, Ludwig. 1958. *Philosophical Investigations*, 3rd edition. New York: Macmillan.
Yanagisako, S.J. 2002. *Producing Culture and Capital: Family Firms in Italy*. Princeton: Princeton University Press.

— Chapter 4 —

FACING TWO CRISES

The Disembedding of Society and the Economy in the Furniture-Caravan District, Valdelsa, Tuscany

Francesco Zanotelli

Introduction

The large amount of research dedicated to Italian industrial districts originally examined the specific factors leading to their creation, development and successive modification (Trigilia 2002). Over time, the tendency to consider *industrial district* and *crisis* together on a theoretical level (Becattini and Rullani 1996) was verified on an empirical level by a number of studies carried out during the 1990s (Whitford 2001: 55). In these, scholars tackled the problem of the continuity and transformation of the district, focusing specifically on the emergence of new forms of global capitalism based on the reorganization of larger firms in terms of flexibility. Such literature considered the failure of the districts prevalently in their productive and business dimensions, moving away from the original definition, which considered the study of local integration among entrepreneurial identity, loyalty of workers, specific political and institutional options and culturally well-defined family groups to be essential (Becattini 2003).

In particular, little attention appears to have been paid to the crisis of the districts in connection with the dynamics between local entrepreneurs and the introduction of capital and external organizations into a specific industrialized territory, nor is there much knowledge on how the crisis was viewed by those directly involved and what significance they attributed to it. Economic literature tends to underestimate these perspectives or ignore them completely, concentrating instead on exploring the structural dynamics of the market and, in some cases, the impact on the social structure. To bridge this gap, more attention needs to be dedicated to the various dimensions (ideal, social and economic) of the processes of disaggregation suffered by a territory in connection with the specific productive organization of the district. These difficulties are particularly interesting in cases where the industrial districts had previously been considered models of performance and development.[1]

In line with this approach, my aim is to analyse the critical phases of a specific territorial economy, that of Valdelsa, an industrial area of Tuscany, extending uninterruptedly from the southern part of the province of Florence to the northern part of the province of Siena. Valdelsa is well known in sociological and economic literature dedicated to the so-called 'Third Italy' (Bagnasco 1977) because it represents an emblematic case of premature transformation, during the years following the Second World War, of the agricultural society of central Italy. Traditionally based on sharecropping, it evolved into an industrially dynamic territory, founded on small and medium-sized businesses, in this specific case for the production of furniture (Becattini 1978; Bagnasco and Trigilia 1984). Subsequently, the economic crisis and the decline of the furniture industry, which began after the oil crisis of 1973 and developed in the 1980s, resulted in industrial reconversion into an engineering and wood-processing sector for the assembly of chassis and interior furnishings for motorized caravans. This reaction indicates a continuous capacity for transformation, generally attributed to the precious heritage of productive know-how acquired by the local skilled workers.

From the early 1990s onwards, the success of some important motorized caravan firms and the suppliers connected to them, consisting of small and medium-sized firms, had attracted to Poggibonsi and the outlying towns a growing number of new workers, predominantly from Senegal, Eastern Europe and southern Italy.[2] These contributed to a revival of demographic dynamics, with a tendency to expansion similar to that registered during the economic boom following the end of the Second World War.[3] Since 2008, however, a reduction in orders has led company management to make use of Extraordinary Temporary Lay-Off Schemes (Cassa Integrazione Straordinaria), permanent voluntary dismissals and early retirement. The French Trigano S.p.A., one of the major groups producing motor caravans in the district (and leader in Italy in the motor caravan sector and well-established in the European market), has reorganized its business based on a more flexible use of the workforce, orienting its production towards making to order rather than making to stock. Between 2008 and 2010, when the freefall in motorized caravan sales was evident, the company decided to dismiss 31 per cent of the shop-floor workers and 21.4 per cent of the office employees.[4] Today it would be an exaggeration to predict an epilogue for the motor caravan district in Valdelsa or even the deindustrialization of the area, bearing in mind also the recent upward trend in business and employment following the severe crisis which hit the area after 2008, which will be discussed later. However, a number of indicators make it advisable to pay attention to these territories, precisely because of their previous ability to regroup and react.

In order to offer an interpretation of the social and economic process as it took place, I therefore propose to adopt a diachronic perspective, first considering the previous crisis involving small and medium-sized firms specializing in furniture production, which made the fortune of this territory during the two decades of post-war rebuilding, only to suffer a drastic slump in the late 1970s and 1980s. A comparison between two crises that are not only distant in time but also, as we shall see, resulting from very different economic processes, will prove an extremely useful instrument with which to interpret the social changes involving the territory. Moreover, a view of the two different crises will make it possible to give a clear picture of the impact of global capitalist reorganization on the social and economic staying power of the local industrial district. Finally, on a heuristic level, this comparison will permit us to assess the effect of a diachronic view of the district on the theory of social and economic integration. For this reason, I will describe the sequence of events, defining the internal hierarchy of the economic field of the district from a historical point of view (Bourdieu 2005). At the same time, using ethnography and the anthropological perspective, I will highlight the changes that took place in terms of social, political and family cohesion, in a territory where the secret of success was based on the integration of these elements.

This chapter will focus on the active role of the subjects present in the territory when faced by a decline in the market, on their personal roles during the crises, on the strategies they adopted to survive the changes and on their attempts to understand them. More precisely, the difficulties experienced will emerge in particular from the entrepreneurs, even though up until now, economic anthropology has commendably focused on the tactics adopted to react to the crisis; however, attention is also given to the behaviour and cultural prospects of those considered to be the main victims of the adjustments resulting from the most severe aspects of every industrial transformation: shop-floor workers, temporary workers and the unemployed.[5]

The personal views of the two crises offered by the subjects involved will serve to reconstruct the many facets of the local moral economy. In particular, the points of view of the subjects reinforce in their conclusions the interpretation of the processes that took place in the district, that is, the *disembeddedness* of the same. In other words, I intend to apply the historical view of Polanyi (1968) in order to interpret the phenomenon of the two crises as a move towards the disintegration (de-institutionalization) of the political, social and economic dimensions that together had once created a peculiar social and economic system.

From a theoretical point of view, I will attempt to ascertain whether the model of integrated capitalism of the 'Third Italy' is still valid or has become obsolete as a result of the reorganization of production in terms of a more rapid and lighter financial capitalism, based on the neoliberal model. I will also assess whether the social and economic crises in the territory may be explained by the frictions and cultural differences emerging among the representatives of the subsequent generations in local families; this could have affected both the field of political representation and the business organization of the district's economy; meanwhile, the literature has underlined the harmonious aspects of integration, thereby playing its part in concealing the theoretical weaknesses of the model.

The Limits of the Model

The industrialized areas of central Italy, including the Valdelsa district that is the home of the furniture industry, have been presented as interesting examples of the growth and success of a specific type of socially integrated capitalism. If we consider that at the end of the Second World War, over 70 per cent of the buildings had been destroyed in 1944 by the Allied bombardments, between the 1950s and 1960s this territory demonstrated an unexpectedly good performance in terms of economic recovery and productive development.

The historical and economic data are unequivocal, especially given the reduced population in this specific context: the small town of Poggibonsi, which represented the productive and commercial centre of the area, counted 12,000 inhabitants in 1940, but over 17,000 at the beginning of the 1960s. Now it counts approximately 28,000. This increase was due both to considerable urbanization within the province and to internal migrations from southern Italy. In addition, from the outbreak of the Second World War to the beginning of the 1960s, the number of industries in Poggibonsi employing more than eleven people quadrupled, while the number of employees tripled. Within this trend towards expansion, industries specializing in furniture and furnishings underwent an exponential growth: in this sector the number of firms with more than eleven employees increased from three in 1940 to fifty-eight in 1960, while the number of employees rose from sixty-two to 1,736 (Bianchi 1999: 68). From an economic point of view, the astonishing development of local industry was favoured by a phase of expansion in the market, with a demand above all for widely used consumer goods: furniture production, with its limited need for technical specialization, immediately fitted into this category.

The success of this 'model' based on small and medium-sized firms located in a single area has led scholars of the economics, sociology and history of the districts (and more recently anthropology, focusing on the history of industrialization) to recognize in Poggibonsi, with its timely and rapid affirmation on the Italian scene, an emblematic case study. Local-area literature (Becattini 1978; Bagnasco and Trigilia 1984; Bianchi 1999; Dei 1999; Ginsborg and Ramella 1999; Zanotelli 2013) has defined a series of useful elements with which to identify local development:

- social and fiduciary networks among friends or immediate and extended family members, as a factor in organizational support for family businesses and funding for workers' salaries;
- a strong connection between the social requirements of the population and the political and ideological direction of the Italian Communist Party and the local government;
- a common vision, within this ideological framework, of a modernist perspective, oriented towards industrial development, shared by institutions, workers and small and medium-sized firm entrepreneurs;
- a perfectly balanced mix of individual aspirations and affirmations, and the willingness to share risks and profits through collective corporate firms;
- a system of good relations between entrepreneurs and workers, based on the concrete prospect of passing from one social condition to another within a single lifespan;
- finally, a historic phase of the market, with its expansive nature conferred by the quantity of both internal and international demand.

This formula was accepted so rapidly and widely as to assume the nature of a solid explanatory theory, a sort of generally adopted model to explain the secret of the success of small and medium-sized Italian firms.[6] However, rather than adopting the characteristics of this model *a priori*, it is advisable to evaluate its limitations, monitoring not only the birth but also the evolution of the territorial economy. It is in this way possible to discover that, over the twenty years following the world energy-oil crisis of 1973 and the rebuilding of Fordist capitalism, the furniture district of Poggibonsi suffered a severe decline. In the introduction to a volume published in 1999, the historian Paul Ginsborg and the sociologist Francesco Ramella reconsidered the Valdelsa area following the preliminary study of 1984 by Bagnasco and Trigilia, noting that:

> During the first half of the 1980s Poggibonsi underwent a difficult and painful process of industrial readjustment which, as a result of the decline in the furniture sector, redefined its sectorial profile, bringing to light the dynamism of the engineering firms. A parallel vigorous growth in tertiary employment accompanied this development. (Ginsborg and Ramella 1999: 14–15)

Employment and local entrepreneurship are therefore redefined in the direction of the services sector and of engineering industries, specializing in particular in the production of machines for wood processing and of both motorized caravans and their single components. The latter development is particularly interesting because it is during this recent phase, from the 1990s up to the present day, that the Poggibonsi territory has assumed a new identity from the point of view of its economy. This process has been mirrored in a significant way on both the political and economic planes, since the local political representatives are seeking an institutional recognition for Poggibonsi as the official national district for the production of the Italian motor caravan. It is not merely a chance development that one prevalent industry (that of furniture) should be replaced by another (that of motor caravans) in the same territory. The skills acquired and shared over two generations, first in the field of wood processing for furniture and later in that of the mobile home industry, constitute a specific *technical environment* within which, if necessary, such skills may be redefined, refocused and redirected.[7]

Ginsborg and Ramella also pointed out that the supposed harmony and integration that existed among the elements of the social landscape of Valdelsa were in fact far more conflictual, revealing an undercurrent of division: for example, in the considerable presence of families that the authors defined as *alienated*, that is, positioned outside the framework of social, political or economic representation (1999: 18). In the field of cultural consumer preferences and identity options, Dei (1999) also noted a gap between those who were the protagonists of the industrial boom in the furniture sector and the subsequent generation. Ginsborg recently returned to this subject, seeking to trace the historical development of the Valdelsa industrial district and thereby to envision its destiny today.[8] To follow his example implies verifying the interaction among the social and economic subjects of the industrial district, reconsidering the case of Valdelsa society with the use of a diachronic lens, also focusing on the changes and the fractures.

The First Crisis: The Local Moral Economy of the Furniture Entrepreneurs (Late 1970s–1980s)

In this section, I will use the ethnographic data to analyse the various dimensions of integration (or disintegration) of the furniture district: relations among the firms in the area; between firms and family connections; and between firms and political institutions.[9] Rather than producing data on the negative economic performance of the sector in the decades of its decline, I will use the words of the entrepreneurs involved to explain the causes of crisis, basing my analysis on their memories, which will naturally be filtered by hindsight through the present perspective. These oral accounts will offer a more complete picture than cold figures and will make it possible to glimpse a specific and intimate moral economy of the local context, which their personal view of the crisis renders easier to interpret.

A first element of analysis of the crisis concerns the parabolic curve of entrepreneurial development and the reasons for its decline in Poggibonsi. Bruno M., owner of a furniture firm that began in the early 1960s, sums it up briefly:

> Some workers [who were] employed in different firms created their own small business without any money … then built it up little by little … for about twenty years. Then, after twenty years, the collapse … and what was terrible about the collapse was this: all those little firms, they would buy a machine, for example a sander, it cost millions, they would use it for one day a month … you see? So a machine costing all that money … well, it should have been used at least … almost day and night, to pay for itself … and as there were about fifty or sixty sanders in Poggibonsi, doing the work that could have been done by three … so that was the waste and then … we all drowned.[10]

According to Bruno, the collapse was caused by the poor local organization of the firms, due to their inability to form a network, conversely one of the characteristics frequently quoted by economic literature in singing the praises of the district. Nevertheless his conclusion is the fruit of direct personal experience linked to the short-lived attempt to create a consortium that would have supplied the firms with a structure of services and marketing channels, as well as the advantage of economies of scale.

Over time, the flawed productive organization was aggravated by the problem of keeping up with technological change:

> From around sixty, sixty-five … technological progress began … the bandsaws were out of date, there were … excavators, and … good God … multiblade saws … so that with one saw you could cut six or seven pieces, all together. Yes, yes … transform … we needed money to buy the things, space to use them, and we needed also … to sell more, to create the conditions for selling.

Bruno attributes these shortcomings to a general *lack of a head for business*, which is not to be confused with the *will to work*, which instead was plentiful – as if to say that the phenomenon of mass capitalism lasted until the first difficulties came along, then collapsed into a number of individual destinies. He continues: 'we got by up to a certain point, but then we couldn't go on, because of our mentality, our skills, our lack of business … of a head for business … all because … and there is no way out, that is the price to pay'.

Similar opinions are expressed by Sergio M. and Elio B., respectively a former entrepreneur and a former shop-floor worker. Both underline further shortcomings in the productive sector of Poggibonsi: Sergio expands on the lack of skilled workers capable of upgrading quality in a moment of market crisis: 'because in Poggibonsi, the … technical part has always been lacking, outside the firm, because … we could go up to a certain level … but … well, we couldn't go to a skilled worker and say, hey, have a look at us … because … there weren't any'.

According to Sergio, they were also lacking in administrative skills: 'what we needed was administrative know-how, because even on the level of accountants, there was nobody who could help us. And as for designers … technical ones … there weren't any, you see?'[11]

Elio, on the other hand, underlines the rough and ready nature of a large number of improvised entrepreneurs who had little interest in the quality of their products. According to this interpretation, therefore, the crisis assumed a selective function, permitting only the best to survive on the market: 'here in Poggibonsi, in my opinion, the furniture crisis … this is the way I see it … because the … better qualified firms survived, the ones producing … a better quality of product … while the ones producing … poor quality products went under … products that didn't even last … they weren't even fit to sell'.[12]

The inside view of the crisis not only focuses on its causes, but also speculates on the possible destinies of those who were directly involved. Thus, if we excluded those who succeeded in remaining active in the furniture market or who switched to the tertiary sector or to that of engineering supplies, some potential future occupations emerged and were commented on by those interviewed.

One of these possible occupations was that of small-time entrepreneur, represented for example by the brother of Elio, who after two attempts at running a business, first alone and later in partnership, went back to being a shop-floor worker:

> Then he did other jobs, he made picture frames, but he never took anyone on, eh! … he always worked alone, then he went into partnership with someone, but the partnership came to nothing, lasted two or three years then they split up (laughs) and my brother went back to the shop-floor. He retired as a shop-floor worker.

Another possible destiny was that of the entrepreneur who, having made his money in the years of development, chose to liquidate the firm at the first signs of the crisis, holding on to his capital. Sergio G., interpreting one of the attitudes of the time, declares:

> When there is a considerable fortune involved, the person is maybe older, and doesn't have much affinity with the next generation, that is, his kids are not interested, he retires from business. So he says: 'what's the point? I might as well hang on to what I've got and that's an end to it'. And this was one of the ways out.[13]

Moral judgement turns into open criticism at the point where the capitalist firm is considered as a chance to make an exclusive profit without any positive social impact on the community. Thus, Elio continues ironically:

> E.B.: The firms didn't raise their standards, in the sense that … they didn't innovate, they didn't buy new machinery, they didn't renew anything; they had containers full of workers and nothing else.
>
> Author: And … sorry, but what did they invest the profits in?
>
> E.B.: Well … they were probably invested in something different (smiling).

Author: And could you see that?

E.B.: Yes, well, you could in … (smiling) I don't know if they built themselves a villa or bought themselves a farm … something like that.

As we can see from the interviews quoted, the crisis brought to light a multifaceted industrial area, where the many very different ways of realizing personal business ventures were interwoven with the necessities dictated by capitalistic competition, although these necessities were not always met. It was indeed possible to go back to the shop floor, tracing a concrete path across the social categories, or to choose to liquidate the firm and invest the profits in other sectors, such as vineyards and wine production, or simply to dissipate the capital accrued.

Added to the poor capacity of firms to create a network in the moment of crisis was a further element often quoted in the literature as an integrating factor in the district: the supposedly important family links in the industrial organization, deriving from a multiple family (more precisely, a polynuclear patrivirilocal extended-family aggregate) very typical of the former sharecropping system.

One might wonder why the problem of the lack of generational succession mentioned by those interviewed was not solved by the following generation, which, in such a moment of systemic difficulty, might have taken the destiny of the district in hand, making the necessary innovations. Above all, however, there is concrete evidence that the success of the Valdelsa district was originally the creation more of urban entrepreneurs and craftsmen than of farmers and sharecroppers; this is true at least of the first generation, corresponding to the development of the furniture businesses during the 1950s. Moreover, the creation of a widespread climate of reciprocal loyalty and trust, which was fundamental in the initial phases characterized by limited funds, was fostered by the relations among equals established among city acquaintances rather than by relationships based on the kinship hierarchies typical of a rural farming society. The data obtained from the Archives of the Siena Chamber of Commerce point in this direction: over a period of twenty-four years, from 1946 to 1969, out of 1,138 firms created in all the sectors in the town of Poggibonsi, only 231 (about 20 per cent) were owned by members of the same family. Instead, there is a prevalence in the new start-ups of individual firms and de facto societies, most of which were composed of partners not related by blood. While local social cohesion was certainly a fundamental element for the formation and development of many firms in the 1950s and 1960s, this cohesion was not based prevalently on the solidarity of family and relatives, but rather on that of friendship and intragenerational connections. This explanation appears important for understanding one of the reasons why most of the firms terminated their activity so swiftly during the crisis of the 1970s and 1980s. In the view of the first entrepreneurs, the hypothesis of building a business dynasty made little sense, contrary to what appeared to be the ideal of entrepreneurs of the silk business in Como, as studied by Sylvia Yanagisako (2002). The model to be imitated was therefore that of a personal business or partnership, something to be built with their own hands, those same hands that later would bring about its decline.

This reading of the lack of generational succession corresponds to what, going back to the point of view of the younger generation, was remarked on by both Dei (1999) and Bianchi (1999). The analysis of these authors of the different directions followed in Poggibonsi by the sons with respect to the fathers, not only in the field of cultural consumer choices but also in educational, professional and political choices, reveals those *underground fractures* in the social context of the district that yet again underline its fragility. This correspondence is commendably summed up by Sergio G., born during the 1950s, a witness who first embodied a line of political dissent against the local ruling class in the 1970s (he was an active member of one of the extra-parliamentary student groups), and later took up important political positions in the Italian Communist Party and in the Town Council of Poggibonsi. Sergio G. declares that 'the first generation of industrial entrepreneurs … were incapable of … transferring their knowledge, and did not have the courage to take the second generation into the firm, their sons, for example … most of whom in any case were not interested in their fathers' businesses, so there was also a generation problem'.

This last quotation allows us to introduce the third dimension – that of the relations between the economic district and the role of the local institutions – which completes the framework of the integrating factors in the district theory. The analyses performed with regard to this dimension have focused on the role of the local branch of the Italian Communist Party (PCI), which, in line with that of the national party directors in the 1950s, aimed to create an alliance between the small and medium-sized business entrepreneurs and the working class against the monopoly of the large industries (Bianchi 1999: 88–89). As revealed by the historian Bianchi, and as confirmed by a close examination of the documents in the town archives of the PCI,[14] such an alliance was effectively formed and indeed proved by the presence of workers and small-time entrepreneurs who enrolled together in the local branches of the PCI, even at the highest levels. In reality, however, on many occasions this was the cause of internal conflicts and problems of consistency in the political approach of the Party.

The entrepreneurs, for their part, criticised the local institutions for the delays which they saw as damaging the industrial potential of the area. Communications and infrastructures were all public initiatives or participations that the subjects interviewed considered overdue: indeed, they were not completed until the crisis of the furniture sector had already led to its disastrous conclusion. Sergio recalls a further episode that gives a clear idea not only of the criticisms aimed at the institutions by the entrepreneurial classes, but also of the high level of expectation and therefore confidence in those same institutions:

> I remember, for example, during the first half of the 1980s, in the period of … the big crisis in the furniture industry … practically they were closing down one by one … there was a group of industrialists from Poggibonsi … the only case in all Italy … an … attack, we should say like … an invasion, of the Town Council offices by the industrialists, headed by Confindustria … I remember this perfectly (smiling) now I come to think of it, I believe it was in 1983, we were … I was on the Town Council, I was a councillor, we had a Council meeting in the evening about six and there was … about fifty or sixty industrialists came up to the door of the council offices … sort of … a pacific invasion … but to bring … that is … mmm … to inform the public administration of the problems they were facing… and because of these the economy of all Poggibonsi was in difficulty … and that the whole country was, in fact the next day in the daily *Il Sole 24 Ore* … reported the event (raising his voice) on the front page … it reported it… 'Industrialists of Poggibonsi invade the Council offices' etcetera etcetera … anyway this is to show you the connections they had with … the territorial and local dimension … the close connections, so they were complaining to the Town Council because they said that the local government had not done anything to … in this crisis.

The Second Crisis: Disembeddedness and Industrial Hierarchies (2008–)

Thirty years after the first crisis, local society, or at least that part of it that was dependent on the industrial sector, once again went through a period of instability and uncertainty, aggravated by the international crisis and by the reduced internal consumption. From 2008 to 2012, the caravan industry suffered a decline that led in Italy to a loss of 30 per cent in new orders compared to the previous performance in 2007 (Simeoni 2013: 55). This negative trend, which has only recently shown signs of recovery, resulted in the loss of many jobs in the territory and the closing down of a number of local firms directly or indirectly connected with the caravan industry.

Below we will see how a number of important caravan businesses reacted to the crisis, and how their reactions give an indication of a historical process: the progressive *disembedding* of the district economy from the local social context.

Originally, the local caravan industry was a contemporary of the furniture industry. The trend was initiated by a number of firms founded by local entrepreneurs, who in the 1960s had already stood

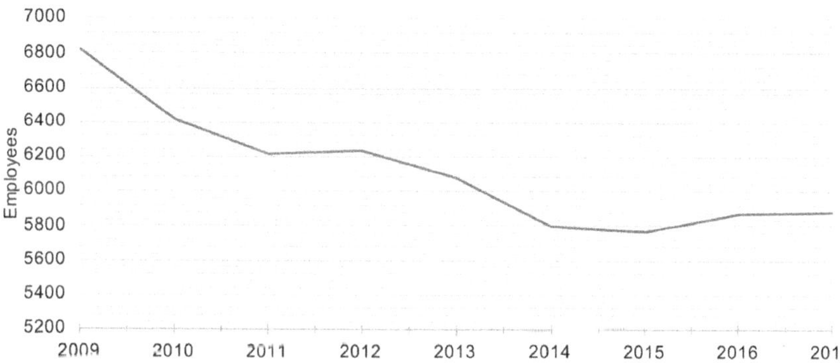

Figure 4.1. Employees in the Valdelsa industrial district, 2009–17. Source: Unioncamere, Siena.

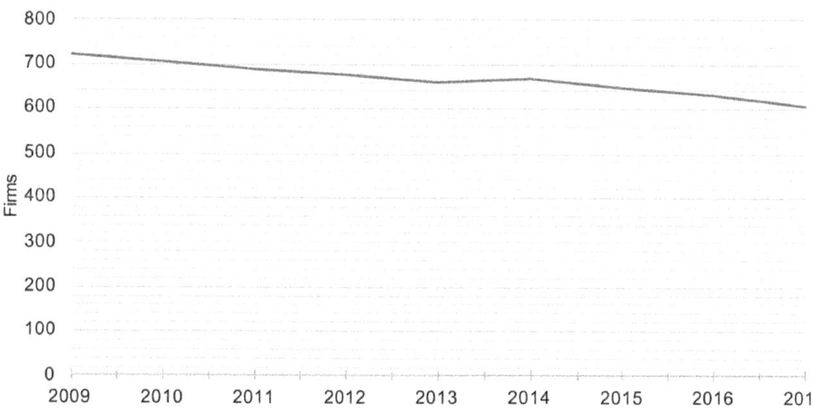

Figure 4.2. Firms in the Valdelsa industrial district, 2009–17. Source: Unioncamere, Siena.

out from the mass of furniture producers, directing their activity towards nautical furnishings and the caravan industry. Etna, for example, an iron processing company founded in 1959, converted to furniture production in 1961 and, just a year later, switched again to the production of caravans, in which it remained active until it became insolvent in 1968. A year later, another company, Rimo, was born out of this experience, and this led to the creation, in a kind of filiation process, of the most important local firms in the caravan sector. The same origins may be traced for the Mobilvetta company, which started up in Valdelsa in 1961 as a furniture business and converted in 1976 to the *plein air* market.

The industrial transformation of the Valdelsa territory, from furniture production to the prevalent supply of parts for motorized caravans, appears to have maintained unaltered the intrinsic characteristics of the district, based on a network of small businesses with a high level of specialization in the sector.

In spite of this, the apparent continuity in fact conceals deep changes involving the degree of cohesion among the relations within the district: once again, we will concentrate on the relations within the entrepreneurial plan, between firms and families, and finally among entrepreneurs, workers and local government.

From the point of view of relations among firms, the flourishing Tuscan caravan district, which developed during the 1990s, attracted the interest of foreign financial groups, which purchased majority shares from the local owners and subsequently sold them on to large industrial groups. As a result, while as recently as 2013, 90 per cent of the firms comprising the Italian motor caravan industry were still concentrated in the valleys between the provinces of Siena and Florence,[15] the main owners are now German (Hymer) and French (Trigano) industrial groups that over recent years have swallowed up important national firms, including some of those from the Valdelsa area, such as Caravans International and Mobilvetta.

From the 1990s onwards, the transformation within the district has had two important implications, the first of which concerns the new relationships among firms: local supply firms act as sub-suppliers to the major industries in the area, whose capital is for the most part owned by sources external to the region. The district therefore begins to resemble more closely those peripheral territories selected by the major industries for delocalized production, dependent on the decision, beyond local control, to invest (or disinvest) capital – what is defined in economic literature as colonization of the district (Bagnasco 1999: 99). In this phase of crisis in demand, the competitive and investing potential of the large international groups may still represent an advantage in terms of their capacity to reach foreign markets and therefore to (partially) safeguard the jobs of the Valdelsa workforce. However, it is also clear that the social constraints of an external agent with regard to the territory are lessened and, in the long run, this also leads to a weakening of the integration among the local firms in the district.

The second implication can be seen within the factories, where from 2008 up to the present day, the progressive fall in sales has led managers to reconsider the organization of production in order to create a new line: the decision in favour of flexibility, which implied a slimming down of the operative phases, has resulted in the need to reduce the workforce, by means of transfers, dismissals, voluntary resignation or early retirement. Indeed, this process had already been set in motion at the start of the new millennium by an increasingly intensive use of employment agencies, even in those industries with continuous industrial activity, for the recruiting and assignment of workers (Zanotelli 2008). The temporary and precarious nature of employment and the rapid turnover of workers is a further indication of social and industrial disaggregation within the working population itself.

Transferring the focus from a structural to a subjective perspective, an analysis of the present crisis offered by the entrepreneurs in the caravan sector reveals some common elements.

Pier Luigi is probably the entrepreneur with the longest experience in the caravan sector; he has run a number of firms since 1970. He succeeded in building up a small empire, which he then sold in the late 1990s to a German financial group; after a few years, this group in turn sold it to the French colossus Trigano. Invited to make a comparison between the crisis in the furniture sector of the 1980s and the present motor caravan crisis, Pier Luigi states that 'this time it's coming from far away, this time it's finances that have ruined everything … this time it [the market] slowed down because Lehman Brothers in America caused people to lose thousands of millions'.[16]

As we can gather from this and other testimonies, the crisis of 2008 is a phenomenon that locals see as coming from *far away*, with causes that can be attributed to international financial pressure or the institutional lack of development strategies for the national market. In any case, compared to the first crisis in the furniture sector, the role of local subjects has now become almost invisible.

In reality, as shown in the short extract from the interview with Pier Luigi reported below, he himself admits as the interview progresses that although the crisis cannot be attributed to these decisions, the involvement of local factory owners, including himself, concerned the capitalization of profits by means of selling their companies to a number of international financial societies; these later acted as intermediaries to introduce the French and German companies into the Valdelsa area. The European leaders in the sector operated by means of corporate unification, productive integration and transformation, moving towards a wider and wider oligopoly of market supply.

> Here we are in East Africa now. We are a land colonized by foreigners ... there are a number of financial societies, people with a certain amount of capital, who keep an eye on the market. If they see that some sectors are doing well, they wait for the right moment to buy up these things ... But it's also true that these financial societies, these merchant banks, because some of them are really colossal, their investments last at the most from five to seven years, then they sell ... They said: 'you must really just go on in the same way' and I fell for it. I listened to what they said and I thought to myself: 'I'll just go on in the same way'.

The difference between the local entrepreneurs and the large international groups that monopolized production in the area is underlined by F.C., a trade unionist, who describes the technique of each in establishing relations with the workforce at the time of the severe recent crisis of 2008:

> When you are faced with an entrepreneur who belongs to the territory, he is in his context, the human resources are a part of the business investment, when he gets to the point of laying off the workforce he suffers the pain of it. When this entrepreneur lays off his workers, it is because he can do nothing else. With the [big financial] groups the situation is completely different. Belonging to a big group has certainly allowed the business, has offered it the chance, has protected it better, has given that context the possibility to hold on a bit longer. With one difference: the aim of the group is the long-term bottom line, even if there is a loss in the short term. There have been workers who have taken home as much as forty or fifty thousand euros in exchange for voluntary resignation.[17]

What emerges is the potential lack of interest of the multinational companies in the destiny of the local territory, something that also emerges in the words of G.C., who is in charge of production for the biggest group operating in the caravan sector in Valdelsa: 'The crisis arrived in 2008 and it arrived unexpectedly. And as we were an important group, quoted on the Paris stock market, we had to take steps right away. And the first steps we took were to offer incentives [to the workers] for leaving.'[18]

In reality, the foreign company directors never seriously considered abandoning their factories in Valdelsa, partly because they were aware of the specialized assembly know-how originally built up by the workers in the area and partly thanks to an innovative decision regarding productive organization, first tried out in Valdelsa and based on the principle of the lean factory. As G.C. explains further:

> Our managing director had arrived in 2008 … and he introduced us to lean production… And I can say, quite proudly, that other firms copied us, attempting to produce at 8:1. This means that … well, if we go on to the line you can see that the motor caravans are different from one another … one has an upper floor, one is profiled, one is a motorhome, one has a fold-down bed, one is a different colour … on the same line of forty phases, but one after the other… I have one motorhome which takes … mmm … 90 hours to assemble, and another that takes 70 hours to assemble; and the ones that take 90 hours, I can't make more than three or four a day, and in between each two of them I make seven or eight vehicles. This is the system of production at 8:1. Practically, it is the line we follow when there is a crisis, to reduce the stock and reduce the raw materials. We work on what we can sell … and this has saved our lives for two reasons: first, because we obviously saved money. And second, because we are part of a group. At the moment the group … has companies assembling pretty well all over Europe: Germany, England, France, Spain, recently also in Slovenia, with very different labour costs in each country … So, you know the logic of multinational societies perfectly well: they say … if I move to Slovenia, if I move to Spain, it'll cost me half as much. Nevertheless, this gave us an identity in the group. We are the only ones who work on 8:1.

Viewed from this perspective, the crisis represents a complex series of frictions and adjustments between the prevalently economic and financial interests of the transnational groups and the complex system of alliances between workers and local company managers. The aim of the local managers appears to be more long-term than the contingent one of the destiny of the present workers, with the objective of keeping the industry, and its connected businesses, in the territory. The progression towards a grouping together, in a small number of external hands, of the firms that had previously been in the internal hands of a larger number of local entrepreneurs, leads to a loss of balance and to a higher level of dependence, both rendered more evident by the crisis. I will discuss this aspect further in the concluding section, introducing the concept of 'economic field', proposed by Bourdieu, parallel to that of 'embeddedness' typical of the literature of the Italian industrial district, as it becomes crucial to our interpretation of the process of interaction among the (dis)integrative factors of the district and its external subjects.

Faced with the business decisions described above, the strategies of the workers to combat the crisis led them to fall back on the family. Basing his observations on the data supplied by the workers of Trigano S.p.A., Dinubila (2011: 8) noted that the original family background represented a support for the worker, not only in terms of accommodation, through the practice of cohabitation both before and after marriage, but also in terms of regular financial aid. Family ties continued to represent an important factor throughout the social and economic history of the territory. During the economic boom of the 1960s, connections other than those relating to the family (friendship, neighbourliness, generational similarity) were more effective in fostering the starting up of new companies, while family ties served more to offer financial support or a home to live in. Today, at a time of severe cutbacks in the Welfare State, alongside financial crisis and unemployment, the family network, in spite of its demographic reduction, is once again looked to for support. Research carried out in the province of Siena also confirms the importance of family connections and intergenerational exchanges, especially from father to son, in both practical and symbolic terms (Grilli and Zanotelli 2010).

Finally, let us examine the changes that took place in the relations between entrepreneurs and the local political and institutional context. When I met Pier Luigi at his caravan business in Colle Val d'Elsa in January 2014, our conversation was frequently interrupted by telephone calls concerning an attempt to create a consortium among owners of the few remaining local firms. This attempt later proved unsuccessful, leading rather to further centralization, following acquisitions by the French group Trigano S.p.A. Despite his advancing years (he was eighty at the time), Pier Luigi supported this initiative with enthusiasm, spurred on by his personal desire for consistency with his ideals of social solidarity and his strong attachment to the territory.[19] He was also encouraged by the local and regional political administrators, who were concerned for the destiny of the connected industries that, even in 2013, kept seventy-five firms in business and provided jobs for around 1,500 workers (Simeoni 2013: 82).

In spite of these concerns, we observe less involvement of the local political representatives in defence of the economy and employment in the district during the second crisis compared to the first; this was in line with a general pattern of withdrawal of the institutions from the economic field. At present, bearing in mind the difficulties faced by local administrations in balancing their own budgets, political interventions seem to act in terms of social support, taking care of the more severe cases of social and occupational difficulty, providing housing for low-income families and offering guarantees for bank credit.

Conclusions: The Industrial District as a *Field*

The bridge traced between two moments of crisis occurring against the same social, economic and political background gives rise to some final considerations regarding events taking place in a specific social context. But this is not all. The importance of the Valdelsa case study in the literature regarding Italian industrial districts, and regarding the peculiarity of Italian capitalism, in the context of international literature focusing on embeddedness in social, economic and political processes, leads us to place the events of a micro-context on levels of a wider significance.

Faced with the original question regarding the implications of economic crises for the social staying power of the districts, I first took a methodological decision. Having opted to follow a diachronic perspective, it was possible to avoid false dichotomies, such as those that would view a homogeneous and harmonious local economic district in conflict with aggressive external market forces. The analysis (albeit a summarizing one) of the role of businesses, families and political institutions, in the local society of the same territory in two separate historic moments, offered the opportunity to bring to light pre-existing elements of weakness and fragility that an exclusively synchronic perspective would have overlooked.

The use of oral sources proved to be a further methodological advantage. The accounts given of the two crises by their protagonists have made it possible to introduce an 'inside view' offering unexpected interpretations. In fact, a clear difference emerges between the first crisis and the second: the first crisis (like the economic boom preceding it) is explained by the behaviour of the local subjects, their inexperience, mistakes and shortcomings: from their point of view, the propulsive power behind the development of the area is an endogenous one, as endogenous as the crisis itself.

However, the second crisis is explained in purely economic terms as a more generalized decline in the market, faced with which the business decisions, if not justified, are at least described as 'external', beyond the reach and control of society and local institutions. Today's crisis of the caravan sector is measured on the basis of exogenous factors linked to the international crisis brought about by financial capitalism.

I am convinced that the different perception of the two crises by members of the community analysed offers a fairly close approximation of the reality of the processes experienced. I therefore intend to show that the first crisis was represented as the consequence of behaviour within the district because the level of participation in and control of the economic processes in that historical phase was effectively closer to the local reality. The interaction of economic, political and social agents, albeit overrun with contradictions and elements of potential disaggregation, represented a form of protection capable of guaranteeing alternative solutions to the entire community: a return to being employed by others, a transfer to the tertiary sector for the next generation and a redefinition of technical skills in the new caravan district. Yet, in the case of the second crisis, the opportunity to play a part in seeking a solution locally appears more remote.

What may help us to explain this process is the concept of the economic field coined by Bourdieu and specifically defined with respect to the economic field of the firms in a specific market space.

Agents, in this case firms, create the space (that is, the economic field), which exists only through the agents that are found within it and that modify the space in their vicinity, conferring a certain structure on it. In other words, it is in the relationship between the various 'field sources' – that is, between the different production firms – that the field and the relations of force characterizing it are engendered (Bourdieu 2005: 193).

If the notion of the economic field is applied to the Valdelsa caravan district, the present critical situation proves to be the symptom of a double process. This concerns the transformation of the geometry of the economic field of the district, which has assumed a strongly hierarchical shape: the power relations within this specific field work to the advantage of the leading firms in the sector, which are increasingly distant from the context in terms of ownership and capital, and local firms act as subcontractors or have even been absorbed by transnational companies. This produces a lack of equilibrium, leading to a risk of de-industrialization in the area should the crisis produce such severe effects as to convince the leading firms to delocalize or close down.

The second aspect of the process, which is certainly connected to the first but is not exclusively dependent on it, concerns the reciprocal disarticulation of the social, economic and political dimensions of the local industrial district. This disarticulation, as we have seen, originates in medium-term processes, both inside and outside the field (this time not only economic but also social and political). The crisis in the 1980s highlighted the internal weaknesses in the productive structure of the small companies, but it also underlined their endogenous capacity for regeneration. It was this latter development that attracted the attention and the financial capital of the leading international firms in the sector. From the point of view of the relationship between family and firm, generational change led to a discontinuity in the management of a number of local firms and a loosening of the ties linking these to local society. Finally, the transformation in a neoliberal sense of the productive processes resulted in a greater use of temporary work agencies and consequently a weakening of the bargaining power of the trade unions. The cohesion among local political leaders, workers and entrepreneurs continued to exist, but was no longer able to offer an effective solution to the local impact of the international crisis.

Today, the transformation of the economic field in a hierarchical sense represents a concrete risk at a moment when, were there to be an interruption in production or in capital investments, this would not only place the economy in a critical state, but also leave a society internally more wearied, less resilient: family and relational links, thus, while continuing to play an important part in local society, would nevertheless assume a merely supportive role, while the political institutions would be more discredited.

Francesco Zanotelli is Associate Professor at the COSPECS Department of the University of Messina. He has published extensively on debt and the moral economy in neoliberal Mexico and on kinship, work, migration and welfare in Italy. He is the author of *Santo Dinero* (CISU, 2012) and is the coeditor, with Simonetta Grilli, of *Scelte di famiglia* (ETS, 2010). He is currently undertaking research on the interaction between the environmental turn in the global economy and its interaction with local political dynamics, with a special focus on Oaxaca, Mexico.

Notes

1. Both Smith (2006) and Narotzky (2007) have underlined how, in the scientific literature on this subject, the idyllic image of the district model has prevailed over its critical aspects.
2. The towns in the area involved in the production of motor caravans and connected industries are Poggibonsi, San Gimignano, Colle Val d'Elsa, Monteriggioni, Barberino Val d'Elsa and Casole d'Elsa.
3. For the successive migrations involving the province of Siena over the last fifty years, see Zanotelli (2008) and Grilli and Zanotelli (2015).

4. Research with a special focus on Trigano S.p.A. has been carried out by Elena Dinubila (2011), to whom thanks are due for the permission to use her unpublished data.
5. In a similar fashion, Magdalena Villarreal coordinated the project 'The Art of Coping: Debt Economy and Social Compensation Practices in Western Mexico' (in which I played an active part), which was dedicated to the daily practice of the rural population of the state of Jalisco, reacting to the 1992 crisis and to the subsequent neoliberal adjustments of 1994. Recently, the European Research Council (ERC) project 'Grassroots Economics: Meaning, Project and Practice in the Pursuit of Livelihood', coordinated by Susana Narotzky, investigated the everyday forms of livelihood in specific areas of Mediterranean Europe following the crisis of 2008, including entrepreneurs among the subjects of the crisis. Both these projects have placed ethnography at the centre of their methodology and research theory.
6. In his study of 1999, Bagnasco underlines the advisability of abandoning both the idea of 'recipes deriving directly from a single case and a general theory of development, capable of explaining every process' (1999: 104). This advice does not appear to have been followed in the main literature.
7. On the concept of *technical environment*, we may refer to a long tradition of research, especially in France, from the works of André Leroi-Ghouran, through Balfet and on to Warnier (see Lai 2012: 64–71). In Poggibonsi, the skills linked to wood processing date back to the beginning of the twentieth century, when the important Fassati company was established, specializing in the transformation of Chianti wine and its marketing for export. The creation of a connected industry to provide wooden crates for the transport of the characteristic Chianti bottles may be considered one of the key factors in the development of the *technical environment* based on wood processing.
8. He returned to the question during the 'Anthropology of the Industrial District: Cultures of Work, Families and Politics in Poggibonsi and Elsewhere' Conference, held in Poggibonsi (Siena) on 5 and 6 November 2010.
9. I carried out ethnographic research in Valdelsa from 2005 to 2009, with some follow-up in 2013 and 2018. Together with the group of archivists, anthropologists and oral historians that I worked with and coordinated, we conducted around fifty interviews with entrepreneurs, workers, institutional and administrative officers, and union representatives. We also worked on archival sources, analysing the historical, economic and political process. The main archives we worked on are: the archive of the Camera di Commercio, Industria, Artigianato e Agricoltura della Provincia di Siena and the Historical Archive of the local branch of the Italian Communist Party (PCI) in Poggibonsi. All the people involved in the research process were very kind and generous in trusting us and helping us with their time and suggestions.
10. Interview with Bruno M., retired entrepreneur, in Poggibonsi, 8 February 2007.
11. Interview with Sergio M., furniture entrepreneur, Poggibonsi, 28 March 2007.
12. Interview with Elio B., retired shop-floor worker, Poggibonsi, 18 January 2007.
13. Interview with Sergio G., former local administrator, Poggibonsi, 23 March 2006.
14. My analysis of the historical sources is based on the research performed by Antonio Fanelli in the local archives of the PCI. I thank him for allowing me to use his unpublished data.
15. According to Simeoni (2013), these were Autocaravans Rimor S.p.A., Industrie Giottiline S.p.A., P.L.A. S.p.A., Laika Caravans S.p.A. and Trigano S.p.A.
16. Interview with †Pier Luigi A., caravan entrepreneur, Poggibonsi, 22 January 2014.
17. Interview with F.C., local trade unionist, Colle Val d'Elsa, 30 July 2018.
18. Interview with G.C., responsible for production at a multinational caravan company, Valdelsa, 8 October 2018.
19. Pier Luigi was budget assessor on the Poggibonsi Town Council twice during the 1980s, when the PCI governed the city. Unfortunately, he passed away recently. I dedi-

cate this chapter to his memory, to his free-traveller spirit and to his regret at being trapped in a game he could no longer control.

References

Bagnasco, A. 1977. *Tre Italie. La Problematica Territoriale dello Sviluppo Italiano.* Bologna: Il Mulino.

———. 1999. *Tracce di Comunità.* Bologna: Il Mulino.

Bagnasco, A., and C. Trigilia (eds). 1984. *Società e Politica nelle Aree di Piccola Impresa. Il Caso della Valdelsa.* Milan: Angeli.

Becattini, G. 1978. 'The Development of Light Industry in Tuscany: An Interpretation', *Economic Notes* 7(1): 107–23.

———. 2003. *Industrial Districts: A New Approach to Industrial Change.* Cheltenham: Edward Elgar.

Becattini, G., and E. Rullani. 1996. 'Local Systems and Global Connections: The Role of Knowledge', in F. Cossentino, F. Pyke and W. Sengenberger (eds), *Local and Regional Response to Global Pressure: The Case of Italy and Its Industrial Districts.* Geneva: International Institute for Labour Studies, pp. 159–74.

Bianchi, R. 1999. 'Il Centro in Periferia. Società e Politica nella Valdelsa Contemporanea (1900–1980)', in P. Ginsborg and F. Ramella (eds), *Un'Italia Minore. Famiglia, Istruzione e Tradizioni Civiche in Valdelsa.* Florence: Giunti, pp. 32–108.

Bourdieu, P. 2005. *The Social Structures of the Economy.* Cambridge: Polity.

Dei, F. 1999. 'Strategie della Distinzione. Giovani, Governo Locale e Politiche Culturali a Poggibonsi negli Anni Settanta', in P. Ginsborg and F. Ramella (eds), *Un'Italia Minore. Famiglia, Istruzione e Tradizioni Civiche in Valdelsa.* Florence: Giunti, pp. 155–84.

Dinubila, E. 2011, 'Gli Effetti della Crisi: una Ricerca Antropologica sui Lavoratori Metalmeccanici della Triganò S.p.A.' Unpublished report, Siena.

Ginsborg, P., and F. Ramella (eds). 1999. *Un'Italia Minore. Famiglia, Istruzione e Tradizioni Civiche in Valdelsa.* Florence: Giunti.

Grilli, S., and F. Zanotelli (eds). 2010. *Scelte di famiglia. Trasformazioni Della Parentela Contemporanea.* Pisa: ETS.

———. 2015. 'Il Contributo delle Migrazioni Interne alle Trasformazioni Produttive e Sociali: il Caso della Toscana Meridionale dagli Anni Cinquanta ad Oggi', *Popolazione e Storia* 16(1): 57–80.

Lai, F. 2012. *Spazi Locali, Spazi Globali. Un Saggio sul Concetto di Economia Mondo.* Milan: Angeli.

Narotzky, S., and G.A. Smith. 2006. *Immediate Struggles: People, Power, and Place in Rural Spain.* Berkeley: University of California Press.

Narotzky, S. 2007. 'The Project in the Model: Reciprocity, Social Capital, and the Politics of Ethnographic Realism', *Current Anthropology* 48: 403–24.

Polanyi, K. 1968. 'The Economy as Instituted Process', in G. Dalton (ed.), *Primitive, Archaic and Modern Economies: Essays of Karl Polanyi.* Boston: Beacon Press, pp. 139–74.

Simeoni, F. 2013. *Il Settore del Camper: Struttura, Analisi Competitiva e Comportamenti Strategici Emergenti.* Milan: Giuffrè.

Smith, G.A. 2006. 'When the Logic of Capital Is the Real Which Lurks in the Background', *Current Anthropology* 47(4): 621–39.

Trigilia, C. 2002. *Economic Sociology: State, Market and Society in Modern Capitalism.* Oxford: Blackwell.

Whitford, J. 2001. 'The Decline of a Model? Challenge and Response in the Italian Industrial Districts', *Economy and Society* 30(1): 38–65.

Yanagisako, S.J. 2002. *Producing Culture and Capital: Family Firms in Italy*. Princeton: Princeton University Press.

Zanotelli, F. 2008. 'Molti e Diversi. I Lavoratori Meridionali tra Dipendenza e Autonomia', in F. Berti and F. Zanotelli (eds), *Emigrare nell'Ombra. La Precarietà delle Nuove Migrazioni Interne*. Milan: Franco Angeli, pp. 105–37.

———. 2013. 'Per un'Antropologia Storica della Genesi di un Distretto Industriale. Le Fonti Orali, i Post-Mezzadri e la Piccola Impresa a Poggibonsi', *Lares* LXXVII(1–2): 59–88.

— Chapter 5 —

The Global Enterprise from a Peripheral Perspective

The Crisis and Its Meanings in Two Generations of Metalworkers in the Case of FCA-SATA in Melfi, Basilicata

Fulvia D'Aloisio

Anthropology and Globalized Work

In the Melfi valley, which extends from the Vulture volcano to the industrial area of San Nicola, the road sign that indicates FCA (Fiat-Chrysler Automobile) seems a bit strange in this large agricultural setting, off the beaten track even for tourists. Since 2014, Fabbrica Italiana Automobili Torino (FIAT) has become FCA, with its business headquarters situated in the Netherlands and its most important plant in Detroit. The Melfi factory, called SATA (Società Automobilistica Tecnologie Avanzate)[1] was founded in 1993 as FIAT's last Italian plant, and now has almost 7,500 employees; 6,000 workers were employed in 1993/1994, when the factory began its production (5,542 in 2013, prior to the merger with Chrysler; Bubbico 2014). Afterwards, 1,500 new metalworkers were employed in 2014/2015 after the international merger in order to produce a new car model, the Jeep Renegade, which was primarily intended for the American market.

At first glance, the two generations of metalworkers are already different in many respects: age, education, first employment in the factory and presumably also their motivations and aspirations. An underlying factor consists of the new multinational structure of the FCA Company, increasingly projecting the Melfi factory on to the global division of work and production scene. However, in the progress of the factory, in its alternation between full production and temporary slowdowns, many similarities seem to emerge that lead us to reflect, in line with the focus of this volume, on the implications of the crisis, on the ways of facing it and on the future perspectives of different workers inside the factory, tracing differences and similarities.

From the perspective of the anthropology of the enterprise, the production and work sites, and the contexts in which they operate, lend themselves to an effective reading regarding the way in which the economic processes of the global level are grafted onto local contexts, helping to transform them. In the genesis of this perspective, some scholars in France, such as Selìm and Sugita (1991), initially focused their attention on the opening of possible spaces for collaboration between anthropologists and companies.

About fifteen years later, some scholars expressed a viewpoint that is of great interest for the purposes of this chapter: in the face of the idea of globalization as a growth of homogeneity, produced essentially by the circulation of goods, Didry and other scholars argued that: 'Contrary to popular belief, what we face in the process of capitalist globalization is not the search for a new thought of the homogeneous. This process leads to a refined perception of the multiple, to grasp, under the diversity of the phenomenal forms of work, a freedom and inventiveness that irremediably resist modeling and put in the hands of the workers often unsuspected resources, sometimes obscured by the social sciences, to shake the chains of capitalism' (Didry et al. 2004: 10; Althabe and Selim 2000).

Later on, taking up a critique of the notion of post-Fordism, which they considered a generic, unifying and threateningly vague category, such scholars recalled how it becomes increasingly difficult to identify a single capital/work relationship; rather, it seems, attention must be directed towards different paths that testify to different forms of capitalism, and even more specific local syncretisms of economic processes, which give rise to different and sometimes original configurations of production and work (Selim 1996; Althabe and Selim 2000).

In the ethnographic case study presented here, we talk about a type of work, the metalworking industry, which Mollona defines as old-fashioned, meaning that it is now out of the mainstream of social research on work, numerically decreasing in terms of employees, even in some respects overcome by the new forms of so-called cognitive work (Rullani 2004; Negrelli 2013); currently, the research increasingly focuses on services, on new jobs and professions, and on less stable and localized work. In the hypothesis that we propose here, the case of Melfi helps us to go beyond the traditional categories and distinctions and to outline a nonhomogeneous working class, maybe similar to other situations of subalternity and exploitation, but different in its internal composition. On the one hand the local metalworkers can be anchored to old conceptions of the metalworker class, and on the other they are in a state of considerable transformation. The profiles of the workers in Melfi and their strategies in the face of the crisis and the future, investigated with the help of ethnography, can be read as representing a useful peripheral work-force that, through various events, has contributed and reinforced the new global aspirations of FCA.

The Foundation of the Factory in Melfi: Distant Echoes of a Myth

Twenty-five years after its foundation in 1993, the FIAT-SATA factory in Melfi has had a profound effect on the Basilicata region, starting from a strong entrenchment in national economic history that considers FIAT as a symbol of Italian modernization and development. At the same time, from 2009 to 2014, the FIAT-SATA inserted itself into the international framework, with the acquisition of the US company Chrysler and then with the creation of the new FCA Group.

From an anthropological point of view, the longitudinal ethnographic research that this chapters proposes is articulated in different phases of fieldwork (the first from 1999 to 2003, the second from 2011 to 2014 and the last since 2018); it is therefore able to offer a glimpse into the evolution of the factory and the transformation of the local work model, inspired by Toyota and also reflecting the new general structure of automobile production and engineering work.

In 1993, the Melfi plant was at the heart of an industrial revision plan that had its origin in a long-standing crisis, in the automotive sector and also in the FIAT company. Starting with the oil crisis of 1973, there was a substantial change in the balance of the global automotive market, both in terms of the drastic drop in demand and in terms of supply, due to the need for new investments in processes and product innovations. Twenty years later, in the 1990s, what Volpato called 'the arrogant advance of the Japanese manufacturers' was in turn combined with a new scenario for the international automotive industry, that is, 'the first time the production potential exceeds the demand in a structural way, a situation that determined the exit from the market of companies in a weaker and marginal position (Volpato 1993: 15). The Melfi factory thus constituted the answer, in organizational and production terms, that FIAT Auto intended to give to the new characteristics of the market, with the aim of overcoming the old Taylorist/ Fordist production model. It was a series of transformations, on the whole based on the principle of limited rationality, which aimed to mark the detachment from the previous model known as absolute rationality, with the explicit target of controlling the uncertainty and variability of a different production situation. The main objectives, inspired by the Japanese model, were thus to correct the defects (according to the principle of total quality), shorten the time spent on solving problems, follow a 'just in time' production model, that is, with an already-existing demand for cars, and finally bring about a spatial unification between company and supply chains (Bonazzi 1993; Cerruti 1993; Ohno 1993). The realization of this organizational revolution, based on 'inverse thinking' (Coriat 1993), was to be carried out in a so-called 'green field' area (see below), where there was no entrenchment of the old Fordist organizational structures. The green-field label, which was used in the advertising of the industrial operation in Melfi, constituted an effective synthesis of some basic local characteristics directly related to the location choice of the plant: first of all, the absence of industrialization in the area and therefore of a Fordist memory, the great accessibility of labour from unemployed school leavers and the absence of organized criminal networks (unlike some other southern Italian regions).

In short, all the characteristics of an industrially virgin area have been useful to the complete realization of the new organizational model and its success, emblematically transforming historical local shortcomings into effective prerequisites for the construction of the new factory. The economic literature did not fail to underline this contradiction, often tracing it as such, sometimes with a celebratory tenor that was an echo of the presentation of the project by Alberto Pianta, President of SATA in 1993:[2] the green field, the symbol of the operation, found its precise environmental reference in the beautiful green valley of San Nicola, about 20 km from Melfi, where a complete plant for the production of motor vehicles was built in just over two years: a total area of two million square metres, with four departments: taping, body-in white-shop, painting and assembly, the latter with two assembly lines (D'Aloisio 2003, 2014).

Big industry in Italy has presented, since the post-unification period, some characteristics of a specific configuration within the framework of global capitalism: among these, in the opinion of Amatori, are the weakness of the internal market, the close interconnection with the state and a historical entrepreneurial attitude that has been less cautious in terms of cutting unit costs and more prone to political and state support, useful in obtaining both economic and legal support (such as budgets for new investments or measures to support the demand for cars that accompanied the history of FIAT in Italy) (Amatori 1999).[3]

The origins of FIAT, which was founded in 1899 by a group of aristocrats and professionals from Turin, did not deviate much from this picture. It immediately began large-scale production ('making like Ford' was the motto of the leader, Giovanni Agnelli) and also diversified production in several sectors, such as marine engines and industrial vehicles, given that the characteristics of internal demand would not have allowed for the creation of a mass market. To mention just a few steps in the company's history that were deeply intertwined with the history of the country, FIAT's superiority over other car manufacturers was such that its share of Italian production soared from 5 per cent in 1905 to 50 per cent in 1914. The inauguration of the 'Lingotto' establishment in 1923, the result of investing profits gained through orders during the war, and the arrival of managers such as Ugo Gobbato and Vittorio Valletta made FIAT a company with strong vertical integration, with an extensive sales network and all the characteristics of a modern company (Amatori 1999: 713).

In order to better understand, through some fragmented steps, the role of FIAT in the national context, while not forgetting the myth surrounding the evolution of the company, we have only to think about the postwar project, sustained by the company's president Vittorio Valletta: 'Getting in line with the automotive world: producing small-displacement cars, between 500 and 1,000 cubic centimeters, thus increasing not only the foreign demand but also the national one' (Berta 1998: 15). So, the '500' and '600' car models became not only the most popular models for Italian families during the 1960s, but also the symbols of modernization in their lives, thanks to the increasing mobility in their free time and new forms of leisure, such as travel and tourism. At the same time, the Mirafiori plant became the emblem of Taylorism and of the standardization of tasks, aimed at reducing costs and increasing productivity, a transformative movement led by FIAT and a few other Italian companies.[4]

These signs serve to highlight the salient features of a company that, although now in crisis, when the Melfi factory was established back in 1993 carried with it the echo of a glorious past of economic development and modernization, as well as that anticipatory socialization of thousands of southern migrants who had improved their lives by working in Mirafiori – a passage that for them, coming from the construction industry, had marked the arrival of a better paid, better protected and, above all, safer job (Alberoni and Baglioni 1965; Signorelli 1995). This legacy carried considerable weight in terms of the expectations and impact of the factory, and was still detectable in local memory among the population of Melfi at the end of the 1990s, when the first phase of ethnographic research began. SATA's arrival was an almost messianic event in the local area, connoted by the expectation of all-round economic development, an event able to produce a long-awaited modernization. However, with insight, we have seen that these aspirations have remained largely disregarded (D'Aloisio 2003: 54).

Perceptions of Time during the Crisis: Uncertainty and New Precariousness

The Japanese of Melfi, or even the 'Melfi boys' as the workers were called by the press and the local people, were hired between 1993 and 1994, all with an apprentice training contract, which provided tax relief for the recruitment of young people under the age of thirty-two. They were mostly university graduates, unemployed, dedicated to small odd jobs, often undeclared work, for whom recruitment at the factory meant stability, regular wages and the possibility of planning for the future. In this sense, the red line that emerged from the first interviews was undoubtedly the time gap between the years of job insecurity and new future prospects opened up as a result of joining FIAT.

The conception of time is an exquisitely anthropological theme: a key element of the 'modifying intervention' typical of cultural action (Remotti 1993: 45), as well as the conceptual category with which social subjects elaborate their own being in the world (De Martino 2002). In the hypothesis that has inspired this writing, the conception of time is an effective category for observing, using the tool of ethnography, the transformation of Melfi's industrial plant from the role of being the driving force behind the renewed automobile production to its new location within the international geography of production, which responds to the new global company FCA (Fiat Chrysler Automobile, from 2014).[5]

The timeframe we are talking about is not merely the objective and objectifiable time of the clock, or a psychological time, but a social time, shared by the body of workers at Melfi, first marked by the opposition between work time and free time, which has assumed a changing connotation in recent years and consequently has contributed to producing a different self-conception and world vision in the workers. The long-term effects of the 2008 crisis began to be felt in Melfi in the autumn of 2011, with a decline in production and, consequently, in the number of working days: three days a week, in the first phase, with the support of an unemployment benefit provided by the Italian state, the so-called CIG (Cassa Integrazione Guadagni).[6] On a different scale, if we look at the sense of time within the long term, the crisis introduces a new sense of precariousness and uncertainty: a condition already known, in the past, to the workers of Melfi when the majority of them were unoccupied or engaged in temporary jobs, but this time experienced through different and unexpected facets. It is worth remembering that the experience of time, according to the definition given by Cavalli (1985), is also the essential dimension of self-perception for social subjects, through what remains identical to itself and what changes: therefore the role of work, in its change, maintains a close connection with identity and with the projection of the self in the future.

After the first phase of decline in production in 2011, a restructuring phase began in February 2014, with the intended goal of producing two new models; thus, the number of working days reduced even further, with a sort of a weekly shift rotation. Full production then resumed in January 2015. The work shift (two days or three, or stopping for a week) was communicated to employees, each time, only on Sundays (and often in the evening), via a mobile phone text message.

In the autumn of 2011, my second phase of fieldwork began in Melfi, and in the first few months workers felt no sense of worry or regret; on the contrary, there was a certain relief expressed, linked to the reduction in pressing productive rhythms, judged by all the workers in Melfi to be increasingly unsustainable. The working time inaugurated in Melfi (called TmC2) had made it the most productive plant in Europe; subsequently, the introduction in 2010 of the new time-calculation system, the so-called ERGO-UASS, constituted a production regime in which the reduction of working days was undertaken in quite a contradictory manner.[7] The most contradictory aspect was represented by the permanence of the rhythm of production, however intense, which some trade unionists calculated in terms of a decrease in total production of only 30 per cent, but which did not correspond to the reduction of the working week from six to three days (i.e. 50 per cent).

To understand the widespread fatigue in the first phase of the CIG, it is useful to look at a survey conducted by the trade unions inside the factory that shows the pathologies diffused among the workers (FIOM-CGIL 2010).

These, together with ethnography, draw the picture of a working class deeply weakened in body and mind, afflicted by tendinitis, problems of the spine, sleep disorders and anxious-depressive syndromes, as evidenced by the widespread use of sleeping pills, anxiolytics and antidepressants. Most of these illnesses (physical as well as psychological) were often not even officially declared by employees, a trend that became even more acute in the new phase of precariousness, on the one hand due to fear of losing their assigned job positions and on the other due to fear of being seen as more vulnerable in view of possible cutbacks in manpower:

> With the redundancy fund, we are working three days. So, they say, given the fact that we work three days, in short, I don't know if the other interviewees have already told you these things, I don't want to be repetitive. They say that, since we do three days, as there is no absenteeism, people are all in the factory, that is, there isn't anyone who stays at home, who takes a day off, in short, there is no absenteeism in the factory and therefore they can produce more. So, on this basis they raise the bar to the maximum, and then they make you do the same production as you did before, maybe, when you could work all week, when you produced 220 pieces per shift, those were the number of cars you did. They had already begun to intensify the line a bit before we all passed to the three working days a week. And then with the three days of CIG they progressively increased. They said yes, all right, you can work hard this week, because next week you're off.
>
> (Cristina, forty-nine, first-level degree, assembly line worker, widow, one son, 2012)

That the first phase of workers accepted the reduction in their working hours with a sense of relief was not openly stated in interviews, but was simply admitted to off the record. The temporary relief soon faded, being replaced by a growing concern for what, day after day, has become an increasingly limited and restricted lifestyle, which involved adapting to a salary reduction and the growing difficulties of meeting daily living expenses, which were stretched to the maximum by the end of the month. The widespread use of loans for purchases of various kinds by the workers shows that the salary, initially, was considered as continuous and secure, while gradually the reduction in workers' salaries led to restrictions in daily life , with increasingly narrow economic limits that, over a long period of time, also shortened the future perspective:

> Bad, honestly, we're not doing well, because economically we can't cover all the monthly expenses, because we have commitments and other things. What happened was, we took on commitments with a normal salary, now there is less money, but the commitments aren't fewer than before, you must still make the payments regardless of everything, and so. But we hope it's a momentary thing, hopefully! Because in Melfi, projects for other car models at least at the moment aren't foreseen. This is our fear. Because as long as it's a month, two months, three months, one tries to survive, but if it's seven, eight months, ten months, it means that we'll go under a little bit. And it'll take time to resurface. That's if we can!
>
> (Sara, forty-three, high school diploma, paint worker, separated with three children, 2013)

Workers' reduced working activity, their growing awareness regarding their reduced income and the restrictions this placed on their daily lives during these long months increased their uncertainty in relation to the future, and also the concern for the prolonged reduction of work. Since February 2014, the ordinary CIG was transformed into an extraordinary CIG, linked to a restructuring in the factory: the production of two new models, the Renegade SUV and the 500X, which were planned for Melfi, while the Punto, the first model produced in Melfi, was gradually phased out of production. In this way, the conception of time was directly connected to the new FIAT-Chrysler set-up in the global economic scenario:

> At the beginning of this 'novelty', and this drastic reduction of working hours and therefore with the physiological lowering of … let's call it income, at the beginning it was seen as a way to rest, because you know, the years have gone by for everyone. I must tell you, however, that after two years, I'm beginning to see people seriously worried: I can tell you that some of my members, some people close to me, who turn to me for personal reasons, because we trade unionists often become a bit like confessors to workers because we manage to present ourselves as balanced and able people willing to listen to them. And I have tell you that there's a terrible situation, and it derives from the fact that the level of debt in this area is very high: being relatively young, those who signed up for a mortgage years ago, today have to pay it, and maybe if they chose variable mortgage rates, today they have a daunting instalment to pay. At the moment the law allows us to put on hold the mortgage for a year or two and so block time.
>
> (Marcello, forty-five, high school diploma, assembly worker, single, trade unionist, 2013)
>
> Now we go forward with many uncertainties. A few years ago, we never thought that we would arrive at the point of working three days a week. Now it goes on, you know, with fear, you don't know how many days you'll be

> working next month, as a matter of fact, now we're in November and I don't know how many days we'll work this month. Now we start next Wednesday working, on Wednesday it'll be the 8th, from the 1st to the 8th we haven't had a single day of work. There's a lot of worry. Concern for the future, also because here, the area where we are is also a fairly poor area, if we lose even the little we already have. FIAT in Melfi has brought a lot of wellbeing to the area; if this factory fails it would be a tragedy.
>
> (Michele, forty-three, middle school, assembly worker, single, 2013)

Uncertainty in relation to the future is not a new feature in Melfi; it is an integral part of the work experience of most of the local workers. In fact, almost all workers, before entering SATA, had experienced precarious or undeclared work, but they believed they had permanently moved away from this by being employed by FIAT: this is what clearly emerged in the first phase of this study (D'Aloisio 2003: 161–62). If at the time of recruitment, working in a big factory marked the achievement of a safe and protected working status, twenty years later, when the workers were in their forties and early fifties (as noted above, all those hired were under the age of thirty-two), they found themselves dangerously projected into a new form of precariousness, a process dictated not only by the decline in production but also by the uncertainties related to the recovery. This latter point, in fact, depended not only on the trend in car demand not failing, but above all on the new, different position that Melfi was taking on in the FIAT-Chrysler global production scenario. In short, in the first phase of factory work, when the Melfi plant represented the cutting edge in Italian production, the local workers experienced the kind of work that Accornero defines as 'capital-w work', that is, safe and guaranteed work, fundamental to one's existence and identity; after which, in this phase of crisis, they find themselves again in a time of a new, but different, uncertainty, bringing them back to 'small-w work' (Accornero 2000; Fumagalli 2011).

By 'capital-w work', Accornero indicates the work that characterized the twentieth century: an increase of volume and value of labour products, the increase in the number of workers on a secure salary and an increase in wages across the board. However, so-called 'small-w work', typical of the twenty-first century, is instead a form of work based on a progressive normalization of the variability of production: a work that is subject, much more than was the case beforehand, to new unpredictability and alternating phases. So in this phase, in which it is normal to rapidly acquire and use information on production and the market (in a way which was unthinkable in the past), it becomes even more necessary to learn promptly what will happen tomorrow, because the demand of goods is more unstable, and production requires varied and fast solutions in response to contingent problems (Accornero 2000: 101–2). To cite a fitting example, in the new productive phase at Melfi, normality is manifested in an assembly line with a constant range of different car models, in which the workers no longer follow the same continuity, but manage a discontinuous flow of models and activities.

Biographical time, once again characterized by 'small w-work', has substantially changed the structure of workers' existence, directly linked to the dimension of the global company, a dimension that is not only more extensive, but also more widespread and uncontrollable, within which the production cycle is distributed and organized outside the confines of a single factory: this is the vector set of flows described by Fumagalli that is neither enclosed in a single factory nor in a single organizational work model. At the same time, the whole production cycle is no longer articulated within a single nation, but in a wide and composite geography of closely connected production sites. On the one hand, this configuration is perceived as dangerous because of its spread, which allows fast productive movements; on the other hand, it remains inexplicable, distant from the experience and daily lives of workers, as much of the literature has emphasized (Chicchi and Leonardi 2011; Standing 2011; Marsh 2012; Moretti 2013):

> And the future, I don't know, really, where we're going to end up! Fulvia, in ten years' time they'll be off to Poland, they'll be off to Libya, they can go wherever they want. There the cost of labour, I heard on the TV the day before yesterday, the cost of a worker's job in Italy is two euros and a bit, and in India it's 80 cents, right! They'll go there, to India, they'll find people who work fourteen, sixteen hours without saying a word. Whichever way, they'll have their production. Of course, it's risky for them, because going to these countries, social unrest can break out at any moment, there have been so many companies that have left, they've moved to Morocco, Tunisia. Many factories that went to Tunisia, for example Valeo, then they found themselves in serious difficulty, because of these social revolts: going to these countries that are so poor, there is no security of democracy, so at any moment they can be in a right mess.
>
> (Cristina, forty-nine, first-level degree, assembly line worker, widow, one son, 2012)

During its first twenty years, the Melfi factory progressively assumed a new position in the production scenario, and therefore new and different connotations: the experiences of productive delocalization have multiplied (from Poland to Serbia), the Italian plant of Termini Imerese (Sicily) closed in 2011 and Melfi has been transformed into a branch of the new global company, whose destiny is seemingly becoming less clear and more nebulous. In Garibaldo's opinion, the international market could be a big problem for FIAT, with the majority of its production focused on the medium-size car sector of the market, its power plants located outside of Italy, and its luxury brands, such as Ferrari and Maserati (property of FIAT), which in turn are in direct competition with German brands such as Porsche, Audi and BMW (Garibaldo 2014). In Garibaldo's view, this competition may perhaps be pursued and implemented, but it is hardly credible that it will constitute a substantial part of the European market for FIAT. The problem of how to provide work (and therefore sufficient employment) to Italian factories remains an open one.

The Second Generation of Metalworkers: New Enthusiasm for a Short Future

The acquisition of the US company Chrysler by the FIAT CEO Sergio Marchionne in 2014 constituted, in Berta's view, 'a departure from the orbit of Italy of the most emblematic of its companies' (Berta 2011:14). It was, as noted above, a long path started from afar, and a necessary act for the repositioning of Italy among car manufacturers (FIAT-Chrysler was ranked seventh in the global automotive group rankings: Berta 2014; Trombini and Zirpoli 2013). The first consequence of the merger was the assignment to Melfi of production of the Jeep Renegade, the new model that has achieved (up to now) a good positioning on the market. Between 2014 and 2015, the recruitment of new workers began (Grandi and Greco 2013). Three years later, in the summer of 2018, the second production line began to be dismantled, due to the stoppage of Punto production at the end of 2017.

In January 2015, the Italian press announced the news of 1,500 new positions at Melfi: one article was entitled 'FIAT-FCA Starts Again from Melfi', while others also welcomed the event.[8] The recruitment, according to the new law on labour, was for a contract for six months, with the subsequent possibility of being made permanent. In a little more than twenty years, a new wave of 'Melfi boys' wore the metalworker overalls, which in the meantime had changed colour to white in all the factories of the group (D'Aloisio 2003). They were young graduates and postgraduates, between the ages of twenty and thirty, whose attitude towards the factory was informed once again by the search for job stability, which was otherwise impossible. However, many attitudes of these new workers differ compared to those of previous workers at the plant, such as their view of the future and also their approach to everyday life. The enthusiasm shown for the expansion of the workforce, both locally and in the media, can be traced back, albeit with some differences, to the enthusiasm that surrounded the factory at the time of its founding and the beginning of production (D'Aloisio 2016). In May 2015, the visit to the factory of the then Prime Minister Matteo Renzi, CEO Sergio Marchionne and FCA President John Elkan also seemed to reaffirm an old partnership between FIAT and the Italian government, which was reported in the press in tones of paternalism and approval.[9] In reality, the new multinational positioning leaves behind the old Italian policy which in the past played an important role in financing and supporting FIAT.

In September 2018, the phase of the so-called solidarity contract began in Melfi. This meant that the local unions had reached an agreement with the company such that the decline in production, due to the end of production of the Punto model at the plant, was spread amongst all workers, with a shift rotation. The local reaction to the new phase of lay-offs is very interesting and constitutes a first level from which we can analyse the meaning of work and the experience of time in Melfi. First, as in the phase of reduced production levels, which started in 2011 following the global crisis, workers showed yet again some relief, linked to the possibility of having longer breaks and more time for themselves in the framework of rigid shift work. At the same time, also in a similar way to the phase that began in 2011, the abstention from work, in a few months, also forced workers to deal with a salary reduction. In this regard, a difference can be seen between the two generations of workers: the old employees and the new ones who started working at the plant in 2015. For the latter, who had not experienced the 2011 crisis in the factory, the stop was mainly a circumstantial and transitory event; their opinion was that work goes on and that the Jeep was holding up well on the market, while the large multinational company opened up unexpected spaces and prospects beyond the local situation compared to the past.

Marika (thirty years old), who graduated in biotechnology, applied to work at the factory because she couldn't find a job with her degree; she was looking for economic independence and she wanted to make plans for the future with her partner. She decided to apply, was hired in June 2015 and after a year of work on the assembly line became a team leader. Regarding her relationship with older workers, this is how she put it:

> They tend to overwhelm you if you're weak. So you need to develop a macho character, you have to be strong, well I think you do. Then it depends what you want to do in there, because if you want to do your job, be a worker, just do your hours and that's all. But if you want to go a little further up the ladder, you must obtain respect. Because anyway, you have to consider: you're the last in, so young, because they have this prejudice, there was a little prejudice, there still is perhaps, that you are the last in, before you were a temporary worker, you're not like them with a fixed contract, they can't be fired! Let's say that, in their opinion, you have to do what they tell you to do, because you have no experience, because you are the last rung on the ladder, and you can't possibly understand all the dynamics. On the one hand it's also true, experience counts, but we have brought a breath of fresh air, because technology has advanced, not everyone can keep up with the changing situation, because they have their ways of seeing things; instead, we have a more open mentality.
>
> (Marika, thirty, graduated in biotechnology, team leader)

The generational distance is evident in this quote: on the one hand, young people, with different skills in relation to new technologies, associated with greater physical strength and greater speed in learning the job, as well as a greater readiness to try anything new, associated with the first substantial and stable salary they have received in their life; on the other hand, the resistance of the older metalworkers (now approaching their fifties), faced with new changes, fatigue resulting from years of work in the factory, disenchantment towards the promises of future stability, the financial hardships caused by lay-offs linked to their borrowing for home loans and the need to support their children. Young people, at the height of their physical and mental energies, reassured by the new salary, feel happy in bringing about renewal and new enthusiasm, as the image of the 'breath of fresh air' mentioned by Marika suggests. For their part, the older workers express a vision of shift work that partly attributes responsibility to young people: the new employees, in actual fact, are only partially protected by the trade unions against dismissal, as far as their new work contract allows, and are deprived of the protection that the older workers have. As one worker told me, many say that it is because of them that there is now work rotation and unemployed benefit, and because of the production of only one car model, the workforce taken on in 2015 was in reality no longer needed; others were more tolerant, specifically those who had a child or whose child had been hired at the factory, and in this case their perspective is obviously different.

For their part, many young people feel they have to demonstrate their skills and abilities to their elders in a competitive situation, which in many cases is resolved in favour of the younger workers for the reasons mentioned above. A young 25-year-old team leader, who runs an invention team of ten people, all about twice his age, described how he makes himself respected in his duties and, when I asked him how he is seen by his workers, he replied:

> No, they respect me. Apart from that, I make them respect me. It's something that you can develop, but slowly. That is, when I started as team leader I couldn't get them to respect me for my role, but then with more experience, you can get into people's heads and make them respect you: you're the one who commands. You are the law, they're not the law. You can be good at filling all roles, but in this case the work is different, you have to be good at inducing people to work, while I'm the one who doesn't have to do anything. In other words, a good team leader is the one who doesn't work; if I sit in my chair, during the shift, the chief tells me I'm doing well. Because it means that the team is fine, you make people work. They are the ones who have to work, you just have to manage.
>
> (Massimo, twenty-five, industrial engineer)

Later on, Massimo explained that he started to work as a wildcard, replacing his colleagues in different tasks, and having learnt how to do the work of each role very quickly, he attracted the attention of the manager, who after a year promoted him to the position of team leader. He also mentioned a very interesting issue: young people are less willing to do things and more inclined to answer back to their supervisors, probably due to juvenile cockiness. Another reason for this is because they are less interested in keeping their jobs at any cost, mainly because they do not have family or urgent economic commitments:

> Do you know how they look at us? They take note that our superiors aren't able to treat us badly, like them, I really don't know. Because we entered in the factory before with a major consciousness of the whole system, because the chiefs already explained to us how it all works, unlike the older ones, who had to create their own experience. Instead we already understood everything. We knew how it worked. So, if the boss tries to cheat you, you already

> know how the system works. So, the young worker refuses. Then you know, they look at us like all the youngsters nowadays: the youngster nowadays wants a job, but wants to do as little as possible.
>
> (Massimo, twenty-five, industrial engineer).

This image that some younger-generation workers give in reference to their own generation contrasts with that provided by some workers from the older generation, who argue that when the younger workers came to the factory for the first time in 2015, they were willing to do anything: they didn't complain about the work shifts, they didn't protest about the workloads or about the last-minute communications regarding the shifts. Moreover, some older people attributed to young people the responsibility for having lowered the level of their workers' rights even further, for having contributed to endorsing the unregulated use of labour and for having further worsened general working conditions:

> At the beginning they looked at us in a bad light, because in their opinion, they did different shifts: they did one week in the morning, one week in the afternoon, one week at night. After we arrived, the shifts were turned upside-down: now they work on Sunday afternoons, they work on Saturday nights, they've never done this before, they saw us like invaders, 'so they come', the young people, they'll throw themselves into doing anything. What do you want from me? Physical strength is different, but it's also right, we're twenty years younger than them, there are twenty-year-old guys, that is to say, just high school leavers, who came to work, who have a physical strength greater than someone of forty-five/fifty years old who has already done twenty years of work, twenty years of shifts. And then they said: you can do everything, you accept everything, then they take advantage of us, because they demand the same things from us. And so, what do you want from me? That's it, the age difference counts! And even the physical age difference is important. Others, on the other hand, look at us as kids, the workers who have children said: ah, if you were my kid! They identify themselves in our situation, similar to their children, the others instead ... nothing.
>
> (Giulia, twenty-seven, high school diploma, worker)

It is clear that these two apparently contradictory points of view tell us firstly of a certain distrust, and also a real reciprocal resentment, between older and younger workers, and tell us precisely how the two generations cannot perceive themselves as being on the same level. On the one hand, older and younger workers are so different in terms of energy, will and expectations, that they can only really diverge, and can create a real generational fracture. On the other hand, both visions are true, perhaps at different times during their presence in the factory: at the beginning, as soon as they were hired, the young workers were more eager to work, more willing to tolerate the factory regime and more submissive, at least until their temporary employment contracts became permanent. Once they had achieved stability, and with clearer ideas on the real conditions of possible disciplinary dismissals, they became more aggressive and brazen than their elders and more inclined to react, also because they had already grown up with a more permissive education, being less attentive to the importance of generational levels, and above all, less vulnerable to economic blackmail (Oppo and Perra 2008). In other words, they seem to reflect some characteristics of Italian young adults, who, in comparison to much of the rest of Europe, stay longer in the family home, form long-term relationships later in life, have children later and continue to enjoy the protection and advantages guaranteed by their parents for longer (Barbagli, Castiglioni and Dalla Zuanna 2003; Facchini 2005; Guizzardi 2007, Donati and Prandini 2008).

Regarding their outlook on the future, both in personal terms and in terms of the factory, and also on the possibility that Melfi production may cease at some stage, one of the younger workers said the following:

> I entered when the factory was FCA. I think things have always remained the same, because the work is always the same. Maybe now there's more communication with other companies outside the country, but otherwise I think nothing has changed. No, for the future I think we will work, because they're making the new model, the Compass, the Jeep. We will work, quietly. That is, they've now made these solidarity contracts because the Punto model is finished, so all the people who worked on the Punto went to work on the Jeep and on the 500, so now there are a lot more workers than in the past. To do the right thing, the company decided to make these solidarity contracts.
>
> (Giovanni, twenty-two, high school diploma, assembly worker)

Marika's opinion on the future of the factory was also very different from both the one she gave at the beginning of the 2011 crisis and the current opinion shared by many of the older workers, for whom the new phase of reduced production seems to inexorably lead to the re-emergence of old problems. This is how the young team leader put it:

> A. I don't perceive the crisis so much, to tell you the truth, I think no. I don't feel this concern, that is, at least I don't live this concern.
>
> Q. Don't you fear that there may be modifications? How do you see FCA? What do you think about it?

> A. No, I think it has evolved, already the fact that it's no longer called FIAT, it's called FCA, it has something international, it's no longer limited only to Italy.
>
> Q. Do you think this is a positive element?
>
> A. In my opinion yes, it's a positive factor.
>
> Q. Why?
>
> A. In my opinion we have to be competitive in the world, not just limited to our area. In my opinion it's a positive factor. That is, it's in line with the times.
>
> Q. Don't you worry because of this big, new dimension?
>
> A. No. I don't know, maybe because we're a new generation I think it's a thing in line with the times, that's right. I think it's really right. In my opinion in the past we were too limited to the Italian context, now you have more possibilities, if you want, if one wants to go abroad, to America to work, there is always Detroit, if I'm not mistaken, and you could go to Turin, there are so many possibilities. For me, FCA means possibility. As I see it.
>
> (Marika, twenty-six, high school diploma, team leader)

The transition to the multinational FCA assumes a radically different meaning for the young workers compared to the fifty-year-old workers. The different existential and material conditions have a strong impact on their present and future perspective: from the point of view of the ability to tolerate the hardship of the shifts and the pressure of the work, the reduced physical resistance of the fifty-year-olds is evident; in relation to the reduction in salaries linked to production trends, the older workers suffer from the cost of daily living, the responsibility of supporting their families and also the disappointment of past well-being, largely failed. On the contrary, the young people are in a phase of upward mobility, experiencing for the first time a higher salary than they had received at their previous jobs and, in the main, not yet having family responsibilities and children to support. This makes them more able to occasionally challenge their superiors, to refuse excessive demands for work and to occasionally use illness more readily to deal with the stress. From the point of view of the older workers, the younger workers become bolder, more carefree and also more confident. If we look at the scale of biographical time and the vision of the future, in actual fact, the multinational FCA assumes different, sometimes divergent meanings for different workers.

Conclusion: From FIAT to FCA across Two Generations of Metalworkers

At the beginning of 2015, when the 1,500 young new workers were hired in Melfi to build the new Jeep model, production in Melfi was fully resumed, with strong organizational and technological innovations, as a result of corporate restructuring. The job, again full-time, required further sacrifices regarding the shift system, as new shifts, on Saturday and Sunday afternoons, were also added. So, a new, very hard phase of work was expected, which would be even harder for the workers aged in their fifties, who had accumulated various physical problems during their time working at the plant. In their view, an even more intense period of production in terms of volume and rhythm did not seem to be compensated for by any long-term reassurance of future job security at the site, which, on the contrary, the new FCA contributed to making more nebulous in the new extensive geography of international production sites. Frequent transfers of workers among the Italian plants (Cassino, Pomigliano and Melfi), as well as the delegation of part of the functions to subsidiary companies (such as Magneti Marelli), indicated the search for new assets by FCA. As illustrated by Herod and Standing, the continuous movements of labour and the separation of production parts (outsourcing) are typical features of international corporations, which increases the mobility and precariousness of work at a global level (Herod 2001; Standing 2011).

The 'green field' Melfi plant therefore represented the prime position in the restructuring of FIAT, and the Melfi factory had marked its break from the Fordist phase and the start of a new production phase. Currently, the situation seems to be marked by cyclical time, with the circular return of phases of decline in production and recurring uncertainty, first with the 2007/2008 crisis, which hit Melfi in 2011, and then with the production stoppage of the Punto model in 2017. With the salary cuts in the CIG phases, the difficulty in identifying themselves in the long term with work and finding the desired existential certainty constituted a key feature in the experience of local workers. At the beginning Melfi represented the growth of production and the achievement of exemplary productivity standards when compared to the rest of the world. Now it has arrived at cyclical precariousness, redundant in its repetitiveness and its similarity, such that the older local workers experience risks and fears of the past which they had hoped, once hired, to have left permanently behind them. The re-emergence of insecurity has had harsher and more tragic consequences for the older workers who have previously experienced it than has been the case for younger workers, who are often still living at home with their parents, without family or mortgages.

The linearity and circularity of the notions of time have been described by anthropologists as always coexisting syncretically and not in opposition, as integrated and never mutually exclusive systems (Remotti 1993). Yet the cyclical precariousness of the older workers clashes with the different view taken by the younger workers hired in 2015, who are living a new linear time, that seems – to their mind – to promise new certainty. The younger metalworkers are planning for their future, about to buy houses and start a family, and are more motivated and optimistic, except in meeting with new and similar disappointments. However, the widespread opinion at the trade union level is that in the new productive geography of FCA, the Italian plants are oversized for the current level of production, which means, for example, that it is not clear whether Melfi will receive a new model to produce in the future.

The subsistence strategies developed in Melfi in this new phase of crisis and change comprise different levels, and produce a mix of undeclared work, small integrative work networks for integrative work activities, and parental support networks. It could be said that we are discussing residues of an old 'culture of poverty', but also of solidarity between the bonds of kinship and community, typical of peasant culture. These residues have come from the recent past and are not quite forgotten, and reappear in order to bring together additional resources, differentiated forms of subsistence and solidarity strategies.

As recent studies have illustrated, work in contemporary corporations problematically combines the destinies and paths of workers who persist in former colonial countries and workers in countries with a longer and more consolidated industrial history, pushing us to wide-ranging considerations (Mollona, De Neve and Parry 2009; Vignato 2010a). The conceptualization of the relationship between Western factories and factories in more recently industrialized countries has a new centrality and relevance in the definition that industrial workers can give themselves today: this view, expressed by Vignato (2010b), makes the local/global link the framework in which we can understand the role of different classes of workers. In this sense, however, in the case of Melfi it is evident that the conception of the global economic space assumes a different value for younger and older workers.

The Melfi factory is now placed in the global space of the international company, and its propulsive business and production centre, even if not clearly defined yet, is certainly not in Italy. The peripheral position of Italy, and of Melfi in particular, is quite clear, since the assembly factories are always the most vulnerable plants in terms of relocation and closures.

For Melfi, therefore, the future still remains uncertain, because of the impossibility of making predictions about the future of the plant and, as a consequence, organizing pertinent strategies. Production is becoming increasingly connected to factories in Eastern Europe and Brazil, but also in the United States, where global production is distributed. In the global geography of production and work, the variables for determining the production constellations are always changing and becoming less clear (Moretti 2013). Maybe the most problematic element of the current configuration of the meaning of work is a sort of temporality circumscribed to an eternal present, which designs day by day the uncontrollable expansion of the space of production and the market. Faced with this, the workers continue to respond to the requests for efficiency, renewed commitment and dedication from the corporate-organizational philosophy, associated with the risks of moving production. For their part, the workers must simply roll up their sleeves, increasingly deprived of the necessary link between their efforts and future results.

Fulvia D'Aloisio is Associate Professor of Cultural Anthropology at the University of Campania 'Luigi Vanvitelli'. Her research activities range from the anthropology of the enterprise and work to the processes of economic and cultural change, with a focus on the north-south gap. Her most important publications include *Donne in tuta amaranto. Trasformazioni del lavoro e mutamento culturale alla FIAT-SATA di Melfi* (Guerini & Associati, 2003) and *Vita di fabbrica. Cristina racconta il decollo e la crisi della FIAT-SATA di Melfi* (Franco Angeli, 2014).

Notes

1. SATA, the name of the new company created by FIAT for the Melfi plant, means 'Automobile Society for Advanced Technologies'.
2. The definition 'green field' appears in an interview conducted by Annamaria Ricci to Alberto Pianta, President of the newly founded SATA Company (Automobile Company for Advanced Technology, controlled by FIAT), interview entitled 'Green Field Operation', *Dimensione* 1 (1993): 23–24.

3. Amatori believes that the role played by the state responded to a particular infrastructural and technological weakness of the country, while the frequent recourse to instruments such as protectionism, public orders, facilitations and, even more so, the rescue as an all-Italian tool produced a dilated public control that is unparalleled in the market economies of Western countries (Amatori 1999: 694–95).
4. Since the 1950s, Mirafiori has undergone an expansion aimed at doubling its size: in 1966 its surface was 2.5 million square metres, with almost 50,000 employees. However, regarding the diffusion of cars in Italy, if in 1952 there were sixty-one Italians for each car registered, this figure had dropped to forty-eight in 1954, thirty-five in 1956 and eleven in 1962 (Berta 1998: 19–20).
5. The theoretical perspective of this research is the anthropology of the enterprise, which in the opinion of Papa (inspired by the French studies of Althabe and Selim (2000) and Selim (1996)), focuses not on the organizational dynamics of the enterprise, but on a conception of the enterprise as a point of intersection between global economic processes and their repercussions in local contexts. More recently, Mollona (2009) has insisted on the old-fashioned character of industrial working-class work, in the public opinion: however, it has not disappeared, but rather has taken on new spatial and temporal configurations, blowing up traditional categories of geographical distribution (north-south) and also ethnic and gender categories, and other 'classical' categories, such as white-collar and blue-collar workers.
6. Founded in the fascist era, the CIG (a redundancy fund) was created to help employees cope with interruptions in production in the factories of northern Italy during the Second World War. Its use spread and consolidated in the second postwar period and underwent various reforms in the 1970s.
7. In the survey conducted by Bubbico (2014), concerning the start of production of the two new models in 2014, the production time issue does not seem to have improved: if the report shows substantial improvements in ergonomics and some substantial transformation of the only assembly line restructured, according to the author, the result is the saturation of 100 per cent work time.
8. On 13 January 2015, the most important national newspapers and television stations reported the announcement by the CEO, Sergio Marchionne, in Detroit that the Melfi plant was about to hire over 1,000 new workers; the following day, the newspaper *Il Sole 24 Ore* clarified that it was specifically about 500 workers from other factories (the Pomigliano and Cassino plants), still in the condition of CIG, and 500 temporary contracts. These candidates, once production and demand trends had stabilized, would become permanent employees on the basis of the new laws (launched in December 2013 by the Renzi government; see Malan and Cianflone 2015).
9. The ancient connection between large family business and governments is a typical feature of the development of Italian capitalism (Ginsborg 1989; Castronovo 2013). During its history, FIAT has enjoyed frequent public subsidies for its industrial plants, and until recent times, the Melfi plant was in fact subsidized to the tune of 50 per cent by the state, around 3,000 billion lire (equivalent to €1.5 million).

References

Accornero, A. 2000. *Era il secolo del lavoro. Come era e come cambia il grande protagonista dell'800*. Bologna: Il Mulino.

Agostinelli, M. 1997. *Tempo e spazio nell'impresa post-fordista*. Rome: Manifestolibri.

Alberoni F., and G. Baglioni. 1965. *L'integrazione dell'immigrato nella società industriale*. Bologna: Il Mulino.

Althabe, G., and M. Selim. 2000. *Approcci etnologici della modernità*. Turin: L'Harmattan Italia.

Amatori, F. 1999. 'La grande impresa', in *Storia d'Italia. L'industria*. Turin: Einaudi, pp. 691–753.

Barbagallo, F. (ed.). 1995. *Storia dell'Italia Repubblicana*, vol. 2, subvol. 1. Turin: Einaudi.

Barbagli, M., M. Castiglioni and G. Dalla Zuanna. 2003. *Fare Famiglia in Italia. Un secolo di cambiamenti*. Bologna: Il Mulino.

Berta, G. 1998. *Mirafiori*. Bologna: Il Mulino.

———. 2011. *Fiat Chrysler e la deriva dell'Italia industriale*. Bologna: Il Mulino.

———. 2014. *Produzione intelligente. Un viaggio nelle nuove fabbriche*. Turin: Einaudi.

Bonazzi, G. 1993. *Il tubo di cristallo. Modello giapponese e Fabbrica integrata alla Fiat Auto*. Bologna: Il Mulino.

Bubbico, D. 2014. *Radiografiat. Indagine internazionale della FIOM-CGIL sugli stabilimenti italiani dei gruppi FCA e CNH Industrial*. Rome: Meta Edizioni.

Carrieri, M., and G. Cerruti (eds). 1993. *Fiat punto e a capo. Problemi e prospettive da Termoli a Melfi*. Rome: Ediesse.

Castronovo, V. 2013. *Storia economica d'Italia. Dall'Ottocento ai giorni nostri*. Torino: Einaudi.

Cavalli, A. 1985. *Il tempo dei giovani*. Bologna: Il Mulino.

Cerruti, G. 1993. 'Automazione e integrazione alla Fiat di Termoli', in M. Carrieri and G. Cerruti (eds), *Fiat punto e a capo. Problemi e prospettive della fabbrica integrata da Termoli a Melfi*. Rome: Ediesse, pp. 169–398.

Chicchi F., and Leonardi E. (eds) 2011. *Lavoro in frantumi. Condizione precaria, nuovi conflitti e regime neoliberista*. Verona: Ombre Corte.

Coriat, B. 1993. *Ripensare l'organizzazione del lavoro. Concetti e prassi nel modello giapponese*. Bari: Dedalo.

D'Aloisio, F. 2003. *Donne in tuta amaranto. Trasformazione del lavoro e mutamento culturale alla Fiat-Sata di Melfi*. Milan: Guerini & Associati.

———. 2014. *Vita di fabbrica. Cristina racconta il decollo e la crisi della Fiat-Sata di Melfi*. Milan: Franco Angeli.

———. 2016. 'Work Inequalities between Global Transformation and Local Embedment: The Case of Fiat-Chrysler and the New Course at Melfi's Factory', *Antropologia* 3(1): 53–68.

De Martino, E. 2002. *La fine del mondo. Contributo all'analisi delle apocalissi culturali*, posthumous edition edited by C. Gallini and M. Massenzio. Turin: Einaudi.

Didry, C., P. Dieuaide, L. Roulleau-Berger, M. Selim and R. Sobel. 2004. 'La mondalisation n'existe pas: regardes sur les expériences singulières du travail globalisé', *L'Homme et la Société* 152/153: 9–16.

Donati, P., and R. Prandini (eds). 2008. *La cura della famiglia e il mondo del lavoro. Un Piano di politiche familiari*. Milan: Franco Angeli.

Facchini, C. 2005. *Diventare adulti. Vincoli economici e strategie familiari*. Milan: Guerini.

———. 2008. *Conti aperti. Denaro, asimmetrie di coppie e solidarietà tra le generazioni*, Bologna: Il Mulino.

FIOM-CGIL. 2010. *Il piano industriale Fiat 2010–2014 e l'industria dell'auto regionale: l'organizzazione del lavoro, le condizioni di lavoro in Fiat Sata e nell'indotto e le proposte della Fiom Basilicata*. Potenza: FIOM-CGIL.

Fumagalli, A. 2011. 'La condizione precaria come paradigma biopolitico' in F. Chicchi and E. Leonardi (eds), *Lavoro in frantumi. Condizione precaria, nuovi conflitti e regime neoliberista*, Verona, Ombre Corte, pp. 63–78.

Garibaldo, F. 2014. 'L'Italia l'anello debole della Fiat?', www.economiaepolitica.it, 13 June.

Ginsborg, P. 1989. *Storia d'Italia dal dopoguerra a oggi. Società e politica 1943–1988*. Torino: Einaudi.

Grandi, A., and F. Greco. 2013. 'Auto, la produzione è tornata ai livelli del 1958', *Il Sole 24 ore*, 24 October.

Guizzardi, L. 2007. *La transizione all'età adulta. Teorie sociologiche a confronto.* Milan: LED.
Herod, A. 2001. *Labor Geographies: Workers and the Landscapes of Capitalism.* New York: The Guilford Press.
Malan, A., and Cianflone M. 2015. 'Fiat Chrysler: a Melfi oltre mille nuove assunzioni e fine della Cigs', *Il Sole 24 ore*, 12 January.
Marsh, P. 2012. *The New Industrial Revolution: Consumers, Globalization and the End of Mass Production.* New Haven: Yale University Press.
Mollona, M. 2009. 'General Introduction', in M. Mollona M., G. De Neve and J. Parry (eds), *Industrial Work and Life: An Anthropological Reader.* New York: Berg, pp. ix–xxviii.
Mollona, M., G. De Neve and J. Parry (eds). 2009. *Industrial Work and Life: An Anthropological Reader.* New York: Berg.
Moretti, E. 2013. *The New Geography of Jobs.* New York: Mariner Books.
Narotzky, S. 1997. *New Directions in Economic Anthropology.* London: Pluto Press.
Negrelli, S. 2013. *Le trasformazioni del lavoro.* Rome-Bari: Laterza.
Ohno, T. 1993. *Lo spirito Toyota.* Turin: Einaudi.
Oppo, A., and S. Perra. 2008. 'Solidarietà tra le generazioni', in C. Facchini (ed.), *Conti aperti. Denaro, asimmetrie di coppie e solidarietà tra le generazioni.* Bologna: Il Mulino, pp. 319–42.
Papa, C. 1999. *Antropologia dell'impresa.* Milan: Guerini & Associati.
Remotti, F. 1993. *Luoghi e corpi: Antropologia dello spazio del tempo e del potere.* Turin: Bollati Boringhieri.
Ricci, A. 1993. 'Operazione prato verde', *Dimensione* 1: 23–24.
Rullani, E. 2004. *Economia della conoscenza. Creatività e valore nel capitalismo delle reti.* Rome: Carocci.
Selim, M. 1996. 'L'entreprise: emprise ideologique, mondalisation et évolution des problématiques', *Journal des anthropologues* 66/67: 19–28.
Selim, M., and K. Sugita. 1991. 'Introduction. Parcours Ethnologiques Dans L'Enterprise', *Journal des Anthropologue, Ethnologie de l'enterprise* 43/44: 9–16.
Signorelli, A. 1995. 'Movimenti di popolazione e trasformazioni culturali', in F. Barbagallo (ed.), *Storia dell'Italia Repubblicana*, vol. 2, subvol. 1. Turin, Einaudi, pp. 589–658.
Standing, G. 2011. *Precariat: The New Dangerous Class.* London: Bloomsbury.
Stocchetti, A., G. Trombini and F. Zirpoli (eds). 2013. *Automotive in Transition: Challenges for Strategy and Policy.* Venice: Edizioni Ca' Foscari.
Trombini G., and F. Zirpoli. 2013. 'Innovation Processes in the Car Industry: New Challenges for Management and Research', in A. Stocchetti A., G. Trombini and F. Zirpoli (eds), *Automotive in Transition: Challenges for Strategy and Policy.* Venice: Edizioni Ca' Foscari, pp. 19–35.
Vignato, S. 2010a. 'Introduzione. Per un'etnografia della soggettività nel lavoro', in S. Vignato (ed.), *Soggetti al lavoro. Un'etnografia della vita attiva nel mondo globalizzato.* Turin: UTET, pp. xi–xxxi.
———. (ed.). 2010b. *Soggetti al lavoro. Un'etnografia della vita attiva nel mondo globalizzato.* Turin: UTET.
Volpato, G. 1993. 'Lo scenario della competizione automobilistica internazionale e la strategia di rilancio del Gruppo Fiat Auto', in M. Carrieri and G. Cerruti (eds), *Fiat punto e a capo. Problemi e prospettive da Termoli a Melfi.* Rome: Ediesse, pp. 11–46.

— Chapter 6 —

Freight Fluxes, Flexibility and Everyday Tactics

Working in Road-Freight Transport in Italy

Francesco Bogani

Nowadays, road transport is the principal method of moving goods in Italy and Europe. More than 70 per cent of goods transported by land in the European Union (EU) travel by truck, and in Italy this figure is more than 80 per cent[1]. The dominant position of road transport can be explained by the effective response it provides to the demands of speed and flexibility on the part of the post-Fordist economy. As the French researchers[2] Patrick Hamelin and Bruno Lefebvre recognized (Hamelin 1997; Hamelin and Rodrigues 2005; Lefebvre 1984, 1985, 1996; Lefebvre, Hamelin and Pouy 1993), road hauliers take the brunt of the friction between the various protagonists involved in the production and exchange of goods. As I will attempt to demonstrate, it is the basic production unit of the sector, the man-truck team, which makes it possible to absorb the stresses. Just-in-time imperfections are paid for by truck drivers with long waits for collections and deliveries, and then recouped through long day-and-night driving sessions. Unlike train rides, these sessions are not set by timetables; as we shall see, they are ruled by tactical choices, which the experience of drivers makes possible, and they can be taken to the limits of physical resistance or – when respected – to the limits of the law.

The arguments that I present are largely the result of ethnographic research on the truck-driving trade that I conducted in 2003–4 (Bogani 2004), and then from 2007–11 (Bogani 2011). The main methodology of investigation that I adopted was participant observation, primarily as an onboard observer during truck journeys with my informants. These were Italian drivers mainly working on international routes.

The hypothesis I put forward here is that the profession of truck driver is an interesting subject for study through the lens of ethnography, not only in relation to the strategic function of road transport, but also and above all because it is the bearer, in an extreme form, of at least two traits that connote contemporary life and work: the imperative (already stated) of flexibility[3] and the lack of a clear boundary between time and space of production and reproduction, or between work and the private sphere of existence. To introduce this second topic, it is sufficient to think about how truck drivers, especially those who work on international routes, spend their hours of rest: away from their homes, in motorway service areas or in the car parks of commercial and industrial areas on the outskirts of foreign cities. Their rest time is enclosed within their work time, placed inside it without interruption, forced into the same space.

I will also advance another hypothesis: that the question of the relationship between work and the private sphere of existence is connected to a question emerging from the fieldwork, a dilemma raised on several occasions by my own informants. The dilemma concerns the measure of the gains, both material and symbolic, which the trucker's trade permits, and of the losses it causes. Almost all of the truck drivers I know claim to have a great passion for trucks and for their trade, and at the same time describe the latter as requiring enormous sacrifices. One of my informants defined it as a job 'that steals your life'. Another asked me if I thought he was 'a fool' to sacrifice friendships and family life for work. However, he reiterated that working as a truck driver has allowed him to buy his own home, something that, in another job, he probably would not have succeeded in doing. This ambivalence in depictions, this representation of an unstable and dangerous equilibrium between the two sides, the trade as a positive possibility of self-realization and as a risk of annihilation, requires investigation.

Finally, a last hypothesis, also linked to the previous hypotheses, is that of a progressive transformation of the profession that is leading towards a reduction of the drivers' control of time and of how they do their job. To describe this transformation, we must begin with stories from the past and then retrace the road that leads to today's world and to the heart of advanced post-Fordism.

They Were Different Times

All the truck drivers I met told me the same thing: it was different in the past. In the stories of the past, truck drivers celebrate an abundance: of earnings, but also of food and drink and in relationships with colleagues. Breaks in company are talked of as moments of celebration, where the community manifests itself and bonds are strengthened.

One of the most beautiful stories about road transport in the past was told to me by Vittorio. A native of Brianza and the son of a truck driver, Vittorio began helping his father aboard his truck as a child, in furniture transport in northern Italy. When he was old enough to do so, he worked for a few years, like his father, employed as a driver. Then he bought a truck and set up his own business, also in furniture transportation. When I met him in 2008, he had eight trucks and employed seven drivers, mainly engaged in transport on behalf of a successful furniture company in Brianza. Of the truck drivers I met, Vittorio is the one who travels on the longest routes, alternating between trips to Northern Europe, mainly to Sweden and Denmark, and trips to Spain and Portugal.

The story in question concerns one of Vittorio's trips in the company of a colleague: Badè. Now long retired, Badè is still famous among the truckers of Brianza for being a great teller of stories and jokes. Vittorio has known him for a lifetime and they are also neighbours. About thirty years ago, Vittorio began to 'do'[4] Sicily, as Badè, older and more experienced, had for years. On his first journey to the island, Vittorio decided to follow his friend and colleague in order to learn the route and its hazards.

So, the two of them left together in their trucks. However, when they neared Rome, the trip took an unexpected turn. Badè brought Vittorio to a tavern in the village of Torrenova: 'for lunch', he said. The people of Torrenova knew his truck and to them it was like waving a flag. Vittorio and Badè were eating when 'the whole village', attracted by the truck parked in front of the tavern, came inside to hear Badè's jokes and stories. In the evening, they were still there. The next day, the same thing happened. People came to the tavern to meet Badè, and they ate and drank too. Vittorio was amused, but also started to become concerned: his truck was expected in Sicily. He thought of leaving by himself, but he did not know the route, so he stayed. On the third day, at noon, they were almost ready to leave when another unexpected friend arrived: a trucker from Brianza, nicknamed Paolin Fantasia. Of course, they had to stay for lunch with him. Only in the evening, after a break lasting two and a half days, did Vittorio persuade Badè to return to the road.

On three different occasions, I listened to Vittorio's story about his journey with Badè. One of these times, after hearing other stories, Vittorio continued with the following reflection:

> They were different times, there was more friendliness between us. We did not have phones, oh, but we arranged meetings! Arriving in Villa San Giovanni: we'd meet there, more or less when you arrived. Maybe you were there two or three hours waiting for him to come … your friend! There weren't any phones, you see? It was another, it was another life Francesco! Now I've told you, my drivers travel a hundred metres apart, they do not even wait for each other!

We know that memory can have distorting effects. My intention, however, is not to investigate the accuracy of this story, and the many similar stories that I have heard, compared to actual experiences; rather, I want to consider them as traditional forms of representation of the trade in the past. The link with the past here is to be understood as a relationship of 'reverse filiation'. The metaphor is by Gerard Lenclud, who, on the basis of the works of Boyer and Pouillon, invites us to overturn the assumption on which we commonly base the notion of tradition: 'it is not the past that produces the present, but the present that shapes its past. Tradition is a process of recognition of paternity' (Lenclud 2001: 113). Attention must therefore be given to the filter that transforms the past into tradition: a selective reappropriation whose criteria are 'rigorously contemporary' and respond to 'a social instance from present time, which has to be interpreted primarily on the synchronic plane' (Mugnaini 2001: 37). In the case under consideration, I believe that the instance that acts as a filter has to do with a lack of something. The abundance of the past is opposed with the scarcity of the present – short in profits and in sociability, but also perhaps in an ingredient that remains implicit and that is intimately linked to the first and second: autonomy at work, the relative freedom in the management of one's time and methods.

Padroncini and Supply Chain Management

When we question the transformations under way in the world of road transport, we are confronted with the problem of scarcity of sources. Despite the central role played by the road-transport industry, the attention given by the social and historical sciences to the sector, in Europe (without prejudice to the aforementioned French context) and in Italy has been very scarce until recent years. However, in Italy, there are notable exceptions, such as the investigations launched at the end of the 1970s and published in the history magazine *Primo Maggio*.[5] These investigations were promoted in particular by Sergio Bologna, who, once the magazine closed down, continued to develop proposals for the sociological classification of the technical and economic evolutions of freight transport. The editors of the magazine were part of the Italian theoretical and political Operaista (Workerist) movement and have had political experience in the extra-parliamentary Marxist organizations Potere Operaio and Lotta Continua. With *Primo Maggio*, they were committed 'to the development of a new, militant history "subordinate to struggle"' (Wright 2001: 185), and transport had captured their attention for its strategic position in the new structure of industrial production. Workers in this sector were indeed identified as the only ones to maintain the power to block the production process, despite the development of outsourcing and the consequent form of industrial organization that began to characterize some Italian regions in the late 1970s.

Camionisti. La ristrutturazione del trasporto merci in Italia, the 1986 work by Gianni Crespi, accompanied by a substantial preface by Sergio Bologna, is in line with *Primo Maggio*'s policy and draws on the research it has produced. Truck drivers' work is described in the broader context of the circulation of goods in Italy, with a specific thesis: the existence of tension between the global structure of freight transport, a sector subjected to increasingly strong industrialization and increasing capital intensity and technology, and the numerically dominant figure in Italian road haulage of the *padroncino*, the small-business-owning truck driver. Crespi and Bologna reconstructed the emergence of this professional figure, starting from the post-Second World War period.

This was the moment in which road haulage in Italy took off: the railway system's infrastructure had suffered enormous damage during the war, the demand for transport was high, and there was a pressing need for exchange between the agricultural central-south and the industrial north. The profession of the road hauler presented itself as an opportunity for the unemployed labour force, and there was a surplus of military vehicles in the trucks left behind by the American army. The truck established itself as the keystone of the exchange system, an essential element of the new social configuration: 'The capillary circulation of merchandise typical of an industrial production of mass consumer goods, the physical circulation of goods, unfinished products and goods intended for companies, the functioning of large commercial enterprises. In short, some of the essential factors for the reproduction of the metropolitan-type Fordist society could not have been carried out without the truck' (Bologna 1986: 40).

In the 1950s and 1960s, road haulage grew incessantly, with two well-defined structural traits destined to persist: the extreme flexibility of work and the high number of small businesses transporting goods for third parties. This very high number of operators and the small size of their businesses creates a contractual weakness for hauliers in their relationships with their clients. According to Crespi, big companies did not simply exploit this characteristic of the supply of transport services, but also played a direct role in its production, prompting employed drivers to become *padroncini*:[6]

> For large haulage companies … the practice of splitting the fleet between workers has been in place since the 1960s, with the increase in operating costs and the first demands on the part of drivers … The managers of the sector, moreover, are extremely explicit: 'the union has created … the figure of an absolutely anti-economic employee driver; giving the truck to the driver meant a doubling of the average productivity from two or three thousand kilometres a month to six thousand!'[7] (Crespi 1986: 273)

This does not mean that the appearance of many small companies was not at least partly the product of a spontaneous process. The failure of numerous small-scale companies produced 'micro-truck units with the sale of the vehicle in instalments to the employed driver' (ibid.). Furthermore, the same market conditions seem to impose a limited dimension on companies: 'The Italian truck driver … to survive must be self-employed … All operators who are forced to over-constrict the general and commercial expenses of their company, to eliminate depreciation from balance sheet items (once the initial financial commitment has been covered) and to make the "labour cost" the real strength of their activity are "constrained to be padroncini"' (ibid.: 277).

In the 1960s, the truck-driver profession in Italy was transformed, while remaining centred on the figure of the self-employed haulier, with the 'multiplication of attraction points for freight flows', the 'standardization of loading techniques' and the 'shocking acceleration … starting with the traumatic overthrow represented by the motorway and the power of vehicles' (ibid.: 23). Then, at the end of the 1960s, the entire freight transport sector entered a phase of transformation on a global scale. The maritime sector was distorted by the introduction of the freight container and the consequent restructuring of docks. A 'fast' model for ports was established and the shipping company 'no longer waits for goods, but seeks them at their origin, at the point of production' (ibid.: 120). Maritime transportation became a capital-intensive industry. Making it possible to adopt industrial methods for the physical flow of goods, the freight container facilitated and accelerated production decentralization and the stretching of the factory in space.[8] The 'assertions contained in the freight container revolution' were brought 'to their extreme consequences' by the development of logistics in the 1980s: 'Decentralization of production has been the technical motivation, market fluctuations have been the economic one, because in the structure of the company logistics acquired a strategic function' (Bologna 1986: 56–57).

Here it is advisable to abandon Crespi and Bologna's text and refer to more recent works. In an essay from 2007, Bologna returns to the role that logistics assumes, starting from the 1980s, in the transformation of the industrial system, with the 'post-Fordist overturning of the relationship between supply and demand … bringing input to production not "upstream" of the process but "downstream", not from capital but from the market, the whole cycle must acquire a very high flexibility' (Bologna 2007: 84–85).

The latest development of this reorganization of production is supply chain management: the system of 'interrelations between companies with the client company at the centre and at the periphery a universe of suppliers or partners arranged according to a hierarchical order based on their assigned function' (ibid.: 89).

Supply routes were organized and reshaped 'through the selection of suppliers and the implementation of privileged partnerships with a limited number of trusted subcontractors' (Damien and Maugeri 1996: 243). Outside this highly integrated system, we find 'a sprinkling' of subcontractors, subject to intense competitive pressure 'because of the banality of the remaining work left over for them' (ibid.: 244).

The overwhelming majority of Italian road-transport companies belong to this 'sprinkling'. In 2017, there were 87,361[9] road-haulage companies operating in Italy, of which over 62,000 had fleets of up to five vehicles. There are more than 27,000 companies with only one vehicle. Most of these carry out subcontracting work[10] for large companies in the sector (Pelizzoni 2004: 134), and operate in the market under price-taker conditions: they are not 'in a contractual position to negotiate with customers', nor are they 'able to control profit margins' (ibid.: 96). This produced dramatic consequences when the economic crisis hit Italy and the freight transport industry.

Profit margins in the sector have been declining since the early 1990s, when Italy was hit by a recession. At the same time, the EU started to undertake the liberalization of road haulage, favouring the increase of the already high levels of competition in the country. However, a much stronger increase in competition occurred in the 2000s, with the enlargement of the EU. Road haulage ended up being 'one of the activities most affected by social dumping' (ANFIA 2018: 22); this is stated in a study by the consulting company Trasporti e Territorio Srl. carried out for the European Commission, which underlines 'how an excessively rapid enlargement of the market exposed operators to competition from countries with more advantageous working conditions and remuneration levels in terms of costs' (ibid.). In this context, in June 2008, the surge in the cost of diesel produced a dramatic increase in operating costs. Nevertheless, the worst was yet to come in the years that followed, with the recession triggered by the Global Financial Crisis. Between 2008 and 2012, Italy witnessed a decline in goods transported by road of over 50 billion tonne-kilometres, passing from 206.4 billion tonne-kilometres in 2008 to 154.8 billion tonne-kilometres in 2012 (Confcommercio 2015: 12). The number of companies active in the sector decreased over the same period by more than 14,000 units (ibid.: 37); substantially, this coincides 'with the expulsion from the market of the self-employed and small-business owners' (ibid.). In the following years, the recession in the sector did not stop: from 2009 to 2017, there were almost 21,000 fewer companies in the sector, with a decrease of at least 70,000 employees.[11]

A Modern Break

When the recession hit Italian road haulage in such a dramatic way, the trading system's new organization had already profoundly changed the truckers' daily lives. To understand how, let us go back to ethnography, to a case of sociability among colleagues very different from Vittorio and Badè's stop at Torrenova: the 'lunch' (the first substantial meal of the day, which took place at five in the afternoon) at which I was present, in July 2007, in the company of two of my informants, Paolo and Angelo. Paolo already had thirty years of experience as a driver, always for small businesses. Angelo, younger than

Paolo, still had twenty years of experience at the wheel, also always for small businesses. Both from Tuscany, in 2007, Paolo and Angelo travelled weekly from Italy to France, as drivers for a company that had eight trucks in all, but no office employees: the owner drove one of the trucks and carried out part of the office work from the cab via a mobile phone.

I was a guest aboard Paolo's truck and we were in France, near Chambray, when Angelo called him. As he was in the same area, Angelo suggested eating in a restaurant at a service station. However, Paolo was too worried and in too much of a rush for detours or stops. It was 2 PM and for me and Paolo, the day had begun at 4 AM near Bourges, in the yard in front of a warehouse, where we had to make the first delivery of the week. We had spent the night there, sleeping as usual in the truck cab. As soon as the alarm went off, Paolo made coffee in the cab, while he was warming up the engine to put the truck on the loading bay. Once the goods were unloaded, after two and a half hours of driving, we had made a second delivery near Auxerre, a third one at Sens after another hour of driving, and after another three hours a fourth delivery near Chambray. The last delivery of the day remained: three pallets of automotive components to be taken to the Sevelnord industrial plant near Valencienne. Here deliveries were made by appointment, and Paolo's delivery was scheduled for 10 PM. If we had delayed and missed the appointment, in all likelihood – Paolo had told me that he knew the establishment well – they would have let us in for delivery only after waiting for many hours, probably even for a whole day. Overriding the insistence of Angelo, who had opted for a service area not only because of the restaurant but also to use the bathrooms for a shower, Paolo set the meeting for lunch directly in the outdoor car park of the Sevelnord plant. Since there were no bars or restaurants nearby, the plan was to cook and eat in the cab of Paolo's truck, as he and I had done since our departure from Italy, two days before. Paolo and I reached the Sevelnord parking lot at 5 PM. We were five hours early for the delivery, but Paolo's concern was justified: when he stopped the engine, the tachograph[12] marked nine and a half hours of driving since the last obligatory prolonged rest stop.[13] Thirty minutes more and Paolo would have reached the legal daily maximum of ten hours, and he would have been obliged to stop along the road, for an obligatory stop of eleven hours, without being able to reach the Sevelnord plant. He would then have missed the appointment and compromised the entire programme of collections and deliveries for the next few days.

Marginal Mediators

A restaurant is a place to eat and rest, to recover strength, and also to build or strengthen social relationships. And a three-day stop in a restaurant is a major break in working time. A truck cab in an industrial area, on the other hand, is only a bubble of personal space within an instrument and a space dedicated to work.[14] And a meal in the cab, in an industrial area, arranged during *dead time* (generated by interference between delivery schedules and driving-hours regulations) cannot be fully considered a break from work. For today's truck drivers, time and rest spaces are incorporated seamlessly into the times and spaces of work.[15] To understand how and why this happens, it is useful to refer again to the analyses of the French researchers Patrick Hamelin and Bruno Lefebvre. As anticipated, Hamelin and Lefebvre note how road transport guarantees the speed and flexibility required for today's goods-transportation operations. Small hauliers and drivers are required to adjust their own work to resolve problems created by the lack of synchronization in and between the production and distribution processes. Hamelin (2005) observes that it is up to truck drivers to oversee not only the moving of goods, but also their collection and delivery, points of intersection between economic processes and categories of workers who obey different logics. It is here that the ability to consider possible problems in advance and to mediate between contradictory requests is fundamental. However, the ability to absorb the tensions produced in the chains of commodity exchange is not just a matter of knowledge or skill. In fact, Lefebvre (1985) observes how it finds a necessary presupposition in the condition of marginality[16] to which the work of drivers is relegated. This marginality must be understood in three different ways:

- spatially, due to the continuous solitary movement implicit in work on roads and in industrial areas;
- legally, for the widespread irregularities in the sector in relation to loads, driving and work times and driving speeds;
- temporally, both because of the irregular rhythms of work and their daily duration (which goes beyond the norms admitted in other sectors) and also because of a confinement in the present caused by the double absence of career opportunities, and a memory or collective history as a professional category.

Resorting to Tactics

To further deepen the relationship between marginality, mediation skills, knowledge and the skills of drivers, I propose using a key passage in the research of Michel de Certeau (1980) on everyday life: the distinction between the notions of tactics and strategy. De Certeau defines the faculty of strategy as a prerogative of those who have their own space: the control of space allows one to capitalize on past acquisitions and to plan for their use in the future. The subjects who move in a space controlled by others cannot rely on such an ability and must resort to tactics: profit from opportunities, acting at the opportune moment, using experience and memory to adjust the present. Only by doing this is it possible to transform uncontrolled circumstances into a favourable situation. This is the condition of truck drivers who, during their travels, move seamlessly through the spaces and the times of production, which are outside their control (the exception is the truck itself, which in some ways offers itself as a strategic bubble: for example, having lunch in the cab).

For truck drivers the use of tactics is essential: both to cut out rest and social bubbles in the continuum of work and to carry out the latter efficiently. Paolo and Angelo's meeting at Sevelnord responded tactically to the first requirement. The move that Paolo made later to move the delivery time of his goods forward responds to the second. As soon as he arrived at the factory, Paolo went to the porter's hut and tried to convince the staff there to let us pass for delivery without waiting for the appointment at 10 PM, but without success. At 9 PM – Angelo had already gone on his way – Paolo decided to try again: he took the transport documents, got out of the truck and walked towards the porter's lodge. After a while, he returned to the truck briskly, started the engine and took off. 'What did they tell you?', I asked. '… can you unload now?' Paolo nodded, continuing to drive. It was 9.10 PM. 'I could be out by half past nine!', he said. At 9.20 PM, the truck was at the ramp. In five minutes the warehouse workers had unloaded the three pallets we had to deliver. We left the premises and stopped in the establishment's outer car park, where we spent the night. Paolo was satisfied. In his diary, where he wrote down all of his work details, he wrote: 'Work finished at: 21:35. Nine hours and thirty-nine minutes of driving.' If we had waited for the appointment, we would not have returned to the car park before 10.30 PM. In being persistent, Paolo had clocked off an hour before the scheduled eleven-hour mandatory break, thus gaining an hour for the scheduled goods delivery the following day. It may seem small, but sometimes it is enough to guarantee the success of a trip, its profitability and the respecting of collection and delivery times requested by clients.

A Work Pushed to Its Limit

A change in the timetable, as simple as bringing forward a break by one hour, as well as the subsequent departure, is not obvious. Its presupposition must be sought in the operational freedom of the basic production unit of road freight transport: the pair consisting of an instrument or mechanical part, the truck, and a person or a living part, the driver. While driving, as in other expert practices that recent anthropology has taught us to observe,[17] the distinction between instrument and person fades. The weight of the load is felt in inertia, in the fatigue of the engine. One has the physical perception of the potential and kinetic energy of the medium that transports us and that we are controlling, which is amplified by one's position: high up, above cars and people. A wrong manoeuvre and you risk crushing them or being crushed by your load. Driving a truck greatly expands the operating ability of the driver, while subjecting him or her to the mechanical behaviour of the vehicle: to the driving posture, to vibrations, to the inertia in acceleration and braking, and to the impacts of the load that are felt on the back when braking. In any case, it is the driver – and only the driver – who ultimately has control of the truck. It is this individual control that determines the possibilities and limits of the ability of truck drivers to act as mediators in the trading system. We are far from the Fordist factory: the vehicle with which the truck drivers work does not resemble the machine that swallows Charlie Chaplin in *Modern Times*. For truck drivers, for example, it is common to take short breaks to rest for fifteen or twenty minutes, when they feel sleepy. This simple action is part of an important repertoire of professional practices, which can be attributed to the management of body capital.

The notion of body capital was elaborated by Loïc Wacquant (2000) during a study of boxing practice, expanding upon the classic inventory of the forms of capital identified by his teacher, Pierre Bourdieu (Bourdieu and Wacquant 1992). Wacquant uses the notion to frame a set of practices and empirical knowledge, essential in boxing, consisting of the ability of the boxer to manage his physical and mental energy, both in the short term in relation to training and in the long term with regard to his career. If we consider that the most widespread cause of driving accidents (serious accidents, to be precise) for truck drivers is tiredness, we understand how the ability to manage their energy supply is essential in the profession. Michael Agar (1986), in a remarkable ethnographic investigation of what we might call American owner-operators, observes that none of his informants like or respect the rules for driving times. But this is not because they do not take seriously inadequate rest and the danger of driving while fighting tiredness (ibid.: 119). The fact is – Agar tells us – that they have less trust in the rules than in what he calls their 'folk safety system', the ability to recognize certain actions as fatigue indicators: delayed braking, changes in engine revs, deviations of the vehicle from the road lane or particular actions such as scratching your head or face. If truck drivers have the task of absorbing tensions and finding solutions to the inconsistencies of the trading system, the refined awareness of their own energy cycles and of the needs determined by them plays a fundamental role in this. It draws a boundary between the maximum work performance possible, namely prolonged driving for as long as possible, and the worst one, when drivers and trucks are involved in an accident, which can lead to the loss of the load, of the work instrument and, in the worst case, to the death of the workers themselves.

Entropy

I also propose the hypothesis that for truck drivers (as with boxers), the ability to manage energy is also essential for the long duration of their careers. Some excerpts from Wacquant's ethnography on boxing help to frame the issue. These are estimates made by his informants as to the energy remaining in their *colleagues*: 'The general consensus is that Curtis should have "finished" his opponent in the second round … O'Bannon confides to me later: "Curtis ain't gonna go too far if he lets hisself get beat up by guys like that, if he don't know how to economize hisself better than that. It's a long road. Guys like that, he's got to dispatch them quickly"' (Wacquant 2000: 146).

And yet, Wacquant reports other judgements about boxers at different stages of their careers: 'He already had too many fights. He ain't got enough pep left in him' (ibid.: 141): 'Tha's a lot of punches and a lotta wear and tear on a young body … too much wear and tear' (ibid.); 'he's washed up, done. Think about it, nobody wanta sign some guy who's already washed up' (ibid.).

Not all fatigue and punishment can be recovered from, and bad management of energy can jeopardize one's career by accelerating the inevitable deterioration of its reserves. Metaphorically we can resort to the notion of entropy as the progressive unavailability of a system to produce work. The notion is transferable by homology to the analysis of other performances that play with the limits of individual resistance.

Vittorio once told me about a younger colleague, a guy who lives in his town and who had started working on the route to Spain. Sometimes they met on that route. Initially the guy was always in a hurry, wanting to go home. Over time, he saw him more and more frequently in the service area at Ventimiglia, resting 'as he should'. 'Eventually', Vittorio told me, 'you must calm down! Otherwise you won't last in this job!' 'Calm down' in this case means, with an apparent paradox, reducing the amount of time spent in one's home: the commitment required by the trade is not negotiable, and the only way to reduce the intensity of energy consumption is to compress the sphere of one's private life, to expand those bubbles of rest that we have seen be incorporated into the time and spaces of work. The inevitable entropy, the finite measure of personal energies, conditions the relationship between work and other dimensions of existence.

The truck, a private space that accompanies the driver on his continuous travels, plays the role of a substitute for home, in a relationship that is at the same time one of continuity and in opposition with the actual home. When travelling, it performs the functions of a dwelling and guarantees a certain isolation from the surrounding space, but remains a bubble in the space of others and is not the equivalent of a house or a proper dwelling. The cab is permeable to family life, thanks to the possible sentimental objects that decorate it, to the food prepared at home and consumed on board, and to the telecommunication devices, primarily mobile phones. But continuity with the home is interrupted when we consider the people physically present: other than in exceptional cases, the only person physically present on board is the driver, and the cab remains an individual space, not a shared one.

The first time I considered a possible homology between the experiences of truck drivers and boxers was when I listened to Paolo's wife, Maria, bring these social figures closer together with a comment on her husband's professional past. We were talking about a twenty-year period that Paolo remembers as his golden age and that he spent employed as a driver for a fish transport company. In that sector, the drivers were required to drive without respecting rest times, driving hours or speed. The wages were high: the turnover was considerable and when the fish was sold on the black market, the drivers returned to the firm laden with banknotes that were the result of sales that were never officially registered. However, the good wages did not prevent the fact that many of the drivers who worked with Paolo paid a heavy price for such a heavy commitment: some, Maria tells me, were left by their wives and remained alone, while others have also lost their sense of clarity. They have been marked by work, she tells me, as 'punch-drunk boxers'.

Marxist thought has recognized the separation of work regarded as 'productive' from the areas of 'everyday life' as a distinctive feature of industrial society and has labelled this one of the roots of alienation. In his pioneering *Critique of Everyday Life*, Henri Lefebvre stated:

> Today what still differentiates country life so deeply from the life of the industrial worker is precisely that inherence of the production activity to every aspect of life. The workplace is located around the home; work is not separated from everyday family life ... The bourgeois society has given work a new value, especially in its ascending phase; but when the relationship emerged between work on the one hand and the concrete development of the individual on the other, work began to take on an increasingly fragmented character. At the same time, the individual progressively engaged in complex social relationships, isolated and closed in on himself ... the man 'as a man' was distinguished from the worker ... Family life separated from productive activity. (Lefebvre 1947: 36–37)

Today, however, we see a new tendency in some professions: a process of domestication of work, of its absorption into the spaces, or in any case in the system of rules,[18] of private life. Sergio Bologna (1997), investigating the social condition of freelance workers, identifies the domestication process as one of the three factors that push them to intensify their working day.[19] If the process of domestication, leading existence back to 'a single socio-affective cycle', somehow overcomes the modern fracture between man and worker, the risk is that this happens through the collapse of the former. It is the risk of what Marco Revelli recognizes as a revolution 'betrayed' by post-Fordism, in the passage from the desired 'incursion of life into standardised work practices, to the totalitarian incursion of work into life' (Revelli 2001: 187).

The peculiar relationship between time and space in work and one's private life that characterizes the work of truck drivers emphasizes the possibility of this incursion. Indeed, the truck can curb as much as favour the processes of subsumption of one's life in work.

Many truck drivers, as proof of the current degradation of their trade, have told me about some big companies that would hire foreign drivers who do not have a home and live in the truck, and then illegally deduct a cab rent from their salary, thus saving on expenses and illegally obtaining an advantage in the market. It is not necessary to ascertain the actual occurrence of this behaviour to consider the prevailing representation that it gives: the presumed condition of the drivers in question arouses great annoyance in those who consider their truck to be a space par excellence of comfort and freedom. With the connection between work and home cut, and with the outrage of having to pay rent, thus reminding the driver that it is not even his own property, the truck breaks any ambiguity and becomes an instrument of slavery.

Conclusions

Truck drivers in Italy grew in number throughout the twentieth century. Their role in the material process of transport has become central to the development of industrial production and mass consumption, and has been further strengthened by the transformations of the industry and of the trading system initiated in the 1970s that is still in place today. In this second phase, however, the transformations of the processes of production and distribution of goods, the saturation of the Italian transport market and the progressive liberalization of the sector in Europe and Italy have reduced the already weak negotiating power on the part of truck drivers with their clients, and have resulted in their adaptation to tariffs and work rates set by other protagonists. The economic gains – and with them the possibility to balance the sacrifices required by the trade – have been subjected to erosion and there has been a move from a greater availability of time, marked by the alternation between working time and social life, to a context in which work is never interrupted and break times cannot be controlled.

We can think of this transformation in the wider context of contemporary logistics, in the development of which Debora Cowen (2014) tracks a progressive extension of Taylorist scientific management from the factory to the entire supply chain. This extension requires a meaningful change from classic Taylorism: in the management of the supply chain, the focus shifts from the concrete bodies of workers to a more abstract plan in which workers' movements and labours are 'aggregated and quantified' (ibid.: 110) to calculate efficacy and efficiency on the new larger scale. The contradictions that this movement of discipline and abstraction can generate are evident. Giorgio Grappi calls it the paradox of labour in the 'political philosophy of logistics': in the management of workers, big logistics companies attempt to increase automation on the one hand and flexibility and reversibility of processes on the other, in a conflictual quest for verticality and dispersion, for control and resilience (Grappi 2016: 72).

On the subjective side of these processes, in truck drivers' experiences we witness an invasion of rest time by the logic of production: as work intensifies and breaks are shifting increasingly away from workers' control, larger portions of time must be transferred from the sphere of private life into the spaces and times of production. In this context, we have recognized the centrality of certain skills identified as belonging to the field of tactics, of a tacit knowledge that informs the practice of driving by treading the fine line between effective performance and danger, and also of a complex balancing game that is entrusted with the distribution of energies between the spheres of production and of private life. These skills, knowledges and practices play a central role in the defence or reassumption of autonomy at work, in the preservation of profit margins and in the possibility of giving a symbolic value to the latter and the former.

However, the same elements also work in reverse, such as in the implementation of a refined process of extraction of labour power, calibrated on subjects with unprecedented precision compared to the dynamics of the work studied in modernity. In this, the truck drivers' work does not seem to be a unique case, and the impression is rather that the road-transport sector has been hit with particular intensity by a process of mutation of work that is more widespread in contemporary society.

Francesco Bogani is a member of the Centro Ricerche Etno-Antropologiche (CREA). He works as a freelance researcher specializing in visual anthropology. From 2003 to 2011, he carried out extensive research on road freight transport.

Notes

1. Source: Eurostat, elaboration of the ANFIA 2018 dossier (ANFIA 2018).
2. Patrick Hamelin, who passed away in 2010, had been working on conditions in the road-haulage industry since the early 1980s and was a research director at the Institut National de Recherche sur le Transports et leur Sécurité (a French public institute under the double protection of the Ministries of Research and of Transport). The first

survey in the world of truck drivers by Bruno Lefebvre dates back to the 1980s, a doctorate thesis carried out under the direction of Robert Cresswell.

3. Organizational flexibility and the precariousness that accompanies it emerge globally as the main features of the recent transformations of work (Standing 2011).
4. The formula composed of the verb 'do' followed by the indication of a geographical region ('doing Sicily', 'doing France', 'doing Germany' and so on) is commonly used by truck drivers to indicate regular routes covered.
5. The complete collection of the magazine has been made available in electronic format and distributed on DVD along with Bermani (2010).
6. The word 'padroncini' translates literally as 'little owners' and is used to indicate truck drivers who own their vehicle, and in some cases a few other trucks entrusted to employed drivers.
7. 'Dr. Furlan, Chief Executive Officer Gondrand, interview, 13 November 1981' (Crespi 1986: 273, footnote).
8. This marks the beginning of the logistics revolution: with 'the dramatic recasting of the relationship between making and moving, or production and distribution' (Cowen 2014: 103) and with 'the disarticulation of production into component parts that can be stretched out and rearranged in more complex configurations' (ibid.), more and more commodities will be 'manufactured *across logistics space* rather than in a singular place' (ibid.: 2).
9. Source: 'Albo Nazionale degli autotrasportatori' (National Register of Haulers), updated to April 2017, retrieved from Rivista TIR (2017).
10. Subcontracted work is indicated in Italian haulage by the term 'subvezione'. Between the customer and material executor of the transport of a load, there are often many subcontractors with various different roles (shippers, large carriers, medium haulage carriers, associations of transporters, owner-operators, etc.).
11. Source: Ufficio Studi CGIA di Mestre (2017). It should be noted here that: 'The main national statistical sources present non-homogeneous data on the numerical size of the road transport sector. We decided to use the Infocamere - Movimprese database because it measures the number of companies in business and, unlike others, has allowed us to build both a historical series and a comparison between regions.'
12. An instrument that records a truck's movements, speed and rest stops to allow law enforcement agencies to verify the driver's compliance with driving regulations and mandatory rest periods. Made compulsory in Italy on board heavy vehicles in 1979, the tachograph has since been the subject of a long history of tampering practices and technological innovations aimed at doctoring it.
13. European legislation on driving times and mandatory breaks for truck drivers has changed many times. In 2007, it provided for a maximum of four and a half hours of uninterrupted driving, which had to be followed by a break of at least forty-five minutes. This forty-five-minute break could also be divided into three breaks of fifteen minutes each within the maximum daily limit of nine hours of driving. In a period of twenty-four hours, it was mandatory to take a daily rest that must be eleven consecutive hours, and this could be reduced to nine consecutive hours for no more than three times in a week. The daily rest period could also be taken in two or three separate periods, one of which must however be at least eight consecutive hours. In this case, the minimum rest period was extended to twelve hours. During one week, one of the daily rest periods was extended, as a weekly rest, to a total of forty-five consecutive hours. It could be reduced to thirty-six consecutive hours when it was taken at the vehicle's usual parking spot or at the driver's place of business, and to twenty-four consecutive hours when it was taken away from the vehicle's usual parking spot. In both cases, the unused hours of rest had to be recovered in the three following weeks, at one time and connected to another rest of at least eight hours.

14. See also Bogani (2013).
15. These considerations mainly concern work over long distances, and their relevance fades when the routes usually covered by drivers and the time intervals that they spend away from the home shorten.
16. Ferenç Hammer (2002) also studied truck drivers and marginality, and conducted a survey in the context of Cultural Studies of how Hungarian truck drivers are represented in culture and how they see themselves.
17. See Warnier (1999) and Julien (2005).
18. It is sufficient 'that the workplace is understood as a place where rules established by the independent worker himself are applied, such that culture and the habits of private life are transferred to the workplace' (Bologna 1997: 16).
19. The two other factors are the unwritten rules of the market, which cut out the worker who does not respect the delivery times requested, and the greater push for the greater gain, which must be related to the size of the business risk, the function of which is also to aim for an increased workload.

References

Agar, M. 1986. *Independents Declared.* Washington DC: Smithsonian Institute Press.

ANFIA (Associazione Nazionale Filiera Italiana Automobilistica). 2018. 'Dossier Trasporto merci su strada'. Retrieved 18 February 2020 from https://www.anfia.it/data/dtracker/anfia_dossier trasporto merci su strada_febbraio2019.pdf.

Confcommercio. 2015. 'Analisi e previsioni per il trasporto merci in Italia'. Retrieved 18 February 2020 from https://www.confcommercio.it/documents/20126/448658/Rapporto+sul+trasporto+merci+in+Italia.pdf.

Bermani, C. (ed.). 2010. *La rivista 'Primo Maggio' (1973–1989).* Rome: DeriveApprodi.

Bogani, F. 2004. 'Uomini e camion. L'etnografia di una professione attuale per un'antropologia della contemporaneità', Master's thesis. Siena: Università degli Studi di Siena.

———. 2011. 'Vite su gomma. Lavoro, pratiche e rappresentazioni nel mondo dell'autotrasporto', Ph.D. dissertation. Siena: Università degli Studi di Siena.

———. 2013. 'Una comunità su gomma. Un'indagine etnografica del mestiere di camionista', *Lares* 79(2–3): 225–40.

Bologna, S. 1986. 'Prefazione', in G. Crespi, *Camionisti. La ristrutturazione del trasporto merci in Italia.* Milan: Franco Angeli, pp 38–60.

———. 1997. 'Dieci tesi per la definizione di uno statuto del lavoro autonomo', in S. Bologna and A. Fumagalli (eds), *Il lavoro autonomo di seconda generazione. Scenari del postfordismo in Italia.* Milan: Feltrinelli.

———. 2007. *Ceti medi senza futuro? Scritti, appunti sul lavoro e altro.* Rome: DeriveApprodi.

Bourdieu, P. 1979. *La Distinction. Critique sociale du jugement*, Paris: Les Éditions de Minuit.

Bourdieu, P., and L. Wacquant. 1992. *Réponses. Pour une anthropologie reflexive.* Paris: Le Seuil.

Cowen, D. 2014. *The Deadly Life of Logistics: Mapping Violence in Global Trade.* Minneapolis: University of Minnesota Press.

Crespi, G. 1986. *Camionisti. La ristrutturazione del trasporto merci in Italia.* Milan: Franco Angeli.

Damien, R., and S. Maugeri. 1996. 'Normaliser pour dominer', *Cahiers de médiologie* 2: 237–45.

De Certeau, M. 1980. *L'Invention du Quotidien.* Vol. 1: *Arts de Faire.* Paris: Union générale d'éditions.

Grappi, G. 2016. *Logistica.* Rome: Ediesse.
Hamelin P. 1997. 'Le transport routier, un mode de production en tension', in C. Debons and J. Le Coq (eds), *Routiers, les raison de la colère.* Paris: Les Editions Ouvrières, pp. 123–48.
Hamelin, P., and A.C. Rodrigues. 2005. 'Conducteurs et conductrices de poids lourds', *Recherche, transport, securitè* 87: 147–73.
Hammer, F. 2002. 'A Gasoline Scented Sindbad: The Truck Driver as a Popular Hero in Socialist Hungary', *Cultural Studies* 16: 80–126.
Julien, M.P. 2005. 'Travail et subjectivité : pistes ethnologiques du sujet', *Ethnologie française* 35(4): 733–37.
Lefebvre, B. 1984. 'Routiers : identités professionelles et représentation de l'espace urbain', *Terrain* 11: 58–59.
———. 1985. *Identités professionnelles et représentation de l'espace urbain des conducteurs de poids lourds dans la région lyonnaise.* Lyon: Recherche pour la mission du patrimoine ethnologique.
———. 1996. 'La ritualisation des comportements routiers', *Ethnologie française* 26: 317–27.
Lefebvre B., P. Hamelin and J.B. Pouy. 1993. *Les routiers, des hommes sans importance?* Paris: Syros.
Lefebvre, H. 1947. *Critique de la vie quotidienne.* Paris: Grasset.
Lenclud, G. 2001. 'La tradizione non è più quella di un tempo', in P. Clemente and F. Mugnaini (eds), *Oltre il folklore. Tradizioni popolari e antropologia nella società contemporanea.* Rome: Carocci, pp. 123–34.
Mugnaini, F. 2001. 'Le tradizioni di domani', in P. Clemente and F. Mugnaini (eds), *Oltre il folklore. Tradizioni popolari e antropologia nella società contemporanea.* Rome: Carocci, pp. 11–72.
Pelizzoni, C. 2004. *La liberalizzazione del mercato dell'autotrasporto merci. Impatto sulla performance del settore e previsioni sull'assetto futuro.* Milan: Franco Angeli.
Revelli, M. 2001. *Oltre il Novecento,* Turin: Einaudi.
Rivista TIR. 2017. 'Albo: ecco i numeri delle imprese', *TIR. La rivista ufficiale dell'autotrasporto,* 16 March. Retrieved 18 February 2020 from http://rivistatir.it/albo-numeri-delle-imprese.
Standing, G. 2011. *The Precariat: The New Dangerous Class.* London: Bloomsbury Academic.
Ufficio Studi CGIA di Mestre. 2017. 'News del 18 Marzo 2017'. Retrieved 18 February 2020 from https://www.lentepubblica.it/wp-content/uploads/2017/03/CGIA-Mestre-Dati-autotrasporto.pdf.
Wacquant, L. 2000. *Body and Soul: Notebooks of an Apprentice Boxer.* New York: Oxford University Press.
Warnier, J.P. 1999. *Construire la culture matérielle. L'homme qui pensait avec ses doigts,* Paris: Presses Universitaires de France.
Wright, S. 2001. *Storming Heaven: Class Composition and Struggle in Italian Autonomist Marxism.* London: Pluto Press.

— Chapter 7 —

THE STRUCTURAL CRISIS OF THE ITALIAN ECONOMY AND INDUSTRY

The Perverse Role of Precarity

Andrea Fumagalli

Introduction

Since the early 1990s, the Italian economy has been in a phase of prolonged stagnation. In particular, in the pre-crisis period (2000–7), Italy registered a weak level of growth (on average, just under 1 per cent per year) and then witnessed a decline in gross domestic product (GDP) in the following seven years, an unprecedented drop in advanced capitalist countries (see Figure 7.1).

The crisis that lasted from 2008 to 2014 hit the Italian economy hard. Nevertheless, the effects of the subprime crisis, the destabilizing consequences on the financial markets and the financial crisis of many credit institutions did not affect the Italian economy in any relevant way, thanks to the low internationalization of the credit system and the weak financialization of the productive structure of the country.

From this point of view, the backwardness of the credit and financial markets, with their traditional corollary of scandals, bad administration and territorial provincialism, was to somehow keep the crisis virus away, with the exception of the two more internationalized Italian banking groups (Unicredit and Banca Intesa-San Paolo). Nevertheless, the reality was quite different. The fall in GDP and above all in industrial production was equal to, if not higher than,

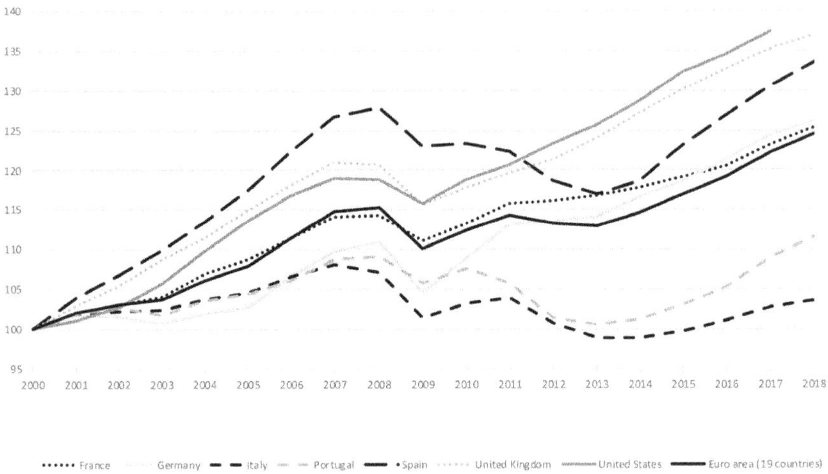

Figure 7.1. Dynamics of real GDP at constant prices in the main OECD countries, 2000–18. Real GDP dynamics is standardised to the value of 100 for the year 2000 (2000=100) for each country (on the left axis). Source: OECD, https://stats.oecd.org/.

that of the economies most affected by the financial crisis. From this point of view, the financial crisis of 2008–9 was like the straw that broke the camel's back in Italy, which – unlike other economies – was already on the verge of saturation.

This is the starting point from which we need to analyse and understand the different texts collected in this volume. With varying intensity, they converge from an interdisciplinary point of view, and not only with the often narrow and tarnished lenses of economic interpretation alone, towards a single conclusion: the failure of the transition of the Italian economy towards the paradigm of cognitive capitalism. It is specifically this aspect that we want to deal with in this chapter. In particular, we will focus on three aspects:

- the dynamics of the labour market, with particular reference to the new forms of self-employment more oriented towards cognitive production;
- the dynamics of labour productivity and production factors in Italy;
- the (non-)technological specialization of the Italian economy.

The Dynamics of the Labour Market in Italy

The analysis of the dynamics of the labour market means, in particular, dwelling on the labour demand of firms and therefore on the variables that characterize the structure of production. In particular, we need to emphasize some stylized facts.

These stylized facts (the dominance of small firms and the relevant role played by autonomous labour and by low-technology traditional industries), jointly analysed, represent an obstacle to the transition of the Italian economy towards a knowledge economy, or, to use a terminology that we consider more appropriate and less neutral, towards the spreading of the paradigm of biocognitive capitalism (Fumagalli 2011).

After the first Gulf War (1991), innovations in the field of transport and information and communications technology (ICT) began to coagulate around a unique and new paradigm of accumulation and valorization. The new capitalist configuration started to identify in the commodities 'knowledge' and 'space' (geographical and virtual) the new cornerstones on which to base accumulation capacity. In this way, two new dynamic economies of scale started to operate, which underlay the growth of productivity (and therefore a source of valorization): learning economies and network economies. The former are linked to the process of creating new knowledge (based on new communication and information technologies), while the latter derive from the district organizational methods (territorial networks or system areas) that are no longer used solely for the production and distribution of goods, but increasingly as a vehicle for the diffusion (and control) of knowledge and technological progress.

The centrality of the learning and network economies, typical of cognitive capitalism, had been questioned since the beginning of the new millennium following the burst of the speculative bubble of the 'Net Economy' in March 2000. The new cognitive paradigm was no longer able to protect the socioeconomic system from the structural instability that characterizes it. New liquidity should be introduced into financial markets. In fact, the capacity of financial markets to generate 'value' is linked to the development of 'conventions' (speculative bubbles) able to create generally homogeneous expectations that push the main financial operators to invest in certain financial assets.[1] In the 1990s, it was the Net Economy, while in the 2000s, the attraction came from the development of Asian markets (with China joining the World Trade Organization (WTO) in December 2001) and from real estate. In recent times, the focus has been on dismantling European welfare following the imposition of draconian austerity policies, and on the diffusion of social networks and the big data sector. Tomorrow, the sphere of green-economy and life policies (biotechnology, pharmaceuticals, increasingly privatized health and education, and big data) could be affected. Regardless of the type of dominant convention, contemporary capitalism is perennially in search of new social and vital areas to be engulfed and commodified: to add economic value to the vital faculties of human beings. This is why in recent years we have begun to talk about the bioeconomy and biocapitalism – hence, biocognitive capitalism.[2]

In this context, we should witness the development of new sectors with high intangible (cognitive-linguistic) productions. But in Italy, this has happened only in some areas of the country – the most metropolitan ones, where there was a conversion of the Fordist industrial system rather than only its dismantling (for example, the Milan metropolitan area, where more than a third of the value added and employment is in the intangible tertiary sector).

This means that labour (especially of the most flexible and less subordinate or autonomous kind) increasingly tends to disengage from the material production of goods; the result is a process of tertiarization that still depends on underlying industrial production and manufacturing (transport, storage, services to companies, more reticular production for flows than for stocks, within a production cycle that, while witnessing a tertiary development, tends to become increasingly more stringent in hierarchical production chains).

This follows a new composition of labour dictated by production needs, characterized by a mix of flexible, subordinate, hetero-creative labour, that tends to innervate the entire cycle of exploitation of intangible products and not only the realization phase with higher added value. In this regard, as a paradigmatic benchmark for the new enhancement processes, we focus mainly on the 'professional-freelance' workers segment, which represents the main component of the composite magma of third-generation self-employment (Fumagalli 2015).

Some research at the European level (Rapelli 2013) defines these workers as Independent Professionals (I-pros). In Italy, they are usually called freelancers[3] or professional workers. These are independent workers without employees, engaged in tertiary and/or intellectual activities that have nothing to do with industry, crafts and retail services. This is a definition that goes beyond the classical and traditional one of registered freelancers.[4]

This autonomous labour of the third generation, the child of the social, economic and organizational transformations of biocognitive capitalism, opens up new contradictions. In the presence of cognitive-relational labour with a purely intangible production purpose, learning and network economies play an even more important role. Elements of self-prescriptiveness and self-performance, especially if labour activity takes place in very competitive contexts, are added to the forms of high hetero-direction (which still remain). Thus, forms of self-exploitation have started to spread. They are stronger where the need for 'recognition' and 'gratification' is more relevant. We are witnessing the emergence of a division of labour that is not dictated solely by the type of job to be performed (as in the Fordist factory) or by positioning along the production chain (territorial/international division of labour) as was prevalent in second-generation self-employment.

The Smithian division for tasks and professional status (worker/employee, employee/independent, subordinate/autonomous) increasingly tends to be replaced by the emergence of a cognitive division of labour, which oscillates between elements of cooperation and elements of increasing hierarchy and command, between processes of individualization and processes of the socialization of work.

Within this new context, two factors have powerfully emerged: merit and recognition. They are the levers of a new form of dichotomy and division that subtly innervates the new labour market, creating the basis for extending and strengthening the precarity trap (Fumagalli and Morini 2013) as a tool for governance and *life subsumption* (Fumagalli 2019).

Regardless of the production context, today the autonomous labour of the third generation is divided between 'those who are worthy' and 'those who are not worthy' (in terms of merit) and between 'those who are successful' and 'those who are not successful' (in terms of recognition), all within a solipsistic (and unconscious) process of individualization/customization of labour activity, even within a process of social cooperation. It is precisely this social cooperation that increasingly becomes the main source of the extraction of a surplus value, which is not distributed, but simply expropriated and extracted in the form of rent. Far from becoming aware of this new labour dimension, these professional workers are struggling in the labour market by engaging in an individual competition that increases with precarity and indebtedness – a condition that makes them more susceptible to income blackmail.

Table 7.1. The percentage growth of I-pros in nine EU Member States, 2004–13.

Countries	Growth 2004–13 (%)
EU	+45%
The Netherlands	+93%
Poland	+88%
France	+85%
United Kingdom	+63%
Finland	+56%
Belgium	+53%
Spain	+51%
Germany	+43%
Italy	+12%

Source: P. Leighton with D. Brown, *Future Working: The Rise of Europe's Independent Professionals (iPros)* (London: European Forum of Independent Professionals, 2013), http://www.crse.co.uk/sites/default/files/Future%20Working%20Full%20Report.pdf.

New powerful businesses are on the horizon: models of socializing jobs such as coworking are also being created to meet people's desire to feel less alone and less alienated, developing corporate forms of proximity. In this way, the spatial dislocation of the autonomous labour of the third generation oscillates between the permanence of *domestication* and the creation of common areas of work. If in the autonomous work of the second generation, domestication is the result of the fragmentation and individualization of work performance, now for the third-generation autonomous worker, domestication is the starting point that regulates the individual use of one's cognitive abilities and relationships, to the point of favouring aggregative moments (which are in any case functional to the development of cooperative forms), but such as not to affect one's individual performance space. Training and knowledge-specialization courses are organized in an attempt to access higher levels of knowledge in the hope that this will allow greater recognition. In the meantime, work is increasingly turning into unpaid work and the promise of employment into mere unpaid *employability*.[5]

From the distribution point of view, monetary remuneration thus increasingly tends to be accompanied by a 'symbolic' remuneration,

Table 7.2. Distribution of I-pros in the main European countries, 2008–11.

	Number of I-pros (in thousands and in %)				Var. (%)
Countries	Q2 2008	%	Q2 2011	%	
Italy	1,705.04	22.3	1,689.00	19.7	-0.94
United Kingdom	1,303.05	17.1	1,625.69	18.9	+24.76
Germany	1,325.07	17.3	1,531.93	17.8	+15.61
France	545.62	7.1	743.21	8.6	+36.21
Spain	608.78	8.0	553.49	6.4	-9.08
The Netherlands	385.20	5.0	398.53	4.6	+3.46
Belgium	171.78	2.2	204.69	2.4	+19.16
Sweden	141.91	1.9	155.15	1.8	+9.33
Finland	79.15	1.0	90.94	1.1	+14.89
Denmark	65.78	0.9	64.71	0.8	-1.61
EU-27	7,638.60	100.0	8,593.30	100.0	+12.50

Source: P. Leighton with D. Brown, *Future Working: The Rise of Europe's Independent Professionals (iPros)* (London: European Forum of Independent Professionals, 2013), http://www.crse.co.uk/sites/default/files/Future%20Working%20Full%20Report.pdf.

through forms of recognition and gratification or the possibility of activating relational capacities that are as exclusive as possible. In fact, it is no coincidence that unpaid labour is increasingly becoming an instrument of possible transition from being 'employable' today to being 'employed' tomorrow, within an 'economy of promise' (Bascetta 2015).

On the basis of these premises, a comparison at the European level is interesting. First, if we analyse the dynamics of I-pros, starting from the 2000s, we can see that this is the segment that has undergone the greatest increase, even in the period of the economic crisis (with the exception of 2008), which demonstrates the growing weight of the cognitive paradigm.

In 2013, research commissioned by the EU and carried out by Patricia Leighton (University of South Wales, United Kingdom) confirmed the remarkable growth of this segment of work, albeit in a nonhomogeneous way. On average, in the period 2004–13, I-pros grew by 45 per cent, with peaks of 93 per cent in the Netherlands, 88 per cent in Poland and 85 per cent in France, but also with some much more moderate increases, as in the case of Italy (+12 per cent).

It should be noted that Italy represents the tail end of the growth of third-generation self-employment, despite being the country with the highest absolute number of I-pros (see Table 7.2) and the higher share of total employment (6.8 per cent compared to an EU average of 3.8 per cent).

If the autonomous labour of the third generation can be considered a proxy for the diffusion of forms of immaterial and cognitive accumulation, the Italian data is contradictory. In fact, Italy in 2011 still presents the highest share of this segment of work, a share that in the early 2000s, when biocognitive capitalism became more and more pervasive (and especially in Western countries), was almost double that of countries that we know are particularly specialized in cognitive and relationship-intensive productions, such as the United Kingdom, the Netherlands and Finland.

This might suggest that in Italy, we witnessed the growth and spread of forms of cognitive capitalism in the new millennium. But in the same period, the increase of the autonomous labour of the third generation was only 12 per cent in ten years, a value that turns out to be a third of the European average, eight times lower than the growth recorded in the Netherlands, seven times lower than that in France and five times lower than that in the United Kingdom.

These contradictory data (high share but low dynamics) are explained, on the one hand, by the high presence of I-pros in Italy, due to the greater weight that independent labour has always had in Italy, and, on the other hand, by the low productivity of this work. It should be noted that the national level of the advanced service sectors is on average lower than the European level, with some significant exceptions linked to the main metropolitan areas (in particular, Milan, as mentioned above). These observations are confirmed by a more in-depth investigation of the autonomous labour of the third generation (the 'professionals') recently carried out by the Bruno Trentin Association, entitled 'Lives for Professionals' and coordinated by Daniele Di Nunzio and Emanuele Toscano.

On the basis of this analysis, we are able to outline a sort of physiognomy of the autonomous labour of the third generation, featuring more drawbacks than clear advantages. If we analyse the traditional parameters that labour economists use to document working conditions, we can conclude that on average, the new autonomous labour of the third generation is characterized by:

- low income and therefore high uncertainty and instability;
- a poor degree of autonomy;
- high work intermittence;
- poor (if not nonexistent) social protection;
- working time that is not always measurable; and
- gender discrimination.

In short, the autonomous labour of the third generation is characterized by a condition of high precarity, which is not only limited to the sphere of work, but also overflows into the existential sphere.

The focus on labour with greater cognitive-relational intensity allows us to provide an unconventional point of view on some qualitative aspects of the dominant accumulation paradigm in the Italian economy. The structural difficulties and the backwardness of the Italian model will be highlighted, and it will be argued that such a model is unable to grasp the opportunities inherent in the transition to biocognitive capitalism.

The Dynamics of Labour Productivity and Production Factors in Italy

The long process towards the deregulation of the Italian labour market, which began in the 1980s and came to fruition thirty years later with the approval of the Jobs Act and the related implementing decrees, has deeply affected not only the job supply, but above all the labour demand and the dynamics of productive specializations of the Italian economy.

The mainstream position underlines the need to activate a policy for economic growth. This objective clashes with two structural problems. The first consists of a perverse dynamic of the distribution of income that, by concentrating more and more into a few hands, is incompatible with a level of final demand able to guarantee high economic growth. The second is the poor productivity dynamic. Let us focus now on the second.

The high share of precarity means that in Italy, labour conditions are basically worse than in other European countries. Further, wage levels are lower and working times are longer. According to the

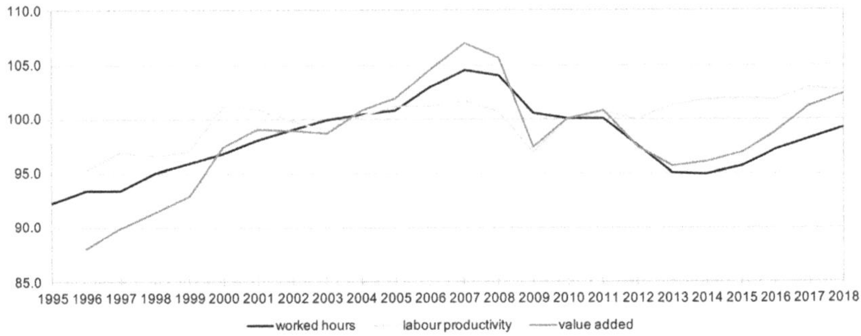

Figure 7.2. Labour productivity, added value and worked hours in Italy, total economy, 1995–2018 (2010=100). All the variables on the left axis (worked hours, labour productivity, value added) are standardized with a base 100 to 2010. Labour productivity is defined as output/per hour. Source: Istat, http://dati.istat.it/.

OECD data on the number of hours worked per year, the stereotype of the lazy and sluggish Italian worker is dispelled. The average number of hours worked is around 1,800 a year. In Germany the equivalent data is little more than 1,500 hours, in France 1,550 hours, and in the Netherlands just over 1,400 hours, in line with the Scandinavian countries. The Italian average working time is similar to that of the United States and slightly below that of Japan. Moreover, the trend of the hours worked follows a pro-cyclical dynamic. In the phases of greatest expansion (relative) –like that between 2005 and 2007 – the number of hours worked remained stationary if not slightly higher, while starting from 2008, they reduced due to the decrease in production dynamics.

The high number of working hours is combined in Italy with lower average wages. At the European level, Italian workers who are employed full-time in a company with ten or more employees receive lower gross earnings than their colleagues in Luxembourg, the Netherlands, Germany, Belgium, France and Spain. In fact, according to Eurostat data, relative to 2012, an Italian worker received an average of €31,272 gross earnings, compared to €51,049 in Luxembourg, €42,673 in Germany, €39,858 in Ireland, €34,604 in France and €21,878 in Greece.[6]

The Italian labour market is therefore characterized by low wage levels (especially for first-time young employees) and higher average working hours. This combination has the effect – not too paradoxically – of providing a productivity of the economic system in terms of added value per employee that is below the European average. Figure 7.2 shows that in the last twenty years, labour productivity

Table 7.3. Added value, productive inputs and productivity statistics, total economy,* 1995–2017, compound average annual rates of growth.

Timeframe	Value added	Hours worked	Capital input	Combined inputs	Labour productivity	Capital productivity	Multifactor productivity
1995–2017	0.7	0.3	1.4	0.7	0.4	-0.7	0.0
2003–15	-0.1	-0.4	0.6	-0.1	0.3	-0.7	-0.1
2003–9	-0.2	0.1	1.7	0.6	-0.3	-1.8	-0.9
2009–15	-0.1	-0.9	-0.5	-0.8	0.8	0.5	0.7
2016	1.9	1.9	0.3	1.4	-0.1	1.6	0.5
2017	2.1	1.3	0.9	1.1	0.8	1.2	1.0

* Net total of real-estate activities of households, of activities of extraterritorial organizations and of all activities of the General government sector.

Source: Istat, https://www.istat.it/it/files//2018/11/EN_Productivity_Statistics_1995-2017.pdf.

has increased only by 0.5 per cent a year and hours worked have increased by 0.2 per cent, with a drastic drop in the period 2008–14, characterized by the economic crisis.

In particular, productivity rose in a very limited way and then started to fall from the beginning of the new millennium. If we disaggregate the data on the basis of the contributions of the various factors of production (see Table 7.3), the 'capital' productivity pushes the total factor productivity downwards, making it always a negative value, except in the three-year period 2015–17. The Italian production system is not able to compete in terms of new technologies and the efficiency of human and physical capital. The Italian economy thus shows a structural deficiency, the result of the choices (or, rather, the non-choices) that have directed the strategies of economic policy in the last twenty years. First of all, it is useful to remember that what in the 1980s and up to the early 1990s was considered the pride of the Italian economy – that is, small enterprises and lower labour costs, with the consequent specialization of production in sectors with low technological intensity (Made in Italy), which positively affected the increase of exports and the emergence of industrial districts – today, after the passage in the late 1990s towards the diffusion of forms of cognitive accumulation with increasing technological intensity and Research and Development (R&D), turns out to be a boomerang, one of the main factors to explain the low level of productivity growth.

Second, the small average size of Italian firms, the prevalence of family capitalism, the difficulties in accessing credit and the pursuit of competitive strategies based on low prices and rarely on the quality of production have excluded Italy from the higher added-value production chains, which today are located on the technological frontier of computer, pharmaceutical, biogenetics and nanotechnology production. The Italian specialization in mature and traditional sectors also makes it particularly difficult to efficiently exploit the dynamic economies of scale that are at the base of productivity growth: learning economies, capable of generating knowledge and innovation, and network economies, aimed at disseminating and exploiting them economically. To this end, the development of a properly prepared and skilled human capital and labour force is essential: an economic and social environment that should be characterized by stability and good wages in order to promote the growth of higher added-value industries on the knowledge frontier. These are conditions that the process of labour market flexibility does not allow to be acquired.

Since the 1980s (after the defeat of the workers' and social struggles of the 1970s, which had contributed so much to the process of modernizing Italy) and especially since the 1990s, a new methodology of economic policy has been the focus: a 'two-steps' policy.

Before going into more detail on this policy, let us pause for a brief historical reflection. It is often claimed, only for purely ideological reasons, that the 1970s was a period of crisis in the Italian productive system, due to the high level of social turbulence, which heavily affected the increase in labour costs (with the corollary of inflationary spiral), and the rigidity of work with depressive effects on the dynamics of productivity.

Figure 7.3 compares the dynamics of Italian productivity with that of Germany, starting from 1970 up to the first years of the recent economic sovereign debt crisis.

It can easily be seen that in the 1970s and 1980s, Italian productivity was not only in line with German productivity, but in some years was even higher. The better German performance began to appear

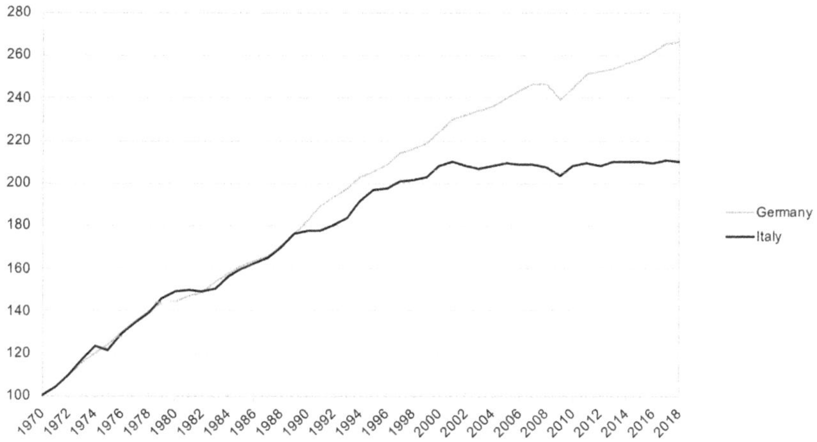

Figure 7.3. Labour productivity index in Germany and Italy, 1970–2018 (1970=100). Source: OECD, https://stats.oecd.org/.

at the end of the 1980s, opening up a gap that tended to increase in the following years. The turning point coincided with the beginning of the crisis in industrial districts and with the diffusion of the first forms of precarity. The combined effect was the positioning of the Italian industry in sectors with a predominantly low added value and low cognitive-technological intensity.

This was the consequence of Italy's exit from the short-term Fordist crisis, fuelled by the need to reduce costs (also following a media campaign on the supposed rigidity of the Italian labour market and excessive wage dynamics that were not empirically verified),[7] which meant that the opportunity for a qualitative improvement of Italian production in favour of sectors with greater added value was not seized. It is in this context that the 'two-steps' policy should be analysed.

The first step is aimed at increasing the competitiveness of the economic system in the process of globalization as the only condition to encourage growth that, in a second step, should – in the best reformist intentions – generate resources to improve the social distribution of income and therefore the level of demand. The measures to create competitiveness, in the context of the dominant economic culture, concerned first of all two guiding principles: the dismantling of the welfare state and its private financings (starting with pensions, then gradually affecting education and now health) and the flexibilization of the labour market, in order to reduce production costs and create the necessary profits to encourage investment growth. The results were not very positive: far from favouring the modernization of the production system, this policy has created precarity, economic stagnation and progressive erosion of labour income, especially after the trade unions' agreements of 1992–93, and therefore a drop in productivity. The second step has not yet begun and we know that, *sic rebus stantibus*, it will never begin.

The 'two-steps' policy took place while a Copernican revolution was underway in the processes of capitalist valorization: immaterial-cognitive production started to assume ever-greater importance, to the detriment of material-industrial production. Today the sectors with the highest added value are those of the advanced tertiary sector and the sources of productivity are increasingly in the exploitation of learning and network economies, precisely those economies that require labour stability, income security and investments in technology. In other words, labour flexibility generates positive results only if it is accompanied by social and economic security (continuity of income) and free access to intangible common assets (knowledge, mobility and sociality). The failure of biocognitive capitalism to take off in Italy is the main cause behind the current crisis of productivity. The current mantra that the excessive rigidity of labour is the first cause of poor Italian productivity makes no sense; instead, reality tells us the opposite. It is rather the excess of precarity that is chiefly the first cause of the problem. *Those who cause precarity die of precarity*. In conclusion, it is the high precarity in the sectors with greater cognitive intensity that precludes an efficient exploitation of the learning and network economies.

It follows that the synergistic binomial – lack of specialization towards the sectors characterizing the new paradigm of biocognitive capitalism, and increasing precarization – creates a vicious cycle that more than any other factor explains why the stagnation and decline of the Italian economic apparatus began about a decade before the onset of the Global Financial Crisis of 2008.

The Italian Technological Trajectory and the Dynamics of Investments

Since the 1990s, the Italian economic system has faced a crossroads, with the end of the advantages brought about by the exploitation of economies of scale based on the externality and on the productive decentralization that had distinguished the spread of industrial districts in the previous decade. A new technological paradigm is globally emerging, driven by the spread of the Net Economy in the

United States. As already mentioned, the increasing return to scale at the base of the new accumulation model is now based on dynamic 'internal' scale economies, linked to learning and network processes. Knowledge and space become the engine of the growth of cognitive capitalism, driven by those sectors where technological intensity is increasingly determined by high levels of appropriability (intellectual property rights) and above all of cumulativeness (innovations that generate innovations). As Paul A. David wrote in 1975:

> technological learning depends on the accumulation of actual experience in production; choices with a limited time horizon on what to produce and in particular on how to produce using known methods, indeed, also determine what is subsequently learned.[8]

Faced with the acceleration of technological progress and the spread of intangible linguistic-communicative technologies, the Italian economic structure, despite the strong innovation process of the 1970s and 1980s, seems inadequate, especially from a qualitative point of view. Yet at first glance, contrary to what is normally believed, the investment dynamics in Italy have been only slightly below the European average, as can be seen in Figure 7.4. The question that arises is therefore not of a quantitative but of a qualitative nature, just as for the productive factor of labour. In this case, in fact, what matters is not the number of hours worked (above the European average), but the qualitative data about relative productivity (lower than the European average). The same applies to investments. In quantitative

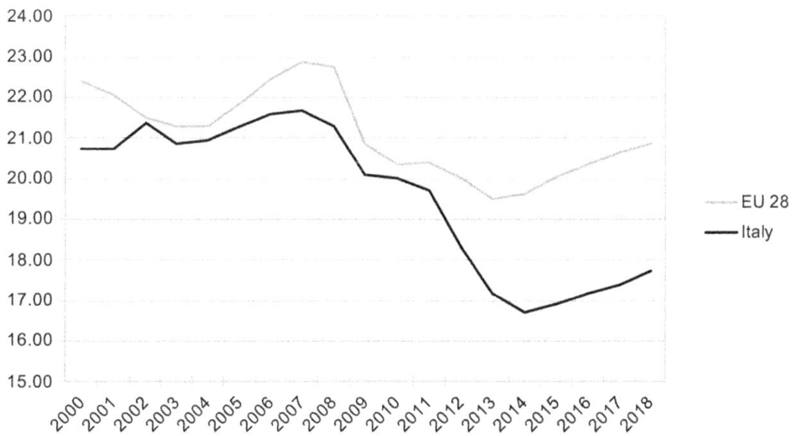

Figure 7.4. Total investment-to-GDP ratio in Italy and the EU-28, 2000–18. Source: Eurostat, https://ec.europa.eu/eurostat/data/browse-statistics-by-theme.

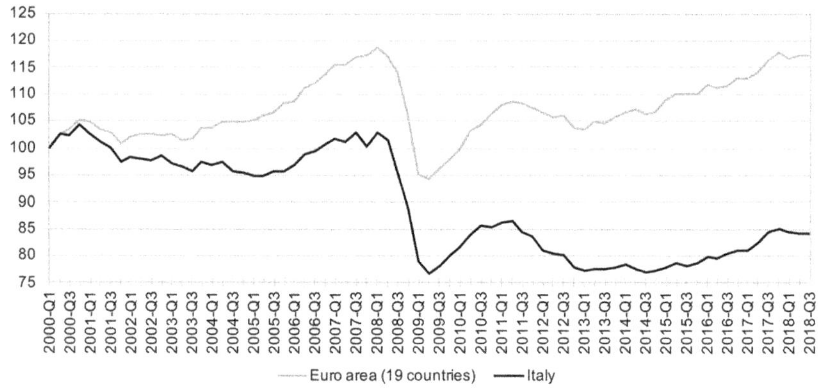

Figure 7.5. Manufacturing production in the eurozone and in Italy, 2000–17 (2000=100). Source: Eurostat, https://ec.europa.eu/eurostat/data/browse-statistics-by-theme.

terms, until 2007, Italy was the only European country that maintained the investment share on GDP over 20 per cent. Even during the economic crisis (2008–13), despite a sharp decline, Italian investments remained close to the EU average, with the exception of 2013.

If we look instead at the trend of Italian production compared with that in Europe as a whole, we can see a completely different and opposite dynamic. As can be seen in Figure 7.5, Italian production, starting as early as 2000, has a decidedly lower trend than that of Europe as a whole, highlighting a gap that, with the passing of the years, and regardless of the crisis situation, tends to increase more and more.

It follows that Italian investments have a lower capacity to affect the growth of industrial production and this confirms the lower productivity of capital compared to other factors of production (see Figure 7.5). However, in order to better understand this aspect, it is necessary to analyse the different components of the investment.

By considering the total fixed gross investment dynamics, Figure 7.6 points out that productive investments in Italy until 2007 present a dynamic that is in line with the European average and more competitive countries, but after 2007, in the years of crisis, Italy had a more contained dynamic than the European one, while maintaining a larger share of GDP.

With reference to investments in machinery and equipment, the dynamic is similar even if the oscillations in the cycle are slightly more pronounced (see Figure 7.7).

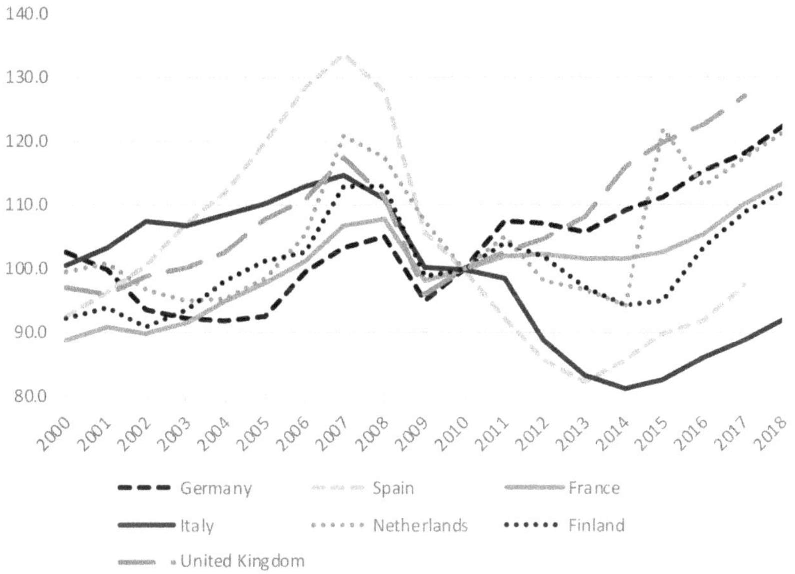

Figure 7.6. Cross-classification of gross fixed capital formation in some EU countries, total fixed assets (gross), 2000–18 (index 2010=100). Source: Eurostat, https://ec.europa.eu/eurostat/data/browse-statistics-by-theme.

Moreover, by considering production investments in R&D, we can see how in Italy, unlike in some European countries, investments in research keep lagging behind. As Lucarelli, Palma and Romano have pointed out:

> Over the last 25 years (1987–2012) the main industrialized countries in Europe have contracted investments in relation to GDP. This was accompanied by an increase in the ratio between R&D and GDP. More specifically the relationship between business research and development (BERD) and GDP indicates a gradual shift of production specialization to innovative sectors with higher levels of research intensity. (Lucarelli, Palma and Romano 2014: 47)

However, at the European level, not all countries showed the same trends, but the general tendency is to strengthen spending on R&D in parallel with a reduction in investment in machinery (Ibid.).[9] To give just a few examples, Finland records a sharp reduction in the share of investment in machinery as a share of GDP (around 8 per cent in 1987 and slightly less than 4 per cent in 2011) and a simultaneous net increase in the BERD (R&D expenditure of the business sector)

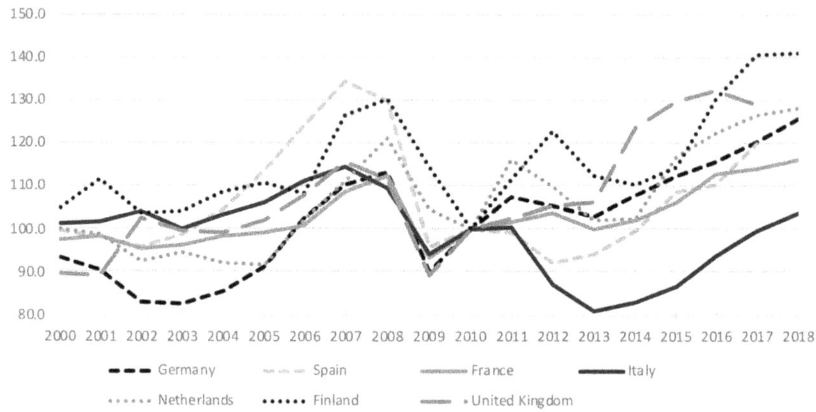

Figure 7.7. Machinery and equipment and weapons systems (gross) in some EU countries, 2000–18 (index 2010=100). Source: Eurostat, https://ec.europa.eu/eurostat/data/browse-statistics-by-theme.

share of GDP (from 1 per cent to about 3 per cent in the same period); Germany maintains a level of the BERD share of GDP of just under 2 per cent, which appears sufficient to ensure a decreasing trend in the ratio of investment in machinery/GDP (from around 7 per cent to around 5 per cent over the period considered). France, like Germany, sees a reduction in the ratio of investments in machinery/GDP (from 4.5 per cent in 1987 to around 3.5 per cent in 2010) and keeps the BERD/GDP share to just under 1.5 per cent.[10]

Italy, on the other hand, shows a stagnation of the BERD/GDP share, which is still below 1 per cent and shows no tendency to grow, but is accompanied by an increase in the ratio of investments in machinery/GDP in the period from 1992 until 2008, and then records a fall, in line with the European figure, in the years of the economic crisis. In 1987, the value of this ratio was equal to 0.66 per cent; it was reduced to values between 0.50 and 0.52 in the period 1998–2004 (in which the growth of the job insecurity process is greater) and then went back to values equivalent to those at the start of the crisis; more due to a decline in GDP than to the increase in BERD investments.

If we look at investments in machinery instead, in Italy the decline in this type of investment was the most contained, second only to the United States. Figure 7.8, analysing the dynamics of the relationship between BERD investments and investments in machinery, describes

Figure 7.8. R&D expenditure (% of GDP) – Italy, Germany, the United States and the EU, 2000–17. Source: OECD, https://data.oecd.org/rd/gross-domestic-spending-on-r-d.htm.

a qualitative indicator of the investment policies that have developed in Italy. It can easily be seen that Italy is at the lowest level of this relationship. With respect to this point, Lucarelli, Palma and Romano (2014: 51) write:

> Italy is a borderline case, but representative of the new paradigm: it is the country that more than others invested in capital goods, but at the same time it is also the country with the worst GDP growth. The Italian economy is characterized by an absolutely stagnant BERD/investment ratio, which leads the country to maintain a high level of capital goods needed for production, and to ensure that demand for capital goods is increasingly less satisfied by domestic production, compared to a production specialization dynamically more and more distant from the technological frontier and therefore insufficient to mobilize adequate technological skills.

We can therefore conclude that in Italy, the effect of substitution between BERD (basically intangible) investments and investments in machinery (capital goods) for the production of intangible and tangible assets has not taken place. This provides further confirmation of the lack of passage of the Italian economy towards production with greater added value typical of biocognitive capitalism, as also highlighted by the lack of correlation between investment and production dynamics (and therefore of GDP).

Preliminary Conclusions

Unlike what has happened in the major industrialized countries since the 1990s, and more recently in a significant group of Northern European countries, Italy has a deficit of efficiency. However, contrary to what one might think, this situation does not derive from a rigidity of the labour market and of a bureaucratic-institutional nature. Of course, the Italian bureaucracy is certainly an element of structural constraint, even if it is functional for the development of an informal economy that, thanks more to fiscal elusion than to evasion and the illegal economy, plays a role in compensating for the growing polarization of income distribution.

However, the most marked inefficiency lies in the low productivity of the Italian economic system. In this case we refer to the inability to fully exploit the productivity of social cooperation in terms of learning and network economies. It is not a question of material productivity, but rather of social productivity, which cannot be measured in a direct way as it tends to be immaterial. But the 'measure' is in some way attributable to the dynamics of financial conventions that animate the financial markets themselves. It is not the rigidity of labour that is the cause of the low productivity. If anything, it is its opposite: the excessive flexibility of labour (and its becoming increasingly precarious) negatively affects the efficiency and productivity of work.

This creates a vicious circle that negatively affects even the potential present in terms of the educational and cultural preparation of the new generation, which is increasingly sacrificed. From this point of view, inefficiency is combined with a high level of waste of human capital. Moreover, this vicious cycle affects the technological specialization of Italy, with the risk of becoming a structural constraint for the trade balance. The increase in the technological intensity of manufacturing imports did not find an adequate balance in the increase in the technological intensity of exports, due to the cognitive backwardness of the Italian industrial system. It follows a structural deficit in the commercial balance of high-tech productions, as an effect of the structural gap between the demand for technology – coherent with that of others with advanced industrialization – and technology supply. It is no coincidence that over the last twenty years, technology demand and supply have been accentuated over the long term. The dependence of innovative processes on the use of capital goods, which are the major component of high-tech productions, has naturally aggravated this failure.

Given the particular nature of the Italian crisis and the general economic situation of this country, it is reasonable to argue that the request for indiscriminate investment could be counterproductive, as it may have the effect of increasing the Italian trade deficit. Italy is therefore structurally weak and exposed to the unstable dynamics of the global economy, a situation that is due to long-standing structural reasons and that today, in the contemporary context, can only be overcome with a decisive inversion in labour policies.

Current labour market reforms, far from representing a potential for improvement or growth in the future, are instead impeding the modernization of the economic system towards a more efficient model of biocognitive capitalism. From this point of view, the adoption of "secur-flexibility" policies instead of a flex-security policy would certainly be more adequate for the purpose of increasing the efficiency and quality of economic activity. It would be necessary to implement income guarantee policies that are able to reduce the uncertainty of life and at the same time to develop the level of independence and autonomy of labour performance, in order to create a situation that allows for greater human potential.

Andrea Fumagalli is Associate Professor of Political Economy at the University of Pavia and also lectures at the University of Bologna. He is the Italian coordinator of the COST European project 'Dynamics of Virtual Work'. He is member of the Associazione Bin-Italia (Basic Income Network) and is Executive Committee of BiEn (Basic income Earth network). He is also a member of the independent research network Effimera and of the San Precario network of Milan. Among his recent publications are *Cognitive Capitalism, Welfare and Labour: The Commonfare Hypothesis* (2019, Routledge); *Lavoro male comune* (2014, Mondadori); *La crisi economica globale* (with S. Mezzadra, 2010, Ombre Corte); and *Bioeconomia e capitalismo cognitivo. Verso un nuovo paradigma di accumulazione* (2007, Carocci).

Notes

This chapter would have never seen the light without the contributions and suggestions of Stefano Lucarelli and Roberto Romano. I also thank Fulvia D'Aloisio for her encouragement. Thanks to the psychedelic support of the music by The Grateful Dead, Jimi Hendrix and Phish. Any errors or omissions are the responsibility of the author.

1. See Orléan 2009.
2. The terms 'bioeconomy' and 'biocapitalism' are very recent and were introduced in the Italian debate. The concept of 'bioeconomy' was introduced in Fumagalli (2004,

2005, 2007). For an interesting analysis of the concept of 'bioeconomy', see also Chicchi (2008) and Bazzicaluppo (2006). The term 'biocapitalism' was instead coined by Codeluppi (2008). See also Morini (2007), Fumagalli and Morini (2003) and Fumagalli (2015). For a survey on the hypothesis of cognitive capitalism, see Lucarelli and Vercellone (2013). See recently Fumagalli et al. (2019).

3. See Allegri and Ciccarelli (2013).
4. Using the European NACE classification, the sectors concerned are predominantly those characterized by information and communication activities (NACE, key J, codes 58–63), financial and insurance activities (NACE, key K, codes 54–66), real estate activities and professional activities (NACE, key L, code 68), scientific and technical activities (NACE, key M, codes 77–82), administrative and service activities (NACE, key N, codes 54–66), educational activities (NACE, key P, code 85), health and social care activities (NACE, key Q, codes 86–88), artistic activities (NACE, key R, codes 59–93) and other tertiary activities (NACE, key S, codes 94–96). See Rapelli (2013: 9).
5. By 'employability', we mean the creation of professional and training conditions to improve access to jobs.
6. It should be noted that before the 2008 crisis, the gross salary of a Greek worker was in line with the Italian salary.
7. It suffices to say that the campaign against the Statuto dei Lavoratori that underlay the growing process of precariousness of the labour market up to the recent Jobs Act (2014–15) was specious. It chose to ignore that the workers for whom this statute has force represented only a third of the total workforce. The job protection ensured by the Statuto dei Lavoratori did not apply to the majority of the labour force, which is still employed in small firms. This dual system of the labour market also explains why Italian real wages were and still are well below the European average and, more importantly, well below that of Italy's main competitor countries (especially Germany).
8. Quotation taken from Lucarelli and Romano (2015: 148).
9. The authors note that: 'For investments in machinery we used OECD data, Other machineries and equipment; for BERD we used OECD data, Business enterprise R-D expenditure by industry. We have expressed both variables in relation to GDP (OECD data, Gross domestic product, output approach).'
10. For a more systematic and exhaustive analysis, see Lucarelli, Palma and Romano (2013). All the data presented here are taken from this source.

References

Allegri., A., and R. Ciccarelli. 2013. *Il Quinto Stato. Perché il lavoro indipendente è il nostro futuro. Precari, autonomi, free lance per una nuova società*. Rome: Ponte alle Grazie.

Bascetta, M. (ed.). 2015. *Economia della promessa*. Rome: Manifestolibri.

Bologna, S., and A. Fumagalli (eds). 1997. *Il lavoro autonomo di II generazione*. Milan: Feltrinelli.

Bazzicaluppo, L. 2006. *Il governo delle vite. Biopolitica ed economia*. Rome-Bari: Laterza.

Chicchi, F. 2008. 'Bioeconomia ambienti e forme della mercificazione del vivente', in A. Amendola et al. (eds), *Biopolitica, bioeconomia e processi di soggettivazione*. Macerata: Quodlibet, pp. 143–58.

Codeluppi, V. 2008. *Il biocapitalismo. Verso lo sfruttamento integrale di corpi, cervelli ed emozioni*. Turin: Bollati Boringhieri.

Fumagalli, A. 2004. 'Conoscenza e bioeconomia', *Filosofia e Questioni Pubbliche* IX(1): 141–61.

———. 2005. 'Bioeconomics, Labour Flexibility and Cognitive Work: Why Not Basic Income?', in G. Standing (ed.), *Promoting Income Security as a Right: Europe and North America*. London: Anthem Press, pp. 337–50.

———. 2007. *Bioeconomia e capitalismo cognitivo. Verso un nuovo paradigma di accumulazione*. Rome: Carocci.

———. 2011. 'Twenty Theses on Contemporary Capitalism (Cognitive Biocapitalism)', *Angelaki* 16: 7–17.

———. 2015. 'Le trasformazioni del lavoro autonomo tra crisi e precarietà: il lavoro autonomo di III generazione', *Quaderni di ricerca sull'artigianato* 2: 228–56.

———. 2019. 'New Forms of Exploitation in Bio-Cognitive Capitalism: Towards the Life Subsumption', in A. Fumagalli, A. Giuliani, S. Lucarelli and C. Vercellone, *Cognitive Capitalism, Welfare and Labour: The Commonfare Hypothesis*. London: Routledge, pp. 77–93.

Fumagalli, A., A. Giuliani, S. Lucarelli and C. Vercellone. 2019. *Cognitive Capitalism, Welfare and Labour: The Commonfare Hypothesis*. Abingdon: Routledge.

Fumagalli, A., and C. Morini. 2013. 'Cognitive Bio-capitalism, Social Reproduction and the Precarity Trap: Why Not Basic Income?', *Knowledge Cultures* 1(4): 106–26.

Leighton, P., and D. Brown. 2013. *Future Working: The Rise of Europe's Independent Professionals (iPros)*. London: European Forum of Independent Professionals. Retrieved 18 February 2020 from http://www.crse.co.uk/sites/default/files/Future%20Working%20Full%20Report.pdf.

Lucarelli, S., and R. Romano. 2015. 'Le tendenze dell'innovazione e il governo della domanda effettiva', in L. Pennacchi and R. Sanna (eds), *Riforma del capitalismo. Per un nuovo modello di sviluppo*. Rome: Ediesse, pp. 145–64.

Lucarelli, S., and C. Vercellone. 2013. 'The Thesis of Cognitive Capitalism: New Research Perspectives', *Knowledge Cultures* 1(4): 15–31.

Lucarelli, S., D. Palma and R. Romano. 2013. 'Quando gli investimenti rappresentano un vincolo. Contributo alla discussione sulla crisi italiana nella crisi internazionale', *Moneta e Credito* 67(262): 169–205.

———. 2014. 'Il sostegno agli investimenti in un'economia tecnologicamente in ritardo'. Retrieved from https://www.economiaepolitica.it/primo-piano/il-sostegno-agli-investimenti-in-uneconomia-tecnologicamente-in-ritardo/.

Morini, C. 2007. 'The Feminization of Labour in Cognitive Capitalism', *Feminist Review* 87(1): 40–59.

———. 2010. *Per amore o per forza. Femminilizzazione del lavoro e biopolitiche del corpo*. Verona: Ombre Corte.

Morini, C., and A. Fumagalli. 2011. 'Life Put to Work: Towards a Theory of Life-Value', *Ephemera* 10: 234–52.

Orléan, A. 2009. *De l'euphorie à la panique. Penser la crise financiére*. Paris: Rue d'Ulm.

Rapelli, S. 2013. *European I-Pros: A Study*. Retrieved 18 February 2020 from https://www.pcg.org.uk/sites/default/files/media/documents/RESOURCES/efip_report_english.pdf.

Vercellone, C. (ed.). 2006. *Capitalismo Cognitivo*. Rome: Manifestolibri.

— Afterword —

FROM THE THIRD ITALY TO UNIVERSAL ALIENATION

Uneven and Combined

Don Kalb

In retrospect, the robustness of the best of social theory of some three decades is striking. Which of our present predicaments, in a general sense, is not somehow prefigured there? Bring, for example, David Harvey's *The Condition of Postmodernity* (1989), Manuel Castells' *The Informational City* (1989), Saskia Sassen's *The Global City* (1991), Enzo Mingione's *Fragmented Societies* (1991) and Giovanni Arrighi's *The Long Twentieth Century* (1994) into the conversation, and so much of what has obsessed social research since then is arguably pretty well sketched out – in a general sense, that is.

A few years after these books were written, around 1999, much of this was condensed, confirmed, condoned and contested in the notion of the neoliberal. This concept quickly turned out to be so effective and in such high demand that it threatened to swallow up all around it: all the foreseen decline of the social, the ongoing commodification, the corporatization, the inequalities, the post-democracy seemed to be wrapped into it (Harvey 2005; Clarke 2008; Smith 2008) – neoliberalizations, again in general.

The retrenchment of the welfare state and the crumbling of the standard employment contract – arguably the *pièces de resistance* of twentieth-century capitalist modernity for the many – were only the most visible demonstrations of this process (Breman et al. 2019). The unstoppable social polarization, the globalization of capital that began feeding into both the localization and the technocratization of politics, the resulting rise of identity politics and populist mobilizations, precarity of various types, the evaporation of hope in the once unbeatable promises of modernity, not just in the poorer parts of the world but also in the richer ones – all of this was already well described as a likely threat in those general analyses of a generation ago. Add to this the dramatic accelerations in climate change, speculative finance and general indebtedness, the swift rise of a billionaires' plutocracy in the United States, the massive advances in technology and oligopoly, and of course the rise of China – things that have become much more visible since the financial crises of 2008–14 – and our twenty-first-century predicament is all but painted in broad strokes. 'Flexible accumulation' flexibly shifted the risks and the price of ongoing accumulation onto the bodies of the working people and the earth. Both people and earth, their talents and resources having been increasingly commoditized, were increasingly appearing almost as free gifts to capital, now being expertly offered up for exploitation by that Janus-faced institution called the national welfare state, by this time a neoliberalized structure, and almost everywhere deeply indebted to capital and therefore practically owned by it. We know that this is true for Italy even more than for most other nations, though Italy is not yet in a category of its own, as Japan or Greece is. However, both Italy's and Japan's national debt is largely owned by domestic capital, which is of major significance for sovereignty. But the sovereignty of whom – the people or the bondholders?

If the seductive idea of modernity was once proposed with the intention of shifting the cognitive focus of the public away from its nasty engine – capitalism – and onto modern urban educated living for all, we can now safely conclude that capitalism is back, while modernity appears as a false and tired promise reduced to its techno core. Capitalism is back as fact, as problem and as public obsession. It is the elephant in the room that has escaped the shackles of the postwar democratic welfare state and has subdued the state's administrative and judicial apparatus to its own priorities, property rights and interest payments on the national debt first of all. And so, all that came with it and had once appeared to be obsolete is back too: class, labour, exploitation, extraction, precarity, the voracious metabolism of capital and the consequent cannibalism of nature, human and nonhuman alike. Even Hardt and Negri, who were once inordinately optimistic about the creative alter-globalist multitudes within and against Empire – a millenarian infliction? – have again begun to talk plainly about capital and class (Hardt and Negri 2019). Even in social movement studies, until recently so well settled around the problem of post-material identities, capital and class are back (Della Porta 2015; Kalb and Mollona 2018b), as is also the case, in fact, within anthropology (Kalb, 2014, 2015; Kalb and Mollona 2018a; Kasmir and Carbonella 2014).

But these are the 'mere' generalities. In contrast, anthropologists (and some sociologists and geographers) have professionally specialized in providing the local and close-on-the-skin particulars. I call this anthropological political economy. Political-economy anthropologists have often tried to provide these particulars in conversation with the wider theoretical literature. Indeed, anthropologists of capitalism, labour and class have once more sought to articulate their local and ethnographic histories with grand history and big theory, in effect seeking to realize visions of what Leon Trotsky called 'uneven and combined' development (Kalb 2018; Kasmir and Gill 2018). They have also blown up the classic distinctions of 'class in itself and class for itself' and have sought a less nominalist, more relationally realist grasp of the hybrid and complex histories that people are living in their habitats as well as on the move. They have thus aimed at describing and understanding in analytic ways the evolving popular moralities and everyday politics of their subject populations, placed within precise and fine-grained relational matrixes of social reproduction, house holding, hierarchies, solidarities, dependencies and variably constituted national, regional and local public spheres (of institutions, media and politics). They have been seeking what I call the critical junctions (Kalb 2005, 2011, 2018a) between global, national and local transformations, trying to picture the intimate as well as large-scale dynamics – cultural, economic, social, geographical, etc – of extractions and impositions by state, private and public formations of capital, those that are obvious and those that are obscured.

The authors in this collection have each joined this important project in anthropology in their own way and from their own local vantage point. They thus update with rich detail Hadjimichalis' (2006) key points: first, that the Third Italy of dynamic industrial districts had never existed in splendid isolation from national and global markets, or, in other words, was never constituted outside of 'global time'; and, second, that the artisanal districts were never the cohesive labouring and entrepreneurial organic trust-communities that a neoliberal governance literature began imagining and then celebrating in the 1980s and 1990s as a general recipe for industrial and regional rebirth vis-à-vis the supposed dead end of Fordist class conflict. In short, they did not exist outside of global capitalism.

My overall impression from the chapters in this volume is that the basic lines of development and involution of the Third Italy as summarized by critics such as Hadjimichalis, Ross (2004) and others in the mid-2000s have been confirmed, updated and further fleshed out in local and variegated detail. But the studies here do add an interesting twist to the timeline. The later 2000s seem to have been fairly good for Italian industrial districts. The general processes that were hollowing out the districts in the 1990s and the early 2000s continued, but they were ameliorated and perhaps temporarily obscured by an exceptionally good conjuncture that endured for a couple of years. This conjuncture was driven by global demand. It was of course not an internal effect of the organic qualities of Italian industrial districts, as the myth-makers might have claimed. Lasting from 2003 to 2008, it was fed by global credit and accelerating overall indebtedness in the core of the global economy, and was driven by the commodity and industrial booms in Eastern Europe, China, the Middle East, Russia and the expanding EU, as capitalism's spatial fixes globalized massively and neoliberals began to celebrate the rise of the 'global middle classes'. The financial crises in the United States and Europe (2007–14) were the result of the contradictions of this sweeping globalizing and financializing drive. The crisis put a sudden end to what turned out to be a short period of breathing space for Italian districts. From late 2008, they all faced mayhem as consumer demand evaporated instantly, in particular in the luxury sectors in which Italian districts were so specialized, from furniture to jewels, clothes, shoes, caravans, etc. Global consumers immediately put on hold unnecessary purchases and then kept a lid on their wallets for a long while in order to pay back debts or save in the face of economic uncertainty. The accumulated anti-value (Harvey 2018) in the system burst and had significant repercussions in labour-intensive consumer-manufacturing localities in Italy and elsewhere. The hollowing out along the lines specified above and by the literature, after a short interlude, then dramatically accelerated.

This calls for a summary view of the critical junctions that have constituted the rise and decline of Italy as a postwar economic location. We need to talk about Trotsky's 'uneven and combined development'. When it comes to global time, it is useful to underline that the basic junctions of Italian postwar history were not different from the general global conditions under which Europe as a whole developed. Until the 1970s, postwar reconstruction and urbanization under varied national Keynesian regimes on the continent enabled the establishment of diverse varieties of capitalism with various industrial specializations. Household formation and population growth were at an all-time high, as was household demand for basic consumer goods such as cars, white goods, furniture and of course fashion.

As is well known, Italy suffered more sharply from spatial inequalities than any of the original EU states. There were in fact three Italies. First, the country was partly composed of a trans-alpine outlier of the old continental capitalist core (Lombardy, Piedmont and parts of the Po valley). Second, there was an extended underdeveloped space, starting somewhere south of Florence, stretching for almost 1,000 kilometres into the Mediterranean, bordering Tunisia and Libya with a short stretch of water in between. Southern Italy provided northern Italian capital with a large internal unskilled reserve army of labour, and therefore a low-paid unskilled proletariat, in a way that did not exist in any other original EU state. Finally, in the middle and the northeast of the country, there were older or newer industrial districts that conformed to the Third Italy model. The central districts were often politically managed by the Italian Communist Party, which had embraced a form of Eurocommunism that was a beacon of light for the radical left in Europe, with flexible local economic policies and substantial inputs into working-class life and social reproduction. The districts were characterized by low capital requirements and skilled artisanal urban/rural labour. They specialized flexibly in labour-intensive light and design-intensive consumer products, with disaggregated production regimes comprising networks of larger and smaller workshops as well as households, all running a sharply gendered division of labour in a very entrepreneurial but also exploitative, hierarchical and informal set-up. Big capital, as Fumagalli and D'Aloisio remind us in this volume, had from its inception always been closely interwoven with the state, as demonstrated by the history of FIAT and the Italian steel and chemical industry. Italian capitalism was a profoundly Gerschenkronian political capitalism, always a bit behind its northern competitors and with a limited home market and private capital base. Small capitals, as the chapters in this volume remind us, were in their turn closely interwoven with the local, often leftist, state. And while a corporatist formal welfare state developed, labour markets and reproductive arrangements were always also deeply infused with informality – an informality that was embedded in ongoing internal (im)migration, as well as hierarchy and patriarchy in the firm, the family and the urban/rural habitats.

While every state in Europe featured all of these elements, Italian history, space and location served to amplify these features to such an extent that Italy appeared to provide the quintessential example. As a consequence of this hybrid spatial and social split, the Italian lira suffered more devaluations than any other continental currency. Indeed, the continued growth of the artisanal export sector remained dependent on these regular currency devaluations as they safeguarded the cost-competitiveness of Italian labour and firms. But it is good to remind ourselves that if Central and Eastern Europe and the Balkans had remained capitalist after 1945, they would have similarly been polarized between cores and peripheries, with ensuing internal migration and continued enclaves of reserve labour. Spatial unevenness is not a specifically Italian quality. However, the industrial district phenomenon could probably not have been replicated in Eastern Europe or perhaps anywhere else in Europe on the same scale and intensity as occurred in Italy (interestingly, parts of Germany and Switzerland might be the exception here). Postwar artisanal districts in Europe depended to some extent on 'premodern' urbanization and the associated spread and specialization of artisanal skills 'before the factory', so to speak. In other words, European industrial districts build on the ongoing presence of old, even early-modern, urbanizations and their artisanal industries. The Third Italy summarizes how such old ensembles were injected with new life during the postwar household consumer boom in Europe.

This general boom came to a halt by the mid-1970s. But the sheer flexibility and technical, artisanal and exploitative capacities of the districts gave them another lease of life until the 1990s, as they kept deepening their export orientation. This may have been their heyday. It was also the period in which the districts became internationally celebrated as a model of post-Fordist industrial and regional governance. But the cracks were already starting to show by 1990, as Michael Blim (1990) pointed out early on. These cracks would only grow bigger as the Berlin Wall fell, the lira became the euro, the General Agreement on Tariffs and Trade (GATT) became the World Trade Organization (WTO), capital and the economy began globalizing quickly everywhere, the EU incorporated Eastern Europe and parts of the Balkans (just over the water from mainland Italy), China became the workshop of the world and immigrants from Eastern Europe and North Africa began substituting in large numbers for internal migrants. And then came the crisis.

This is a global and European story, but it hit the Italian ensemble harder than any other form of national capitalism in the EU (except for Greece and other states in Southeastern Europe, which were at a much lower level of capitalist development), for reasons that have been so well explained in the chapters in this volume. And because of the democratic impossibility of 'internal devaluation' (as against a Greece run by the Troika), it also hit more durably. As the chapters have shown, Italian jobs were outsourced on a large scale to Romania, Bulgaria, India and China, including jobs from the producer circuits of the Third Italy, circuits that themselves were rapidly globalizing too. Fordism came back, as did global rather than local divisions of labour. Italian artisanal labour and small capital, but also big Italian capital, came under immense pressure from the fast-globalizing value regimes. This happened right at the point that they had just lost the economic sovereignty associated with the lira. Pressures towards higher exploitation (the return of an ethos of 'hard work', as Hadjimichalis had already noted in 2006) spread throughout local systems, resulting in sharper internal and external divisions of labour between a male skilled local core and an ever more flexible and exploited female and immigrant pool of labour. Those pressures also pushed all actors to try to move up on the value chain. In the process, small dispersed capital allied and concentrated in a drive to establish bigger and stronger brands such as Prada or Bulgari, with centralized design and sales organizations. Regions that failed to develop such brands became dependent on those that did, or on transnational chains and global capital. In the process, the Third Italy model as we knew it was slipping away.

In this context, a crisis of labour, which was already present in the 1990s, was clearly deepening. This is the picture that the chapters paint in detail. In his chapter, Simone Ghezzi calls this a 'cultural' factor in the decline of the districts. But this cultural factor was just the intimate dimension of the escalating pressures on the reproduction of local labour. It was class rather than culture in the sense of 'local tradition'. It was the stepped-up competition within a now global value regime in artisanal consumer products that was dealing a hard body blow to the working class of the Third Italy. Sons and daughters of local artisanal workers and small entrepreneurs now wanted out. The new white-collar design, administrative and commercial jobs in the transforming local industries would now often be occupied by mobile applicants from other places. The chapters regularly mention that local skills had been disappearing to such an extent that regional employers were forced into collectively providing formal vocational training for the first time in history. The local or nearby service sector became a powerful draw for the children of local artisans and entrepreneurs, like anywhere else in Europe, at least in terms of their imaginations and desires. Many sought a path into higher education. The chapters (in particular that of Michael Blim) also suggest that parents often supported their children, silently or explicitly, in their efforts to find and create lives outside of the industries.

In short, the globalization of value chains and all that it meant – above all, the downward pressure on and the exploitation, precariatization and bifurcation of labour – drove Italian artisanal districts to the wall. The last three chapters of this book take us out of the Third Italy and into other regions and sectors. They show that varieties of this very same experience were in fact quite general, even while the precise circumstances were different.

The modernity that FIAT's move out of Turin and into the new Melfi factory in Basilicata in the early 1990s promised to the Italian South in the end became a great disappointment, as Fulvia D'Aloisio shows. The large cohort of Melfi workers employed since those days, most of whom are higher educated, has since the crisis been hit by short time, chaotic working hours, sharp income reductions, stark speed ups, internal bipolarization and generalized feelings of precarity. All of these workers had families in the 1990s, took on mortgages to finance their family houses and then got stuck, now in their late forties and fifties, with insufficient and insecure income, high debt payments and, as the chapter shows, a high incidence of bad health and nervousness. After the crisis, and after the merger with Chrysler and the consequent move of FIAT's headquarters out of Italy, they are now being played off against a new and much younger cohort of often university-trained and healthy workers. These new workers had been unemployed and in a precarious position for years during the crisis period. FIAT is now promising them global careers. Members of this new cohort, so used to precarity and a shortened timeframe for planning their lives, generally continue to live with their parents and do not have children. This is the same pattern as elsewhere in Italy and in the European South. They seem to have learnt that it can never be known what is going to happen and they do not seek to take on more responsibility than just for themselves.

Francesco Bogani's story of Italian road transport workers and individual truck owners is in its broad outlines and direction not very different. Concentration and a generalized regime of just-in-time production among their clients is leading to sharp competition, long and unpredictable working hours, precarity, uncertainty, self-exploitation and the loss of a private life beyond work. Some of them imagine that the East European drivers competing for their jobs do not even aspire to having a life outside of their trucks, and simply live in them.

Andrea Fumagalli lifts this all to a higher level, nationally and theoretically. Nowhere else in Europe has the crisis resulted in such a loss of industrial production as in Italy (in terms of percentage of GDP). At the same time, the sort of biocognitive capitalism that generates high intellectual content, innovation, patents and new wealth, the sort of capitalism that is rumoured to be taking off in Northwestern Europe, is passing Italy by, with the partial exception of Milan. Italian capital keeps investing significantly more than most other European capitals, but these investments go into machinery rather than research and development and cognitive excellence. Italy is being squeezed between the increasingly cognitive big capitalisms of the North on the one hand and the low-wage mid-tech manufacturing capacities of the emerging markets on the other, from Eastern Europe to India and China. Fumagalli then turns to the conditions of creative-cognitive workers in Italy. As a good anthropologist, he discovers that the Italian cognitive 'entrepreneuriat' (my term) feels a growing pressure to accumulate further professional distinctions in their unpaid time in order to compensate for the absence of paid time and so keep up their hopes for future-time. This should sound recognizable for anthropologists and other academics, and not only in Italy.

This rich anthropological collection has duly focused on particulars; particulars of various Italian industrial districts above all, but also the particulars of southern FIAT workers and of truckers all over the country. This is also true for Fumagalli's explicitly comparative final chapter that seeks, among other things, to highlight Italy's specific path amid further European trajectories. Yet, critical social science visions of a generation ago, if we combine insights from Arrighi, Castells, Harvey, Mingione and Sassen, for example, did add up to a rather robust and reliable general picture of where Western capitalism was heading. While Italian accounts are inevitably particularist, Italy also represents a particular version of a rather universal trajectory. Universal and particular are not an antinomy but a dialectic. I want to conclude with three points.

While the chapters in this collection note that neoliberal global financialized capitalism and its recent crises have been worse for Italy and Italian workers and citizens than for most other Western European forms of capitalism, it may well be that Italy, seen from a vantage point of two decades from now, appears not so much the laggard as a vanguard of sorts: the place where it all began to happen twenty years earlier than elsewhere – the canary in the mine. What may now appear as successful national models of capitalism in Europe – for example, in Germany and the Netherlands – have their own similar but distinct, universal and particular 'secret' embarrassments that echo in a general sense the Italian ones. A total of 25 per cent of German workers are not working under a standard labour contract these days. Female, child and old-age poverty are high. The

Dutch welfare system sustains one million people on disability benefits in a labour market of some seven million, mostly younger people who find it hard to live under the thoroughly flexibilized high productivity regime of the Dutch, which likes to imagine itself as a form of 'top football'. As export champions, both countries also depend on global demand that might evaporate as soon as the next crisis hits or if technological change abruptly devalues existing assets. Dramatic social and regional transformations have been occurring in Eastern Germany and parts of the Ruhr. Immigration is high and is necessary to compensate for similar refusals by younger people to take on responsibilities beyond taking care of themselves, as is the case in Basilicata (the press now calls this 'the demographic time bomb', as if this were a purely demographic phenomenon: it's capitalism, stupid!). Internal transformations within 'successful' regions such as Eindhoven in the Netherlands, site of the former headquarters of the Philips corporation, cannot simply be judged less dramatic than their Italian counterparts. True, the overall sum of growth, job generation and incomes has in the last few decade(s) certainly been better than in Italy, but we cannot simply conclude from this that personal or local suffering must be less, as the Dutch young adult disability figures demonstrate. Just as importantly, deep economic, technological, geopolitical and ecological transformations are in the offing. The German car industry has just announced a potential 400,000 job losses over the next few years as the transition to electric driving is going to hit the country's major industry, with incalculable further ramifications throughout the German economy. The costs of the necessary transition to a low-carbon economy, and the way they will be distributed, are also unclear. In twenty years from now, the German economy may be a story of stagnation and decline compared to its heyday in the 2010s, in a similar fashion to Italy's current position.

While the euro has been a painful story for Italy, although not without its contradictions, there should be no illusions about the extent to which, in the light of the rise of China and the accelerating and probably inevitable imperial competition with the United States, the whole of the EU construction is becoming deeply cumbersome for all of Europe and for the interests of its citizens. The EU, in spirit and in its institutions, embodies the neoliberal free market of the 1990s. It is a market-making construction that sets rules for mutual economic engagement for a grouping of small and mid-sized neighbouring and mutually dependent national economies. The EU is entirely unequipped to play its own role and protect its citizens' interests in a world of two competing technological superpowers, both intent on carving out their own spheres of influence for their technologies and capitals. The deep divisions since the financial crises between the North and the South of the EU, as well as between the West and the East, including the departure of the United Kingdom, may only be the foreboding of a further fracturing. These divisions underline the fact that the EU and the eurozone were not set up to deal with a financial crisis (and still are not). In the neoliberal dreams of the 1990s, such crises could not even have been imagined. Robust agreements in vision and policy among EU Member States in relation to current problems such as the euro and intra-European inequalities are nowhere to be seen, let alone for the future problems of institutionally and legally equipping the EU for an era of global techno-power rivalry. The absence of digital data giants among European capitalists makes this vital issue an even more desperate one. We must also see very clearly that the majority of political desires and knowledge in the EU, steadily offered by the governments of the northern 'successful' Member States, represents a nostalgia for going back to the status quo ante of competitive market economies and pro-capital policy competition, in terms of both politics and economics. There is basically no other social vision on offer. Can the EU ever overcome being a club of small nations quarrelling with each other over the fairness of their internal market with some added EU subsidiarity that is not more than 1 per cent of its GDP? If not, and as mentioned earlier, Italy may well appear as a vanguard rather than a laggard in two decades from now.

Amid the generalities of neoliberal inequalities, precarities, stagnation and decline, right-wing xenophobic illiberal populism has been on the rise everywhere. This is a universal, though certainly variegated, process. The chapters in this book do not pay much attention to local politics, but the particular neoliberal processes and conditions that are playing themselves out in the localities studied here are probably closely intertwined with the collapse of 'old political elites' and the rise of new populist contenders (for anthropological examples of such local accounts, see Kalb and Halmai (2011)). But Italy does not stand out on this point either, despite its clearly significant particularities. Perhaps, in retrospect, the Tangentopoli scandal (1992) may appear as simply the Italian version – a shock version – of the general slow deflation of twentieth-century political ideologies and elites across Europe and the Global North at large, social democrats first of all? Certainly, all the new right-wing populisms differ. Yes, there is sometimes an exciting new left fighting back for a while (Corbyn, for a while; Podemos, which only hesitantly embraced its left-wing positioning; Syriza, certainly, but they blew themselves up; the Sardines in Emilia-Romagna just gave Salvini a bloody nose, but are they left or mainstream liberal, and will they be able to institutionalize themselves?). Nevertheless, there is a general story to tell about the rise of illiberal populist politics. The crisis in Italy, then, is a crisis for us all.

Harvey (2018b) along with Hardt and Negri (2018) have recently argued that the whole of everyday life and social reproduction in late capitalist societies has by now been given up for its 'real subsumption under capital'. Capital thus not only just appropriates the sphere of labour, as in twentieth-century modernist imaginings. In other words, we have moved from the alienation of the product from the producer and, vice versa, to the alienation of and from social life as such – biocapitalism, in a word (Fumagalli also uses this term). Hence, the spread of 'the politics of life itself' comes as no surprise. What if this is the actual, though obscured, core of the current populist rebellion? In their introduction, D'Aloisio and Ghezzi cite the classic work by Ernesto de Martino on southern Italian agricultural labourers, which tells of the way they experienced a 'crisis of presence', the difficulty of connecting their past and present to a future that might be theirs, the experience of being not contemporaneous, of being wrongly synchronized. D'Aloisio and Ghezzi suggest that precaritized workers and small entrepreneurs, who are the subjects of this book, have similarly lost the thread of time and are longing for some shelter. The politics of life, under an unevenly emerging biocapitalism of the globalized and financialized sort, often seems to appear these days as a politics of nostalgia – a nostalgia for a twentieth-century European modernity that is slowly fading in the mists of time.

Don Kalb is Professor of Social Anthropology at the University of Bergen, Norway, where he leads the Frontlines of Value project. He is also a senior researcher at Utrecht University. Until 2017, he served as Professor of Sociology and Social Anthropology at the Central European University, Budapest. His recent publications include *Anthropologies of Class: Power, Practice, and Inequality* (coedited with James G. Carrier, Cambridge University Press, 2015) and *Worldwide Mobilizations: Class Struggles and Urban Commoning* (coedited with Mao Mollona, Berghahn Books, 2018).

References

Arrighi, G. 1994. *The Long Twentieth Century: Money, Power, and the Origins of Our Times*. London: Verso.

Blim, M. 1990. *Made in Italy: Small-Scale Industrialization and its Consequences*. New York: Praeger.

Breman, J., K. Harris, C.K. Lee and M. van der Linden (eds). 2019. *The Social Question in the Twenty-First Century: A Global View*. Berkeley: University of California Press.
Carrier, J., and D. Kalb (eds). 2015. *Anthropologies of Class: Power, Practice and Inequality*. Cambridge: Cambridge University Press.
Castells, M. 1989. *The Informational City*. Oxford: Basil Blackwell.
Clarke, J. 2008. 'Living with/in and without Neo-liberalism', *Focaal – European Journal of Anthropology* 51: 135–48.
Della Porta, D. 2015. *Social Movements in Times of Austerity: Bringing Capitalism Back into Protest Analysis*. Cambridge: Polity.
Hadjimichalis, C. 2006. 'The End of the Third Italy as we Knew It?', *Antipode* 38(1): 82–106.
Hardt, M., and T. Negri. 2018. 'The Multiplicities within Capitalist Rule and the Articulation of Struggles', *TripleC* 16(2): 440–48.
———. 2019. 'Empire: Twenty Years On', *New Left Review* 120: 67–93.
Harvey, D. 1989. *The Condition of Postmodernity*. Oxford: Basil Blackwell.
———. 2005. *A Short History of Neoliberalism*. Oxford: Oxford University Press.
———. 2018a. *Marx, Capital and the Madness of Economic Reason*. London: Profile Books.
———. 2018b. 'Universal Alienation and the Real Subsumption of Daily Life under Capital: A Response to Hardt and Negri', *TripleC* 16(2): 449–53.
Kalb, D. 2005. 'Introduction: Critical Junctions – Recapturing Anthropology and History', in D. Kalb and H. Tak (eds), *Critical Junctions: Anthropology and History Beyond the Cultural Turn*. New York: Berghahn Books, pp. 1–28.
———. 2011. 'Introduction: Headlines of Nation, Subtexts of Class: Working-Class Populism and the Return of the Repressed in Neoliberal Europe', in D. Kalb and G. Halmai (eds), *Headlines of Nation, Subtexts of Class: Working Class Populism and the Return of the Repressed in Neoliberal Europe*. New York: Berghahn Books, pp. 1–36.
———. 2014. 'Class: The Empty Sign of the Middle Class', in D. Nonini (ed.), *A Companion to Urban Anthropology*. Oxford: Blackwell, pp. 157–77.
———. 2015. 'Introduction: Class and the New Anthropological Holism', in J. Carrier and D. Kalb (eds), *Anthropologies of Class: Power, Practice and Inequality*. Cambridge: Cambridge University Press, pp. 1–27.
———. 2018. 'Trotsky over Mauss: Anthropological Theory and the October 1917 Commemoration', *Dialectical Anthropology* 42: 327–43.
Kalb, D. and G. Halmai (eds). 2011. *Headlines of Nation, Subtexts of Class: Working Class Populism and the Return of the Repressed in Neoliberal Europe*. New York: Berghahn Books.
Kalb, D., and M. Mollona. 2018a. *Worldwide Mobilizations: Class Struggles and Urban Commoning*. New York: Berghahn Books.
———. 2018b. 'Introductory Thoughts on Anthropology and Urban Insurrection', in D. Kalb and M. Mollona, *Worldwide Mobilizations: Class Struggles and Urban Commoning*. New York: Berghahn Books, pp. 1–30.
Kasmir, S., and A. Carbonella (eds). 2014. *Blood and Fire: Toward a Global Anthropology of Labor*. New York: Berghahn Books.
Kasmir, S., and L. Gill. 2018. 'No Smooth Surfaces: The Anthropology of Unevenness and Combination', *Current Anthropology* 59(4): 355–77.
Mingione, E. 1991. *Fragmented Societies: A Sociology of Economic Life Beyond the Market Paradigm*. Oxford: Basil Blackwell.
Ross, A. 2004. 'Made in Italy: The Trouble with Craft Capitalism', *Antipode* 36(2): 209–16.
Sassen, S. 1991. *The Global City*. Princeton: Princeton University Press.
Smith, N. 2008. 'Neo-liberalism: Dominant But Dead', *Focaal – European Journal of Anthropology* 51: 155–58.

INDEX

www.ingramcontent.com/pod-product-compliance
Ingram Content Group UK Ltd.
Pitfield, Milton Keynes, MK11 3LW, UK
UKHW021838100926
8556IPUK00004B/415

9 781789 207804